Marxism and the new
imperialism

Marxism and the new imperialism

BOOKMARKS

Bookmarks
London, Chicago, Melbourne

Marxism and the new imperialism
Published July 1994
Bookmarks, 265 Seven Sisters Road, London N4 2DE
Bookmarks, PO Box 16085, Chicago, Il. 60616
Bookmarks, GPO Box 1473N, Melbourne 3001
ISBN 0 906224 81 0
© Bookmarks and International Socialism
Printed by Cox and Wyman Ltd, Reading

Bookmarks is linked to an international grouping of socialist
organisations:
AUSTRALIA: **International Socialist Organisation**,
GPO Box 1473N, Melbourne 3001
BELGIUM: **Socialisme International,**
Rue Lovinfosse 60, 4030 Grevignée
BRITAIN: **Socialist Workers Party**,
PO Box 82, London E3 3LH
CANADA: **International Socialists**,
PO Box 339, Station E, Toronto, Ontario M6H 4E3
CYPRUS: **Workers Democracy**,
PO Box 7280, Nicosia, Cyprus
DENMARK: **Internationale Socialister**,
Postboks 642, 2200 København, N
FRANCE: **Socialisme International**,
BP 189, 75926 Paris, Cedex 19
GERMANY: **Sozialistische Arbeitersgruppe**,
Postfach 180367, 60084 Frankfurt
GREECE: **Organosi Sosialistiki Epanastasi**,
PO Box 8161, 10010, Omonia, Athens
HOLLAND: **Groep Internationale Socialisten**,
PO Box 9720, 3506 GR Utrecht
IRELAND: **Socialist Workers Movement**,
PO Box 1648, Dublin 8
NEW ZEALAND: **International Socialist Organisation**,
PO Box 6157, Dunedin
NORWAY: **Internasjonale Sosialister**,
Postboks 9226, Grønland 0134, Oslo
POLAND: **Solidarnosc Socjalistyczna**,
PO Box 12, 01-900 Warszawa 118
SOUTH AFRICA: **International Socialists of South Africa**,
PO Box 18530, Hillbrow 2038
UNITED STATES: **International Socialist Organisation**,
PO Box 16085, Chicago, Il. 60616

Contents

The chapters of this book are based on articles which originally appeared in *International Socialism*: Imperialism Today by Alex Callinicos first appeared in *IS 50*, Spring 1991 as Marxism and Imperialism today. The New Imperialism by John Rees was published in *IS 48*, Autumn 1990; Class and crisis in Eastern Europe by Mike Haynes in *IS 54*, Spring 1992 and The Return of the national question by Chris Harman in *IS 56*, Autumn 1992.

Introduction

LEE HUMBER

There was widespread optimism among the leaders of the Western powers at the end of the 1980s. The Berlin Wall had fallen and the Eastern Bloc had collapsed. US president George Bush hailed a 'New World Order' marked by prosperity, stability and peace, and policed by US Marines, representatives of the only remaining superpower. Propagandists like former state department employee Francis Fukuyama proclaimed the end of history as liberal democracy took root in hitherto barren territory. The old imperialist order had gone and we were embarking on a new golden age.

By 1994 capitalism has dropped from these lofty ideological heights. Wars rage in the Middle East and Asia, across swathes of Africa, and have returned to Europe on a scale not seen since 1945. In the African state of Rwanda over a quarter of a million people died in the first few weeks of civil war. In Cambodia and Somalia thousands continue to die as the Western powers switch allegiances to first one war lord then another in their search for regional influence and profit. In former Yugoslavia the US, Britain, Germany, France and Russia try to manoeuvre to make the best out of the mayhem there. Dozens of other wars rage around the globe.

The new phase of imperialism has produced a world full of economic uncertainty. The end of the old Cold War hasn't even yielded its hoped-for 'peace dividend'. The arms cuts promised in the late 1980s by George Bush and the then Russian leader Mikhail Gorbachev have turned out to be little more than a restructuring of forces. Instead of launching Cruise missiles from Greenham Common the British Commanders made plans to launch them from the air or sea. The missiles didn't go, they just changed launch sites. Meanwhile older weapons have been sold off to lesser military powers by the major ones. So the Greek army received American and German tanks and its navy Western battleships. The Hungarian ruling class, worried by war in the neighbouring Balkan states has bought $800 million worth of Mig-29 fighters from Russia, while Germany has supplied them with spare parts and equipment from the stockpiles of the old East German army.

The world has never been so well equipped to kill, or so volatile. The political situation in Russia and the countries of the former Eastern Bloc is particularly acute, marked by continued and severe economic crisis, large scale unemployment, civil war and deep alienation from the new political structures. Hungarian workers showed how disillusioned with market economics they were in the elections of May 1994 when the Socialist Party, the renamed Communist Party, was voted back to office. If the new government pushes ahead with privatisation and up to 200,000 job cuts it wants, Hungarian workers will be just as unimpressed with their new leaders.

But perhaps Russia and the career of Boris Yeltsin gives us the most succinct picture of the process of class polarisation and political instability in the region. When he swept to power by defeating a coup attempt against the then leader Gorbachev in August 1991 he swept the mass of the Russian working class along with him. Tens of thousands marched in his support, he was full of optimism for plans for Russia to adopt the market, confident that he could prevent the break up of the old Russian empire. By October 1993, when another coup attempt was made against Yeltsin himself, Russian workers had abandoned him. The years of drastically falling living standards had taken their toll. The workers watched indifferently as two groups of prospective rulers fought it out on the streets of Moscow.

Across Europe, nationalism has re-emerged as one consequence of the protracted economic and political crisis. Fascists have been one of the main beneficiaries of this development as people turn their backs on the old parties. This is true in Russia where the fascist Vladimir Zhirinovsky's Liberal Democratic Party emerged with the largest bloc of seats in the Russian parliamentary elections of December 1993.

It is also true in Italy. Even before the political establishment was shattered in the great corruption crisis of 1993, alienation from the system ran deep. By the late 1980s, in reply to the question; 'Are you satisfied with the way democracy works in your country?' an average 75 percent of Italians said they were 'not at all satisfied' or 'not very satisfied'. The elections of May 1994 saw the fascist MSI National Alliance led by Gianfranco Fini win some five million votes, securing the party a number of places in the government. Jean Marie Le Pen's National Front continues to exert an influence on French politics while in Germany the disorientation and discontent caused by reunification and recession has led to the growth of Nazi parties.

However, the latest phase of imperialism has also helped speed up the tempo of class struggle, as economic and political instability spark off working class resistance. Mass struggle has returned to Western Europe. General strikes preceded the elections in Italy with hundreds of thousands on the streets. Half a million demonstrated against fascism after right wing electoral successes. In France huge strikes and mass protests, including one of over a million against cuts in education, have rocked the right wing government of Edouard Balladur and silenced Le Pen.

These are some of the themes explored in detail in this essential book. The collapse of an old order necessarily implies a struggle to determine the character of the new, this book is part of that struggle.

Marxism and imperialism today

ALEX CALLINICOS

THE WEST'S 1991 war against Iraq showed that imperialism, in the most general sense of the naked use of force to impose the will of major powers on smaller states, is flourishing. This turn of events was all the more remarkable because it came in the wake of the widespread acceptance of the belief that the world was entering a post-imperialist era. Two main reasons provided this belief with its justification.

One was, of course, the expectation that the end of the Cold War would produce what George Bush called 'a new world order' in which disputes between states could be settled peacefully under the aegis of the United Nations. We can now see all too clearly that the new world order is merely the same old imperialist one, with the difference that the collapse of the Soviet Union means that the UN can be used to legitimise military interventions which the United States previously had to make unilaterally.

The second reason for consigning imperialism to the dustbin of history derived from a very commonly held interpretation of the dramatic changes in the world economy over the past generation. The internationalisation of production and the accompanying global integration of capital have, it is claimed, made war obsolete. Thus Tim Congdon, a leading British monetarist, recently declared:

> Economic nationalism, one of the most powerful and destructive forces in the twentieth century, is becoming obsolete. Trade and finance are so increasingly international in character, and business strategy for large companies is so totally globalised, that the idea of the nation-state is losing its relevance.

Congdon made it plain that these economic changes were having political consequences—among them, in the long term, the abolition of war:

> The idea of warfare between Britain and Germany, or the USA and Japan, is, of course, already preposterous. Over time military antagonisms between nations will become literally absurd as the separateness of nations breaks down and eventually becomes meaningless.[1]

The idea that the economic interdependence of states means that it is no longer in their interest to wage war is far from new. During the lead up to the First World War the peace activist Norman Angell published in 1910 *The Great Illusion*, which sought to prove that a general war between the Great Powers would be so destructive economically that it was inconceivable they would undertake so irrational a venture. This analysis was cast into an apparently Marxist form by Karl Kautsky in a notorious article published very shortly after the outbreak of the Great War in August 1914:

> There is no *economic* necessity for continuing the arms race after the World War even from the standpoint of the capitalist class itself, with the possible exception of certain armaments interests. On the contrary, the capitalist economy is seriously threatened precisely by these disputes. Every farsighted capitalist today must call on his fellows: capitalists of all countries, unite![2]

Kautsky indeed went on to argue that economic processes could push capitalists towards global unity:

> What Marx said about capitalism can also be applied to imperialism: monopoly creates competition, and competition, monopoly. The frantic competition among the huge firms, giant banks, and multimillionaires compelled the great financial groups, who were absorbing the small ones, to devise the cartel. Similarly the World War between the great imperialist powers may result in a federation of the strongest, who renounce their arms race.
>
> From the purely economic standpoint it is therefore not impossible for capitalism to live through yet another phase, the transferral of this process of forming cartels into foreign policy: a phase of *ultra-imperialism*.[3]

Kautsky's prediction that inter-imperialist antagonisms could be peacefully reconciled within the framework of a global capitalist cartel proved to be of absolutely no guidance during what Arno Mayer has called 'the General Crisis and Thirty Years War of the twentieth century' between 1914 and 1945.[4] But more recently the idea that imperialism is merely a phase in the history of capitalism, and one that either has been or is being surpassed, has been revived. Perhaps most influential has been Bill Warren's attempt to show that the Third World has experienced since the Second World War not, as dependency theorists such as Andre Gunder Frank claimed, the 'development of underdevelopment' but rather 'a major surge in capitalist social relations and productive forces'. He concludes:

> Within a context of growing economic interdependence, the ties of dependence (or subordination) binding the Third World and the imperialist world have been and are being markedly loosened with the rise of indigenous capitalisms; the distribution of political-economic power within the capitalist world is thereby growing less uneven. Consequently, although one dimension of imperialism is the domination and exploitation of the non-communist world by a handful of major advanced capitalist countries (the United States, West Germany, Britain, France, Japan, etc), we are nevertheless in an era of declining imperialism and advanced capitalism.[5]

Undoubtedly the economic transformations of the past generation—the globalisation of capital, the rise of the Newly Industrialising Countries, the relative decline of both the superpowers—have been enormous. The question which I address in this essay is whether these changes (and associated political upheavals, above all those connected with the end of the Cold War) can still be understood within the framework of the Marxist theory of imperialism. How one answers this question has important practical implications: it will indicate whether the slaughter in the Gulf—and similar, though less spectacular episodes, such as the brutal US-led UN intervention in Somalia—represent the last gasp of an outmoded version of capitalism or the intrinsic workings of a system still liable to give rise to imperialist wars. The first step towards addressing this question is to establish what the Marxist theory of imperialism actually is.

The Marxist theory of imperialism

IMPERIALISM can be defined very broadly or very narrowly—as the domination, throughout history, of small countries by stronger states, or as the policy pursued by the Great Powers in the last third of the nineteenth century of formally subordinating most of the rest of the world to their rule. The classic Marxist definition of imperialism, by Lenin, is more specific than the broad definition, more general than the narrow one. Imperialism is neither a universal feature of human society nor a particular policy but 'a special stage in the development of capitalism', indeed, as the title of Lenin's pamphlet states, 'the highest stage of capitalism'. Lenin sought to characterise this stage of capitalist development by offering the following famous definition of imperialism:

> (1) the concentration of production and capital has developed to such a high stage that it has created monopolies which play a decisive role in economic life; (2) the merging of bank capital with industrial capital, and the creation, on the basis of this 'finance capital', of a financial oligarchy; (3) the export of capital as distinguished from the export of commodities acquires exceptional importance; (4) the formation of international monopolist capitalist associations which share the world out among themselves, and (5) the territorial division of the whole world among the biggest capitalist powers is completed.[6]

Lenin's definition is so often treated by much of the left as a dogma whose truth is undeniable that its limitations are worth stressing. Most obviously it is a list of what Lenin calls 'basic features' of imperialism. But it is not possible to establish from this list the relative importance of these features. This is a serious weakness, since it has become clear that some features are much less basic than others. For example, finance capital, the integration of bank and industrial capital, was far more developed in some imperialist powers than in others, in Germany than in Britain. Moreover, not simply was the relationship between the growth of overseas investment and colonial expansion considerably more uneven than Lenin suggested, but some imperialist powers, notably the US and Japan, were net importers of capital till 1914.[7]

Lenin's basic conception of imperialism, however, emerges from these criticisms undamaged. He was careful to stress 'the conditional and relative value of all definitions in general'. Moreover, *Imperialism* was not intended to be a definitive scientific study but rather, as its subtitle declares, a 'popular outline', drawing heavily on such pathbreaking works as the radical-liberal JA Hobson's *Imperialism* and the Austro-Marxist Rudolf Hilferding's *Finance Capital*. On the basis of these researches Lenin had no doubt what the decisive feature of imperialism was: 'in its economic essence imperialism is monopoly capitalism.' This allowed him historically to situate imperialism, to determine 'its place in history, for monopoly that grows out of the soil of free competition, and precisely out of free competition, is the transition from the capitalist system to a higher socio-economic order.'[8] The antagonisms and wars between the Great Powers were thus no mere aberration, as Kautsky implied, but arose from the dynamic of capitalist development, above all from the tendency which Marx had analysed towards the concentration and centralisation of capital. They could be ended, therefore, only by socialist revolution.

Thus, in Bukharin's more rigorous and systematic version of the theory, imperialism springs from:

> the tendencies of finance-capitalist development. The organisational process, which embraces more and more branches of the 'national economy' through the creation of combined enterprises and through the organisational role of the banks, has led to the conversion of each developed 'national system' of capitalism into a 'state-capitalist trust'. On the other hand, the process of development of the productive forces drives these 'national' systems into the most acute conflicts in their competitive struggle for the world market.[9]

On this account, imperialism has two fundamental features. The first is a consequence of the tendency of concentration and centralisation of capital. The competitive accumulation of capital leads both to the growth in the size of the individual units of capital and to the incorporation, especially during crises, of smaller by larger capitals. Economic power becomes increasingly concentrated. Sectors become monopolised, dominated by a handful of large firms or perhaps only one huge corporation.

Furthermore, industrial capital tends to merge with the big banks to form finance capital. The final stage of this process of 'organisation' is the growing integration of private capital with the nation state, in other words, the emergence of state capitalism. Secondly, however, this national organisation of capitalism takes place in the context of the growing internationalisation of the productive forces. The world economy, which Bukharin defines as '*a system of production relations and, correspondingly, of exchange relations on a world scale*', forms the arena in which the 'state capitalist trusts' compete. Competition between capitals is no longer simply the struggle among private firms for markets: increasingly it assumes the form of military and territorial rivalries among state capitals on a global scale. 'The struggle between state capitalist trusts is decided in the first place by the relation between their military forces, for the military power of the country is the last resort of the struggling "national groups" of capitalists.'[10] Inter-imperialist wars, such as those of 1914-18 and 1939-45, are a necessary feature of a world economy divided between competing capitals.

Bukharin's version of the theory of imperialism is not without its weaknesses. Most fundamentally, he underestimates the extent to which the two tendencies he identifies with imperialism—those towards state capitalism and the internationalisation of capital—can contradict each other. He consequently treats national economies as fully 'organised' state capitalist blocs from which any tendency towards economic crisis (as opposed to war) has been eliminated.[11] Nevertheless, once account has been taken of these errors, we can take Bukharin's theory as identifying the essential features of imperialism as a specific stage in the history of capitalism. We can then summarise the theory of imperialism as follows:

1. Imperialism is the stage in capitalist development where i) the concentration and centralisation of capital tends to lead to the integration of private monopoly capital and the state; and ii) the internationalisation of the productive forces tends to compel capitals to compete for markets, investments and raw materials at the global level.

2. Among the main consequences of these two tendencies are the following:
   i) competition between capitals takes on the form of military rivalries among nation-states; ii) the relations among

nation states are unequal: the uneven and combined development of capitalism allows a small number of advanced capitalist states (the imperialist countries), by virtue of their productive resources and military strength, to dominate the rest of the world; iii) uneven and combined development under imperialism further intensifies military competition and gives rise to wars, including both wars among the imperialist powers themselves and those arising from the struggles of oppressed nations against imperialist domination.[12]

This is a more abstract definition of imperialism than that offered by Lenin, though it captures the core of his conception. One advantage of the definition is that it can be used to show how the dynamics of imperialism give rise to distinct phases in its development. Most of the rest of this essay will be devoted to analysing these phases.

There have, arguably, been three main phases in the history of imperialism: *Classical imperialism, 1875-1945* — the imperialism analysed by Lenin and Bukharin, Luxemburg and Hilferding, Kautsky and Hobson, the imperialism which gave rise to Mayer's 'Thirty Years' War'; *Superpower imperialism, 1945-1990* — the period in which the world was partitioned politically between two militarily competing superpower blocs; *Imperialism after the Cold War* — Bush's 'new world order', in fact a more unstable version of the old.

All such periodisations involve a degree of arbitrariness. As will become clear from the detailed discussion which follows, features of each phase are typically present in a less developed form in the previous phase. Nevertheless, this way of dividing up the history of imperialism in my view helps to illuminate its underlying dynamics and the consequent transformations it has undergone. For obvious reasons, contemporary imperialism will receive the most detailed attention.

Archaic imperialism?

FIRST, HOWEVER, it is worth considering the most sophisticated bourgeois attempt to explain imperialism, which treats it as an essentially *pre-capitalist* phenomenon. This theory is perhaps best known in the form given it by the Austrian economist Joseph Schumpeter. In an essay written during the First

World War he described imperialism as 'non-rational and irrational, purely instinctual inclinations toward war and conquest'. It followed that imperialism was 'atavistic in character', 'an element that stems from the living conditions, not of the present, but of the past—or, put in terms of the economic interpretation of history, from past rather than present relations of production.' More concretely, imperialism reflected the continued dominance of Europe by quasi-absolute monarchies and landed aristocracies the reason for whose existence had always been to wage war. The bourgeoisie was subservient to an essentially feudal 'imperialist absolutism', hence what Schumpeter called 'its wretched weakness in politics, culture, and life generally', while 'a class oriented toward war remained in a ruling position.'[13]

Schumpeter was one of the most sophisticated of the present century's intellectual defenders of capitalism. Interestingly, however, his interpretation of imperialism has recently been revived by the American left-liberal historian Arno Mayer. In his influential book *The Persistence of the Old Regime*, Mayer argues that Europe before 1914 remained 'thoroughly pre-industrial and pre-bourgeois', the landed aristocracy still socially and politically dominant and able to contain the challenge of an industrial bourgeoisie willing to be co-opted into the old order rather than to claim hegemony for itself. Inasmuch as the old order came under increasing pressure at the turn of the nineteenth century, the patrician ruling classes responded by launching a conservative reaction which was the main force driving Europe to war. Thus 'internal conflicts of class, status, and power charged external war with absolute and ideological impulses'. Indeed the race to war must be seen as an outgrowth of domestic class struggles; the pre-1914 'rupture of the international system into two rigid blocs was more effect than cause. Europe's military behemoth, at once enormous and grotesque, was an expression of the general crisis in which ultra-conservatives were gaining the upper hand'.[14] Mayer has sought to continue this analysis in his celebrated attempt to explain the destruction of European Jewry by the Nazis, which he argues must be seen against the background of 'an epoch of general crisis... The elites and institutions of Europe's embattled old regime were locked in a death struggle with those of a defiant new order'. This struggle involved, for example, 'merchant and manufactural [sic] capitalism against corporate and organised capitalism', and 'prescriptive ruling classes against university-trained strategic elites'.[15]

It should be clear enough why this theory of imperialism even when put forward by Mayer, who calls himself a 'left-dissident historian', must be regarded as bourgeois.[16] It is a theory which absolves capitalism of responsibility for the terrible disasters which engulfed humankind between 1914 and 1945. Mayer's study of what he calls the 'Judeocide' is a heroic piece of writing, which seeks to make historical sense of the Nazi slaughter of the Jews rather than merely to treat it as a unique phenomenon beyond analysis. Nevertheless, it explains the greatest crime in human history as the consequence, not of the most serious crisis suffered by capitalism at its highest stage, but of the clash between feudal old order and bourgeois modernity.

Schumpeter makes the apologetic nature of the theory quite explicit, arguing that a 'purely capitalist world... can offer no fertile soil to imperialist impulses':

> In a purely capitalist world, what was once energy for war becomes simply energy for labour of every kind... Wars of conquest and adventurism in foreign policy in general are bound to be regarded as troublesome distractions, destructive of life's meaning, a diversion from the accustomed and therefore 'true' task.[17]

This argument depends on the claim that the state intervention characteristic of imperialism—the most important late nineteenth century measure was the protective tariff—was irrational from a capitalist point of view. This in turn presupposes the kind of capitalism to be found only in the textbooks of neo-classical economics, a world governed by perfect competition in which no individual firm can influence the market for which it produces. Remarkably, Schumpeter, while espousing such a view of capitalism, recognised that 'monopoly capitalism has virtually fused the big banks and cartels into one', creating a powerful class with 'a strong, undeniable economic interest in such things as protective tariffs, cartels, monopoly prices, forced exports (dumping), an aggressive economic policy, an aggressive foreign policy generally, and war, including wars of expansion with a typically imperialist character.' Despite apparently taking over Hilferding's theory of finance capital lock, stock and barrel, Schumpeter continued nevertheless to insist that '[e]xport monopolism does *not* grow from the inherent laws of capitalist development' since trusts and cartels depended on protective tariffs introduced by states which, on the European continent before 1914, were still predominantly pre-capitalist absolute monarchies.[18]

This, of course, begs the question of 'the persistence of the old order'. This is a familiar argument in Britain, notably in the form of Perry Anderson's and Tom Nairn's claim that the political and ideological subordination of the industrial bourgeoisie to the landed aristocracy survived the Great Reform Act of 1832 and indeed has continued into the twentieth century through the central economic role played by the City of London. To some degree, Mayer's argument is a generalisation of this interpretation of English history to Europe as a whole.[19] However, not simply has the theory been demolished in its British version, but even in the more plausible instance of Imperial Germany a persuasive case has been made that the state, though staffed by landed Junkers, operated in the interests of industrial capital.[20] Europe before 1914 was a bourgeois civilisation, where the still considerable remnants of the old landed order were being undermined or assimilated by industrial capitalism, whose development, though uneven, increasingly shaped the entire continent.[21]

The Schumpeter-Mayer theory of imperialism can only be defended through enormous distortions of historical fact. Thus Schumpeter—who, unlike Mayer or Anderson, did not entertain any doubts about the full-bloodedly capitalist nature of British society—argues that imperialism was only a 'catch-phrase' in Britain: not only did colonies become an economic embarrassment during the Victorian heyday of free trade, but it was 'doubtful whether it is proper to speak of eighteenth century English imperialism'.[22] These are astonishing claims. In the first place, during the eighteenth century the British state massively increased military spending to build up a powerful war machine, centred on the Royal Navy, which made possible a series of colonial conquests critical to Britain's growing dominance of the world market.[23] Secondly, the acquisition of what is sometimes called Britain's 'Second Empire' (most of the first was lost in the American Revolution), took place during the Victorian era of laissez faire.[24] While the reasons for individual conquests were often highly particular, the underlying forces at work were sometimes quite visible. Schumpeter dismisses the Boer War of 1899-1902 as 'merely a chance aberration from the trend'.[25] It was, in fact, the biggest war fought by Britain between 1815 and 1914. Recent historical research has confirmed what Hobson argued at the time, that the war was provoked by an alliance of British imperialism and mining capitalists eager to wrest control of the vast gold deposits of the Witwatersrand from the South African Republic.[26]

These and other absurdities (Schumpeter even claims that the US, since it was 'least burdened with pre-capitalist elements' was 'likely to exhibit the weakest imperialist trend'!) should not obscure the significance of the theory of imperialism as an 'atavistic' phenomenon. It represents the most serious attempt to demonstrate that 'capitalism is by nature anti-imperialist.'[27] The political implications are considerable. Not only does capitalism emerge with clean hands from the horrors of 1914-45, but it is a mode of production that has only become dominant in the second half of the twentieth century. Tom Nairn makes the point most explicitly:

> Judged by Mayer's paradigm, the 1914-45 era was a single 'Thirty Years War' of dissolution and revenge. In other words, the European Ancien Regime still isn't ancient and is only just history: the thunder of its collapse is still in our ears, the most characteristic sound of the century, and the dust has only really settled since the 1950s... If the 'triumph' of the bourgeois class and industrial-capitalist values is taken to mean the formation of a number of fairly homogeneous societies regulated by these norms—a stable and pacific state-system at approximately the same level of development—then it has only just come about. We would appear therefore to be living in the first decades of true capitalist ascendancy, and not (as so many left-wing and communist theorists have insisted) in its 'last days'—in something like the full flood of capitalism's social evolution, rather than in an effete 'late bourgeois world' already crumbling into its Socialist nemesis.[28]

This argument appeared before the East European revolutions, but it dovetails perfectly with the idea, widely accepted on the left as well as the right, that these upheavals mark the triumph of free market capitalism and the beginnings of a new era of expansion and prosperity. But if 'capitalism is by nature anti-imperialist', it follows that its predominance should see an end to military competition and war. Schumpeter indeed argues that the 'pre-capitalist elements in our social life' could not indefinitely survive 'the climate of modern life' and that 'with them, imperialisms will wither and die.'[29] Why then has the period since 1945, what Nairn calls 'the full flood of capitalism's social evolution', seen so many wars, even if there has been no general war between the Great Powers? One common explanation on the left has been the attempt to reduce these conflicts to a global 'intersystemic' struggle between capitalist and communist modes of production.[30] But, aside from the inherent difficulty in treating the now defunct Eastern Bloc as any form of socialism, it is hard to explain from this perspective why the end of the Cold War should be so swiftly followed by a major war between the apparent victor and a Third World regional power. There seem to be only two alternatives. One is to deny that imperialism has its roots even in 'past relations of production' and to invoke instead an autonomous process of military competition to explain the persistence of interstate rivalries and wars: this is the course taken by a number of contemporary social theorists, notably Ernest Gellner, Anthony Giddens, Michael Mann, and WG Runciman, following in the footsteps of Max Weber.[31] Or one can turn to the Marxist theory of imperialism as an indispensable instrument in understanding the transformations undergone by the capitalist world system during the past 125 years. This second course seems much more attractive.

Classical imperialism, 1875-1945

1. An economically and politically multipolar world. Modern European history from the fifteenth century onwards is dominated by a ferocious and continuous process of military and territorial competition among the Great Powers. One way of summing up the nature of imperialism is to say that it marked the point at which this process fused with, and was subordinated to, the expansion of industrial capitalism. Eric Hobsbawm remarks of late nineteenth century capitalism that 'the world economy was now notably more pluralist than before. Britain ceased to be the only fully industrialised, and indeed the only industrial economy.'[32] One factor in this change was what William McNeill calls the 'industrialisation of war' in the mid-nineteenth century—the increases in mobility made possible by the railway and the steamship, and the mass production of new weapons such as the breech loading rifle and the machine gun. States' military power now depended directly on their level of industrialisation. The great absolute monarchies of Central and Eastern Europe—Prussia, Austria-Hungary, Russia—were therefore compelled to promote the expansion of industrial capitalism in order to provide the material basis of modern armed strength. At the same time the spread of industrial capitalism exacerbated the rivalries among the Great Powers, particularly as Britain found its industrial and naval supremacy challenged by Germany. The result was a race in naval armaments driven by rapid technological innovation, and Britain's incorporation into one of the two great military blocs into which Europe was now divided. Economic and military competition mutually reinforced each other in a world dominated by a handful of states.[33]

2. *Colonial expansion.* '[C]apitalism's transition to the stage of monopoly capitalism, to finance capital, is *connected* with the intensification of the struggle for the partitioning of the world,' Lenin wrote.[34] European colonial possessions rose from 2.7 million square miles and 148 million inhabitants in 1860 to 29 million square miles and 568 million inhabitants in 1914, and the process of expansion was not yet complete, since the Middle Eastern possessions of the Ottoman Empire were only partitioned between France and Britain at the end of the First World War. Colonial conquest was accompanied by a huge increase in European foreign investment, from £2 billion in 1862 to £44 billion in 1913.[35]

It does not follow, as crude versions of Lenin's theory suggest, that the dynamic of imperialism was provided by the export of capital to exploit colonial slaves. For one thing, the expansion of foreign investment was highly uneven: Britain was the first and by far the greatest exporter of capital, beginning in the 1860s, France followed in the late 1870s, Germany only after 1900, while the US and Japan imported capital before 1914. Moreover, as Hobsbawm points out,

> [a]lmost 80 percent of all European trade throughout the
> nineteenth century, both exports and imports, was with

other developed countries, and the same is true of European foreign investments. Insofar as these were directed overseas, they went mostly to a handful of rapidly developing countries mainly populated by settlers of European descent— Canada, Australia, South Africa, Argentina, etc—as well as, of course, to the USA.[36]

This pattern emerges very clearly from the figures for British overseas investment given in Table 1.

Table 1. Area pattern of British overseas investment, 1860-1929 (%)

AREAS	1860-70	1881-90	1911-13	1927-29
British Empire total	36	47	46	59
Canada	25	13	13	17
Southern Dominions	9.5	16	17	20
India	1.2	15	10.5	14
other	0.3	3	5.5	8
Latin America	10.5	20	22	22
USA	27	22	19	5.5
Europe	25	8	6	8
other	1.5	3	7	5.5

[Source: M Barratt Brown, *The Economics of Imperialism* (Harmondsworth, 1974), Table 17, pp 190-1.]

The colonies nevertheless played a vital economic role. India provided Britain with an annual tribute in the shape of the directly extracted 'Home Charges', along with a trade surplus, interest on investments and other invisible earnings.[37] According to Berrick Saul, 'Britain settled more than one-third of her deficits with Europe and the United States through India'.[38] Avner Offer's outstanding recent study of the First World War has shown that the British Empire played an even more direct role in the process of inter-imperialist competition. Britain and Germany, as the two most industrialised Great Powers by the turn of the nineteenth century, had both developed highly specialised economies heavily dependent on imported food and raw materials. The British ruling class, however, enjoyed a decisive advantage, in that it controlled an extensive empire capable of supplying it with these commodities, while its naval supremacy allowed it both to protect its own sea routes and to deny Germany access to the food and raw materials it needed to import. Planning for economic war therefore formed a major part of British preparations before 1914. The struggle over food and raw materials was an important factor in Germany's defeat in 1918, both because of the impact on the Central Powers of the British blockade and because the German U-boat campaign in the Atlantic brought the US into the war and therefore tipped the balance in the Entente's favour.[39]

The importance of the colonies in inter-imperialist competition was shown once again during the Great Depression of the 1930s, when the world economy fragmented into rival trade blocs. Those powers, such as Britain and France, which could rely on their colonies for protected markets and raw materials, were able to weather the slump better than those, such as the US and Germany, which lacked empires. For both the latter states the Second World War offered a way out of this problem.

3. Militarised state capitalism. Lenin, Hilferding, and Bukharin all seized on the qualitatively greater centralisation of economic power as the decisive feature of the new stage of capitalist development which became evident at the turn of the nineteenth century. In fact, the development of what Hilferding called 'organised capitalism' involved considerable variations—thus Britain lagged behind Germany and the US. Hilferding explained these variations in terms of the uneven and combined development of capitalism. The relatively 'organic' development of British capitalism meant that the funds for investment gradually accumulated in the hands of individual industrialists without the need to resort to banks or the stock exchange to finance expansion. By contrast, German capitalists, industrialising in the shadow of Britain's manufacturing monopoly, could only raise the funds needed through a far higher degree of organisation, provided by the joint stock company and by the role played by the banks in financing productive investment:

> In Germany, therefore, and in a somewhat different way in the United States, the relation of banks to industry was necessarily, from the start, quite different from that in England. Although this difference was due to the backward and belated capitalist development of Germany, the close connection between industrial and bank capital nevertheless became, in both Germany and America, an important

factor in their advance toward a higher form of capitalist organisation.[40]

For similar reasons, both Germany and the US developed an interventionist state much earlier than Britain, for example, introducing protective tariffs to insulate their manufacturing industries from the competition of the Workshop of the World. It took the Great Depression of the 1930s to persuade the British ruling class to abandon free trade, a step taken by their American counterparts 70 years earlier at the beginning of the Civil War.

It is this integration of the state and private capital which explains imperialism's propensity to war: the global economic rivalries among the huge nationally integrated blocs of capital which emerged from the process of organisation analysed by Hilferding and Bukharin could only be resolved by a test of their relative military strengths. But inter-imperialist war served also greatly to accelerate the tendency towards state capitalism. Bukharin grasped this as early as 1915. The mobilisation of resources required by total war tended to transform the economy into 'an organisation *directly subordinated to the control* of the state power'. Thus: 'War is accompanied not only by tremendous destruction of productive forces: in addition, it provides an extraordinary reinforcement and intensification of capitalism's immanent developmental tendencies.'[41]

The war economies of 1914-18 and 1939-45 led to a qualitative increase in the level of state direction of economic life which was not reversed in the succeeding periods of peace. Indeed, the Great Depression of 1929-39 represented a continuation of this process as the world market fragmented into protectionist trade blocs and the major imperialist powers all strengthened their apparatuses of state intervention — a process which reached its climax in Stalinist Russia.[42] One consequence was a decline in the level of global economic integration relative to that attained before 1914. Thus the ratio of trade in manufactured goods to world output only passed the 1913 level in the mid-1970s.[43]

This drive towards economic autarky by the Great Powers served only to exacerbate the tensions among them, since it gave those imperialist states lacking ready access to colonial markets and raw materials — notably Germany and Japan — a powerful incentive to use their military machines to carve out a larger share of the world's resources for themselves. Thus the contradiction which Bukharin had identified between the internationalisation and the statisation of capital produced a second and even more destructive attempt to repartition the globe among the imperialist powers.[44]

Superpower imperialism, 1945-90

1. A politically bipolar, but economically multipolar world. Inter-imperialist competition underwent a fundamental change after the defeat of Germany and Japan in 1945. The European state system ceased to be the fulcrum of world politics it had earlier become. Instead, the European continent was partitioned between, and its states integrated into, two global military alliances each dominated by one of the superpowers, the US and USSR. This state of affairs had been foreshadowed during the epoch of the two world wars. The instability of the European state system which gave rise to the Thirty Years War of 1914-45 reflected an inability to contain the impact of Germany's rise to the status of a world power. Britain's unprecedented dominance of European politics in the run up to the Second World War represented the attempt of the hitherto chief imperialist power to hold together a fatally weakened state system, a role which Britain, whose relative economic decline was brutally exposed by the war itself, could only perform so long as the two great continental powers, the US and USSR, stayed, as Paul Kennedy puts it, 'off-stage'.[45]

In 1941 Operation Barbarossa and Pearl Harbour marked the end of what one historian has called the 'last European war' as the US and the USSR moved to centre stage. The US definitively replaced Britain as the dominant world power, translating its vast economic strength into overwhelming military power. At the same time its rulers used their predominance in the alliance against Hitler to lay the foundations of a post-war world economy open to US investments and exports in an effort to prevent a repetition of the catastrophe wrought on their economy by the trade wars of the 1930s. The main obstacle to achieving this objective was the Russian ruling class: the fusion of economic and political power achieved by the state capitalist transformations of the 1930s meant that integration into a US dominated world market would threaten the dominance of the Stalinist bureaucracy. Thus the basis was laid for the post-war partition of Europe between two rival military blocs.[46]

The Cold War which emerged from the conflicts among

the victors of 1945 involved a new pattern of inter-imperialist competition. In the first place, military and territorial rivalries among states were forced into a bipolar mould. Previously interstate competition had taken place between a plurality of Great Powers who, while they might temporarily form alliances, typically kept their options open in the endless manoeuvres among the chancelleries of Europe which were the stuff of international politics from the fifteenth to the mid-twentieth centuries. The basic axiom of European statecraft was summed up by one of its arch-practitioners, Palmerston, when he said: 'England has no eternal friends and no eternal enemies, but only eternal interests.' Thus Germany and Russia fought two terrible wars in the twentieth century, despite the long standing friendship of the Houses of Hohenzollern and Romanov over the previous century; Britain and France, almost continually at war between 1689 and 1815, were allies against Germany in the two world wars; British war preparations led Trotsky plausibly to predict a conflict between Britain and the US as early as the beginning of the1920s.[47] International politics lost this fluidity after 1945. The European states were locked into the two superpower blocs, a state of affairs reflecting to varying degrees a convergence of interests among the allied ruling classes and the absence of any other choice.

Inter-state politics was more unstable at the system's margins, in the Third World. Egypt, for example, in the post-war period represents perhaps the most dramatic succession of statuses: British semi-colony, neutralist state balancing between the super-powers, the USSR's most important ally in the Third World, the second biggest recipient of US military aid in the world.[48] Nevertheless, the effective partition of the globe into two superpower blocs imposed severe limits to any state's room for manoeuvre. When Egypt, heavily armed by the USSR despite President Anwar Sadat's expulsion of Russian military advisers in July 1972, launched the Arab states' most successful military offensive against Israel in October 1973, the US responded with a huge airlift of munitions to the shaken Israeli army and even at one point placed its own nuclear forces on alert.[49] The Cold War acted as a kind of straitjacket, forcing individual states to align their actions to the interests of one of the superpower blocs.

Secondly, inter-imperialist competition after 1945 did not lead to any general war among the Great Powers. Wars, of course, continued to rage on the system's periphery, just as they had during the nineteenth century European conquest of Africa and Asia: between 15 and 30 million people died in some 80 wars after 1945, but the core remained at peace.[50] Whatever the reasons (most obviously, the possession of nuclear weapons by both sides which, while it did not render a general war impossible, certainly made both Washington and Moscow more cautious than they might otherwise have been), this was a remarkable interruption of the state of almost continuous warfare which had gripped Europe since the rise of absolutism: even the supposedly pacific nineteenth century had seen a convulsive outburst of wars among the Great Powers between 1855 and 1871 whose outcome was the unification of Italy and Germany and the latter's displacement of France as the main power on the continent. The absence of any general war after 1945 increased the rigidity of world politics, since it deprived capitalism of the main lever through which the state system had hitherto been brought into line with the changing distribution of global economic power. At the same time, however, *preparation* for war became endemic.

The arms race between Britain and Germany before 1914 was dwarfed by that between NATO and the Warsaw Pact which began at the end of the 1940s. Unprecedentedly high peace time levels of arms expenditure were sustained, particularly by the US and the USSR, throughout the generation after 1945. At its peak, in the 1950s and early 1960s, this permanent arms economy had the unintended consequence of offsetting the tendency of the rate of profit to fall, thereby stimulating the longest and most powerful boom in the history of capitalism. Between 1948 and 1973 world income more than trebled.[51]

The long boom is closely related to a third peculiarity of inter-imperialist competition in the post-war era. The partition of the world between the superpower blocs was highly unequal, since the Western alliance included not merely the US, by far the biggest economy in the world, but also Western Europe, Japan and Canada. Not merely did this place the Russian bloc at a severe disadvantage, but it gave rise to an increasingly important contradiction in the Western camp. The inclusion of all the advanced economies into a single political bloc, within which the US was overwhelmingly the dominant military power, created a very large economic space in which competition between capitals did not give rise to the military conflicts endemic before

1945. To that extent the pattern analysed by Bukharin broke down, since inter-imperialist rivalries developed within Western capitalism without there being any tendency for these to be settled through what Shakespeare called 'the bloody arbitrament of war'. Economic competition between capitals was thus dissociated from military conflict between states.

This development had, however, long term consequences which were to prove highly destabilising. The first I shall merely mention here, but I shall return to it below: the global economic order erected under US leadership at the end of the Second World War created an institutional framework (the Bretton Woods agreement etc) which promoted a considerable internationalisation of capital. Secondly, this framework was, as I pointed out above, designed to provide the US with markets and sites of investment. However, the recovery during the long boom of the European and Japanese economies from their wartime devastation (a process promoted by the US to provide bulwarks against domestic revolution and Russian military pressures) led to the emergence of capitals increasingly capable of undermining US dominance of the world market.

The high levels of arms spending which were a condition of American politico-military hegemony diverted capital from productive investments; correlatively, West Germany's and Japan's comparatively low military expenditures made possible very high rates of capital accumulation and consequently the progressive erosion of the competitiveness of US manufacturing industry. By the 1960s US relative economic decline was evident; the resulting intensification of competition within the Western capitalist bloc broke up the international financial system and caused a reduction in American military spending. A weakened arms economy could no longer prevent a fall in the world rate of profit, setting the stage for the great recessions of 1973-4 and 1979-82.[52] A profound contradiction had thus opened up between a political order that remained politically bipolar, but which was economically multipolar. The global distribution of politico-military power no longer corresponded to that of economic power.[53]

2. The Third World: malign neglect and partial industrialisation. The most dramatic change outside the Western capitalist core of the system after 1945 was the dismantling of the great European colonial empires. To some degree this change was caused by the decline of the European powers and their dependence on a US eager to gain access to the colonial markets closed to it between the wars; epic struggles for national liberation—in China, Vietnam, Algeria and the Portuguese colonies—also played their part. But decolonisation as a political process corresponded also to the decreasing importance of what came to be known as the Third World to the advanced capitalist countries. The picture which Lenin had painted of an imperialist system based on the export of capital to the colonies—even in his time, as we have seen, only a partial truth—was completely at odds with the reality of international capitalism after 1945. Summing up the immediate post-war experience Michael Kidron wrote in 1962: 'Capital does not flow overwhelmingly from mature to developing capitalist countries. On the contrary, foreign investments are increasingly made as between developed capitalist countries themselves.'[54] As Table 2 shows, this statement continued to hold true for the world economy between 1965 and 1983. The World Bank reported in 1985:

> about three quarters of foreign direct investment has gone to industrial countries on average since 1965. The remainder has been concentrated for the most part in a few developing countries, predominantly the higher income countries of Asia and Latin America. In particular Brazil... and Mexico have received large volumes of direct investment. Within Asia, Hong Kong, Malaysia, the Philippines, and Singapore have been the largest recipients; Singapore alone has accounted for nearly one-half of total Asia; receipts of foreign direct investment in recent years.[55]

These figures directly contradict the analyses of the world system put forward by dependency theorists such as Gunder Frank and theorists of unequal exchange such as Samir Amin.[56] Far from the prosperity of capitalists (and workers) in the advanced countries depending on the poverty of the Third World, the main flows of capital and commodities (by far the largest share of world trade takes place between developed economies) pass the poor countries by. And of course the main concentration of wealth remains in the Western economies. The explanation is simple enough. As we have seen, the colonies' chief importance under classical imperialism lay in the raw materials they provided

Table 2. Direct foreign investment in selected country groups, 1965-83

	Annual average flow ($bn)				Share of flows (%)			
	65-69	70-74	75-79	80-83	65-69	70-74	75-79	80-83
Industrial countries	5.2	11.0	18.4	31.3	79	86	72	63
Developing countries	1.2	2.8	6.6	13.4	18	22	26	27
Latin America & Caribbean	0.8	1.4	3.4	6.7	12	11	13	14
Africa	0.2	0.6	1.0	1.4	3	5	4	3
Asia, incl Middle East	0.2	0.8	2.2	5.2	3	6	9	11
Other countries and estimated unreported flows	0.2	-1.0	0.6	4.8	3	-8	2	10
TOTAL	6.6	12.8	25.6	49.4	100	100	100	100

[Source: World Bank, World Development Report 1985.]

for the increasingly specialised industrial economies of the imperialist metropolis. But the drive to autarky during the Thirty Years War of 1914-45 involved sustained and successful efforts by the advanced economies to reduce their dependence on imported raw materials: thus synthetic substitutes were developed on a large scale, raw materials were used more efficiently, and the agricultural output of the industrial countries vastly increased.[57] Meanwhile, thanks to the permanent arms economy, the developed countries themselves were booming. Nigel Harris spelled out the consequences of these transformations:

> Rising real incomes in the advanced capitalist countries provided expanding markets for the increasingly sophisticated and highly priced output. And it ensured the profit rates on new investment that continuously sucked in an increasing proportion of the world's new savings. Both labour and capital were dragged out of the backward countries to service the economies of the advanced. The trade between advanced capitalist countries provided the dynamo for an unprecedented expansion in world trade and output in the period after 1948, and for an even greater concentration of capital in the hands of the rich countries. What had been seen by the imperialists as the division of labour in the world between the manufacturing advanced and the raw material exporting backward countries was overtaken by a division between the relatively self-sufficient advanced enclave and a mass of poor dependents.[58]

Both Kidron and Harris, when in the 1960s they first analysed these changes in the relations of advanced and developing economies, noted one very important exception to this pattern of declining Western dependence on raw materials — oil.[59] Indeed, the impact of the two great 'oil shocks' of 1973-4 and 1978-9 is in all likelihood, with the rise of the East Asian NICs, the main explanation for the rise in foreign direct investment in the Third World after 1975 (see Table 2, which shows Asia, including the Middle East, increasing its proportion of foreign direct investment from 3 percent in 1965-9 to 11 percent in 1980-3). Nevertheless, oil is precisely an *exception*. The norm in the Third World was not intensive exploitation by the Western multinationals, but rather the effective exclusion of most poor countries from world trade and investment. The workers and peasants of Africa, Asia and Latin America toiled in abject poverty less because the fruits of their exploitation were the main source of imperialist profits than because their labour was irrelevant to the main centres of capital in North America, Western Europe, and Japan—unless, as millions from the Third World did, they followed this capital to its home bases.

It did not follow, however, that, as Frank and Amin claimed, the entire Third World was condemned to permanent stagnation. On the contrary, some less developed countries were able to attain high levels of industrial growth. In particular, the rise during the 1970s and 1980s of the Newly Industrialising Countries (NICs) of East Asia and Latin America marked a significant shift in the world division of labour. Earlier phases of industrialisation outside the imperialist centre had typically involved the production of previously imported consumer goods. The two world wars allowed several of the more important colonies and semi-colonies (for example, India, Egypt, South Africa, Argentina) to take advantage of the metropolitan manufacturing industries' diversion to military production to encourage local capitalists to produce for their own domestic markets.

After 1945 many Third World states sought to continue this import substitution industrialisation, the most ambitious—China under Mao, India under Nehru, Egypt under Nasser—copying the bureaucratic command methods of Stalinist Russia in the hope of building up their own heavy industrial base.

These essays in autarkic state capitalism were generally unable to mobilise from within their own borders the resources necessary for the huge investments on which the heavy industries of the advanced countries rested. Thus Nasser's efforts in the late 1950s and the 1960s to build up state owned heavy industry were made possible by the large reserves of foreign exchange accumulated during the boom in Egypt's main export, cotton, during the Korean War. These reserves financed the imports of machinery, components and other inputs needed to build up Egypt's industrial base. But when the foreign exchange ran out, further imports could only be financed by exports, where Egyptian industry could not compete, or by Russian loans, which were paid for in exports of cotton and rice shipped to the USSR. The failure of Nasser's state capitalist policies lay behind Sadat's pursuit of *infitah*, the opening of Egypt to the world economy.[60]

The NICs of East Asia and Latin America marked a significant divergence from this pattern. Whereas Mao, Nehru and Nasser had sought to follow Stalin in pursuing state capitalist autarky, states such as South Korea and Brazil oriented themselves on the world market. They produced manufactured goods not necessarily (or even, in some cases, primarily) for the domestic market, but for export. And in general they were able to break into world trade in manufactured goods by rigorous state capitalist methods. The South Korean state, for example, exercised centralised direction of private investment, not, however, to attempt to reproduce the kind of diversified industrial economy characteristic of the most advanced countries, but to iden-tify those international markets into which its capitalists could hope to break provided that resources were concentrated on a limited number of industries. The interventionist state, operating frequently in defiance of the free market axioms of neo-classical economics, served as a battering ram into the world market rather than as a means of escaping it.[61]

Does the emergence of the NICs confirm Warren's claim that 'we are...in an era of declining imperialism and advanced capitalism'? Undoubtedly the partial industrialisation of some of the Third World is an event of considerable significance, both be-cause it represents the crystallisation of new, relatively inde-pendent centres of capital accumulation, a development whose political significance I discuss below, and because of the con-siderable expansion of the world working class for which it was responsible. It is, however, essential to stress that the rise of the NICs marked only a *partial* transformation of the Third World. This became very clear with the onset of the debt crisis of the 1980s. In the 1970s Western banks responded to the interna-tionalisation of financial markets, the scarcity of investment op-portunities in the depressed advanced economies, and the oversupply of capital (idle Western funds having been boosted by an influx of oil revenues from the Gulf) by massively in-creasing their loans to the Third World. The onset of a second major world recession in 1979 made it impossible for the debtor economies to generate the export earnings required to repay these loans: the result was the crisis which exploded when Mexico defaulted on its loans in August 1982.

The less developed countries found themselves unable to raise new loans. They were under enormous pressure from their Western creditors to repay a foreign debt amounting to $1,089.2 billion in 1987, 49.5 percent of the capital importing developing countries' gross national product.[62] For much of the 1980s these countries actually transferred more financial resources to the advanced economies than they received in new loans and investment and in foreign trade (see Table 3). The result, for much of the Third World, was stagnation. The United Nations reported at the end of the 1980s:

> During the 1970s, per capita output in all developing countries grew faster than in the developed market economies and the gap was narrowing. In the 1930s, the situation has been more complex. An important group of Asian countries, large and small, has been growing faster, in both overall terms and per capita terms, than the developed market economies... Others, mostly in Africa and Latin America, have been caught in a slow growth trap and their international linkages have been negative rather than positive.[63]

Table 3. The debt crisis: net transfer of financial resources to the capital importing developing countries, 1980-88
($bn; sample of 98 countries)

	80	81	82	83	84	85	86	87	88
Net transfer through direct investment	4.5	0.8	-2.0	-2.8	-2.4	-1.0	-1.3	0.4	4.0
Net transfer through private credit	17.2	7.5	-18.7	-26.5	-33.0	-40.9	-32.1	-34.7	-46.0
Net transfer through official flows	29.0	34.3	32.0	28.6	25.8	16.3	12.7	8.7	8.0
Net transfer	41.7	42.6	11.3	-0.7	-9.6	-25.5	-26.7	-25.6	-32.5

[Source: United Nations, *World Economic Survey 1989*.]

Put more crudely, not merely did the debtor states have to transfer resources to their Western creditors, but they had to submit to IMF-dictated 'structural adjustment programmes' which typically required austerity measures as a way of restricting domestic consumption and boosting the exports needed to fund debt repayments. The worst victim was sub-Saharan Africa. At the end of 1989 the World Bank reported: 'Overall Africans are as poor today as they were 30 years ago.'[64] Parts of the continent had slipped even further back—the Horn of Africa, Angola and Mozambique, where war and famine caused deaths in the hundreds of thousands, even millions. What links remained with the world economy were often of the most primitive kind. Lonrho hired its own private army to guard its plantations in Mozambique. Even the relatively industrialised economies of Latin America went through an appalling experience of stagnation, hyper-inflation and pauperisation. The dynamic East Asian NICs—the 'Four Tigers' (South Korea, Taiwan, Singapore and Hong Kong), were now joined by others, such as Malaysia, Thailand and the Philippines—seemed to be an exception, to be explained in large part by the increasing flow into the region of capital and exports from the most competitive of the advanced economies, Japan.

It would be a mistake, however, to see the debt crisis as simply marking the imposition of a new form of 'dependency' on the Third World. James Petras and Michael Morley have pointed to the phenomenon of capital flight in Latin America— the transfer of locally owned capital to the advanced economies, amounting to an estimated $100 billion compared to Latin America's foreign debt of $368 billion in 1985:

> Large-scale investments and bank deposits by Latin Americans primarily to the USA and Europe—'capital flight'— registered the rise of a new class stratum in Latin America: the transnational capitalists... Local capitalists are transferring their savings to multinational banks which in turn lend capital to Latin American states. These states in turn lend to private capitalists. This behaviour allows private capitalists to protect their savings while risking foreign debt which is guaranteed by the local state. External borrowing and overseas investment have become a lucrative way of life for a small but powerful stratum of capitalists. When local conditions are unfavourable, gains can be maximised through international financial circuits; national productive activity becomes secondary, almost a pretext, for increasing flows of loans and investment. When conditions become more favourable, then capital can shift back from international circuits into local investments.[65]

The debt crisis thus involves not so much a conflict between nation states, rich versus poor countries, but a class struggle, in which the Latin American bourgeoisie, increasingly integrated into international financial circuits, aligns itself with the Western banks and multinational corporations in demanding solutions which further open up their economies to the world market. As Petras and Morley observe, '[a]usterity has a different meaning for those who are able to move their assets outside the domestic environment than for those whose assets or livelihood[s] are immobile and are being directly affected by debt payments and lMF austerity programmes.'[66]

3. Internationalisation of capital. The evolution of the Third World thus reveals the same process evident at the centre of the world system—the increasing international integration of capital. We can say of the two main tendencies in terms of which Bukharin defined imperialism that, if the first, towards state capitalism, dominated in the period 1875-1945, the second, towards the internationalisation of capital, became increasingly important after 1945.[67]

Developing during the long boom, but if anything accelerated in the subsequent years of protracted crisis, this trend towards the global integration of capital had three main dimensions: first, the internationalisation of production through the emergence of what Nigel Harris calls a 'global manufacturing system', organised primarily by the great multinational corporations; secondly, the growing weight of international trade, made possible by the political unity of Western capitalism and the formation and expansion of the European Community, but to a significant degree involving transactions within multinational companies and their outworks of component suppliers; thirdly, the development of international financial circuits largely outside the control of nation states, a process promoted by the growing inability of the US to perform its post-war role as lynchpin of the global monetary system, and accelerated by the manias for deregulation and stockmarket speculation characteristic of the Reagan-Thatcher era.

The most important consequence of these changes was drastically to reduce the ability of the nation state to direct the economic activities taking place within its borders. What Harris calls 'the end of capitalism in one country' was a major factor in the great recessions of the mid and late 1970s. Keynesian demand management techniques proved to be feeble instruments of economic control when profitability sank and money could cross the globe in microseconds. The global integration of the system made itself felt in a variety of ways, from the collapse of the Mitterrand government's attempt in 1981-3 to reflate the French economy at a time of world wide slump to the retreat from autarky by Third World regimes previously bitterly hostile to *laissez faire* such as China under Deng Xiaoping and South Africa under PW Botha.

It was, however, those economies where the tendency towards nationally organised capitalism which proved in the end to be hardest hit by the internationalisation of capital. The revolutions in Eastern Europe and the collapse of the Soviet Union marked the point at which the Stalinist regimes, increasingly disabled by their bureaucratic command economies from reaping the benefits of participation in the international division of labour, finally broke under the strain, cracking open to allow the incorporation of these states into the global market. It was obvious to all (except the eccentric Dr Fukuyama dreaming of the end of history) that a new epoch in world history had begun.[68]

Imperialism after the Cold War

1. Back to a world that is politically as well as economically multipolar. The Eastern European revolutions marked the end of the Cold War, in the sense of the partition of the globe into two competing imperialist blocs. The replacement of the Stalinist regimes by governments which, whether liberal, authoritarian or neo-Stalinist in political coloration, were committed to policies designed to push their economies deeper into the world market and the disintegration of the Warsaw Pact as an effective military alliance amounted to the collapse of any coherent Eastern Bloc. A large chunk of Central and Eastern Europe suddenly tipped into the Western sphere of influence. At the same time, a variety of factors—arms negotiations between the superpowers, the economic crisis in the USSR, domestic isolationist pressures in the US, the unification of Germany, and the second Gulf War led to a rapid rundown of the huge concentrations of troops and weapons on the Central Front in Europe. Meanwhile, outside Europe, a weakened USSR had already been compelled in the late 1980s to make massive concessions to Western interests in various regions, perhaps most notably Indochina and southern Africa. The fall of Stalinism left Third World regimes and movements which had previously been able to rely on Russian support isolated.

One popular interpretation of these changes has been that they have allowed the US to assume a position of global predominance even greater than it had enjoyed in the aftermath of the Second World War. Particularly with the onset of the Western assault on Iraq it became popular to proclaim the US the 'lone superpower'. The *Independent on Sunday* asked:

> Where are the Germans and Japanese now? They are not to be found in the Gulf, unless as businessmen. How very clever, some will say, to go on busily manufacturing motor cars and computers while America and Britain sacrifice themselves on behalf of the West. But what is the end of the sacrifice? In America's case it could be an apotheosis of her military and economic might. It must be dawning on the world that no other country could design and produce so many wonders of technology and then ship them on such a scale halfway across the world and use them to such apparent effect. No other country would want to; certainly not the Soviet Union, preoccupied in trying to hold itself together. That is the point about being a superpower. It is a matter of ability and of will. Only the United States has both.[69]

Arguments of this kind are not wholly invalid. The immediate impact of the Eastern European revolutions was to increase the global political and military weight of the US. But proclamations of a 'one superpower world' wholly mistake the real tendency of events. The collapse of Stalinism was an episode of world historical importance precisely because it broke up the rigid bipolar division of the world characteristic of the post-war era and thereby allowed a return to an era of much more fluid inter-imperialist competition, in which a plurality of Great Powers dominated the stage rather than the two superpowers. The economic preconditions of this political transformation were laid in the Cold War era: the relative economic decline of both the US and the USSR, the increasing domination of world trade by other major capitalist powers, notably Germany and Japan, and the emergence of the NICs represented marked shifts in the global balance of forces which had increasingly destabilised the system in the two decades after 1968. But it was only after the disintegration of the Eastern Bloc that the political contours of this new phase of inter-imperialist competition became clear.

Germany, already the world's largest exporter and the dominant force in the European Community, had re-emerged as a world power thanks to unification and the retreat of Russian influence in central and Eastern Europe. Japan's dynamic export economy had made possible in the 1980s a huge surge in foreign investment, including much of the loans needed to fund America's foreign debt. The USSR's collapse helped to make more visible the growing tensions between the US and the other major Western powers, especially the German-led EC. The German ruling class, their political confidence boosted by the Federal Republic's astonishingly rapid absorption of East Germany, seemed increasingly willing to shake off Washington's reins: thus Chancellor Helmut Kohl settled the question of unified Germany's membership of NATO in bilateral negotiations with Mikhail Gorbachev in July 1990, without bothering to consult the Bush administration. More threateningly, Bonn was instrumental in holding the EC to the hard line which caused the collapse of the GATT trade talks in December 1990, conjuring up fears of a tariff war comparable to that of the 1930s. Finally, Germany's and Japan's reluctance fully to endorse US policy in the Gulf threatened to make their 'disloyalty' to the Western alliance a major issue in American domestic politics.

The growing conflicts among the Western capitalist powers highlighted the contradictory position of the US itself. The Reagan administration of 1981-9 had sought to reverse America's relative economic decline. In fact, its effective economic policy, increased public and private spending financed by large scale borrowing, served instead further to reduce US competitiveness and to create the 'twin deficits'—on state expenditure and the balance of payments—which transformed America into the world's greatest debtor. In the 1980s the US came to depend on a net transfer of financial resources from the rest of the world, rich and poor alike (see Table 4). The most notable domestic economic trends were a vast speculative investment in real estate and the stock market— exciting in the height of the junk bond boom in the mid-1980s but resulting in the almighty hangover of the Savings and Loans crisis, which involved by 1990 some $500 billion of bad debts— and a reorientation of manufacturing industry towards military production, a shift which reflected the huge increase in arms spending begun by the Carter administration at the end of 1970s and continued under Reagan.[70] This 'military Keynesianism' itself exacerbated US capitalism's long term problems by diverting resources from productive investments which might have enhanced American industries' competitiveness. Indeed, it highlighted the US economy's growing dependence on imports. According to one Congressional study, over 80 percent of the semi-conductors used in the high tech weapons systems so widely praised as a sign of America's technological prowess were in fact produced in Asia, mainly in Japan.[71]

Nevertheless, the expansion and reconstruction of the US military apparatus in the 1980s gave the American ruling class the means to pursue strategies designed to compensate for economic decline by reasserting their military and political leadership of the Western capitalist bloc.[72] These strategies were pursued along various dimensions. First, Reagan sought to use the period of heightened confrontation with the USSR after the invasion of Afghanistan in 1979 to force Japan and Western Europe into line — for example, attempting to sabotage the USSR's gas pipeline deals and to impose sanctions on Poland after the December 1981 coup. Secondly, and more successfully than these fiascos, Washington promoted the development of right wing guerilla movements — the Nicaraguan Contras, and UNITA in Angola — which were intended, along with economic pressures, to subvert hostile Third World regimes.[73] Thirdly, a series of efforts were made to overcome the 'Vietnam syndrome' — American domestic opposition to direct military intervention abroad — with a growing measure of success: Lebanon 1982-3, Grenada 1983, Libya 1986, the Gulf 1987-8, Panama 1989-90.

The American naval build up which allowed Iraq to defeat Iran in the first Gulf War was probably the most important of these interventions. In the first place, the Gulf, containing 54 percent of the world's oil reserves, is the most important economic region outside the core areas of North America, Western Europe and Japan. Secondly, the Iranian Revolution of 1978-9 was second only to the Vietnam War among the defeats US imperialism suffered during that decade. It was in response to this humiliation that Jimmy Carter announced in January 1980 the doctrine bearing his name, under which the US declared its willingness to go to war if its interests in the Gulf were threatened. In line with this policy the Rapid Deployment Force was established. Renamed Central Command it provided the framework

Table 4: US financial dependence: net resource transfers to the US, by regions, 1980-88* ($bn)

	1980	1981	1982	1983	1984	1985	1986	1987	1988
Canada	-0.3	0.8	8.3	9.4	12.7	13.4	10.6	9.8	7.7
Japan	9.8	14.9	15.9	23.2	36.2	42.8	54.5	56.2	50.5
W. Europe	-16.6	-9.0	-2.9	5.8	23.3	32.5	36.3	35.5	22.4
(of which) W. Germany	1.8	2.4	4.8	7.8	12.8	15.4	18.9	20.2	
Latin America & Caribbean	-0.9	-4.4	6.3	20.0	22.8	18.7	15.2	16.9	11.8
(of which) Mexico	-2.4	-5.1	4.5	10.4	8.3	7.9	7.9	8.8	
Major oil exporters of Africa & Asia	36.1	26.6	7.6	2.7	6.2	4.0	2.5	7.6	4.7
Other developing countries	-2.5	0.7	2.2	11.0	21.3	22.4	32.7	41.4	46.4
European planned economies	-2.5	-2.8	-2.7	-1.5	-2.0	-1.1	0.2	0.0	-1.3
Other countries	-0.1	-4.7	-3.4	-5.9	-3.7	-2.9	-1.9	-3.2	4.5
TOTAL	23.0	22.1	31.3	64.7	116.9	129.8	150.1	164.3	127.8

* i.e. balance of payments on goods, private transfers and services other than investment income, with sign reversed.
[Source. United Nations, *World Economic Survey 1989.*]

of the US military build up in the Gulf in the summer of 1990. Thirdly, the methods used by the Reagan administration to defeat Iran in 1987-8—for example, the use of the United Nations Security Council (and hence the tacit compliance of the USSR) to sanction the American naval build up and close co-operation with key Arab states such as Saudi Arabia and Egypt—foreshadowed Bush's strategy against his erstwhile ally Saddam Hussein, namely the construction of a UN-approved international coalition to legitimise the US's first real ground war since Vietnam. As Robert McFarlane, formerly Reagan's National Security Assistant, noted when Iran finally sued for peace in July 1988, 'we ought to remember how we did it, for we may have to do it again.'[74]

Bush's decision to 'do it again' on a far greater scale by going to war against Iraq did not simply mark Washington's effort decisively to break the Vietnam syndrome or even the policy, implicit in the Carter Doctrine, of preventing any other power from acquiring a dominant position in the Gulf. The second Gulf War is only intelligible against the background of the more fluid and unstable period of inter-imperialist competition opened up by the East European revolutions. As Bush and his advisers made plain in numerous speeches, the war drive in the Gulf was a means of reasserting American global political and military leadership. Seizing the opportunity offered by the USSR's retreat on the world stage and implosion into an all absorbing domestic crisis, Washington sought to use the Gulf crisis to demonstrate to the world's ruling classes that the stability of the global economy depended ultimately on the military power of the American state. The message was aimed most specifically at Bush's restive allies in Tokyo and Bonn both to remind them that only the Pentagon could guarantee the security of their oil supplies and to bind them more tightly to US diplomatic leadership.

In fact, the immediate effect of the second Gulf War was to intensify the conflicts within the Western Bloc. The rows provoked by Washington's demand that the European and Japanese allies should contribute to the costs of the war, Germany's reluctance to come to Turkey's aid should the latter NATO state be drawn into the war, France's equivocal stance in the final days of peace—none of this seemed to augur the beginning of the new Pax Americana predicted by some commentators.[75] The fact that the Bush administration expected to raise $36 billion of the estimated $50 billion cost of the war from contributions from Saudi Arabia, Kuwait and other allies only indicated how far the US had declined from its global economic predominance after 1945.[76] The US had come a long way from the days of Lend Lease, when it financed the Allied war effort against Germany and Japan. As Noam Chomsky sardonically observed, America seemed to have become less the world's policeman than the world's mercenary: 'We carry out the intervention, and other people pay for it.'[77]

2. The rise of sub-imperialisms in the Third World. A key factor in the development of a more pluralistic and therefore more unstable world order has been the rise over the past two decades of the sub-imperialisms — that is, of Third World powers aspiring to the kind of political and military domination on a regional scale which the superpowers have enjoyed globally. The Middle East, as the most unstable region since 1945 (the second Gulf War in 1991 was the seventh major war in the area; there have in addition been several civil wars and protracted insurgencies), is unfortunate enough to have the largest number of contenders for this role — Israel, Iran, Iraq, Egypt, Syria, and Turkey. But there are others elsewhere: India, Vietnam, South Africa, Nigeria, Brazil, and Argentina are among the most important examples. A conflict between two of these powers — Iran and Iraq — led to the first Gulf War (1980-88), the longest period of conventional warfare this century. Soon the US found itself fighting the victor in that earlier war. Plainly the nature of the sub-imperialisms is a crucial issue in any attempt at understanding contemporary imperialism.

Behind the phenomenon of the sub-imperialisms lies the partial industrialisation of the Third World and the consequent emergence of new centres of capital accumulation outside the imperialist core. As in the case of the original emergence of imperialism in the latter part of the nineteenth century, the possession of a developed industrial base has typically been a pre-requisite for building up regional military power. Typically, but not universally: Vietnam emerged after the final defeat of the US in 1975 as the dominant power in Indochina, even though its economy had been shattered by war and was to be further weakened by the Western trade and aid embargo orchestrated from Washington. Nevertheless, the rise of the sub-imperialisms poses in its acutest form the question of the political consequences of the development of industrial capitalism in the Third World.

A fairly widespread response on the left has been simply to deny these trends any significance. Typically this has involved invoking what has been the orthodoxy among left nationalists and Third Worldists for the past generation, namely the idea that de-colonisation represented a purely superficial change in the rela-tions between rich and poor countries. The ties of economic dependence on the advanced countries have, on this account, kept the ex-colonies in effectively the same position as they were before independence. Constitutionally these 'neo-colonies' or 'semi-colonies' may be sovereign, but the real relations of global power mean that they are still finally subordinated to the West-ern imperialist countries. The term 'sub-imperialism' was orig-inally coined within this theoretical framework. Thus Fred Halliday wrote of the Middle East in 1974, when he was still in-fluenced by Maoism and a firm opponent of imperialism:

> The stability of the imperialist system in the area has rested on building up a set of intermediate capitalist states which are in general populous and strong enough to play a major regional role. These are sub-imperialist states, intermedi-aries in the exploitative whole. The armies and ruling classes of these states are the major agents of imperialism in the area, while imperialism itself maintains bases and pro-vides covert aid.[78]

The obvious difficulty with this kind of approach is that it is just implausible to describe capitalist states such as Is-lamic Republican Iran and Ba'athist Iraq—which have been prepared to defy and even, in the latter case, to fight the US—merely as 'agents' of imperialism. Some Third World ruling classes plainly have a considerable degree of autonomy from the imperialist powers. In the reaction over the past decade or so against dependency theory and related notions such as neo-colonialism, quite large sections of the left have moved to the opposite extreme. Bill Warren, for example, argued: 'The con-cept of dependence has always been imprecise; such signifi-cance as it has relates almost entirely to political control of one country by another.' An implication of this claim, which Warren tacitly drew, was that the attainment of political inde-pendence provided the bourgeoisie in the Third World with the means to end their dependence on the advanced economies.[79] In line with this kind of thinking, some Iranian socialists adopted a defeatist position during the First Gulf War, even after the US intervened in the summer of 1987, arguing that Iran was a developed capitalist power in essence comparable to the US. Without even the excuse which the Iranian left had of having suffered at the hands of the mullahs' secret police, *New Left Review* adopted a similar stance in the lead up to the second Gulf War, declaring: 'The Left should not support the military ambitions of any of the predators now confronting one another in the desert.'[80]

There is something pretty absurd about equating Iraq, with a population of 17.8 million and a GNP per capita of $2,140, and the United States, with a population of 245.8 million and GNP per capita of $19,780.[81] How then are we properly to measure the difference between them? Let us note first the elements of truth advanced by Warren and other opponents of dependency theory. In the first place, the formation of a constitutionally independent state undoubtedly can act as the focus of crystallisation of an autonomous capitalist class: even a venal regime heavily dependent on external support is likely to promote some economic development in order to widen its social base and increase the national income from which state revenues can be extracted; and activities designed to consolidate the territorial power of the new state—for example school and road building—will also create the conditions for capital accumulation. The imperialist carve up of the Middle East after the First World War, when most of the modern states in the region were created under the aegis of London or Paris, provides illustrations of this process. Thus Hanna Batatu writes of Iraq under Faisal I, who had been summarily removed by the British from the kingdom of Syria he had proclaimed after the Arab rising and placed instead on a new throne in Baghdad in 1921:

> Though a creation of the English, the Hashemite monarchy was, in the first two decades of its life, animated by a spirit inherently antithetical to theirs. Owing to the initial intimate interweaving of its dynastic interests with the fortunes of the pan-Arab movement, its basic instinct in the period 1921-1939 was to further—to the extent that its status of dependence permitted—the work of nation-building in Iraq.

Thus Faisal drastically expanded the education system as a means of forging a sense of national identity in a highly diverse population, as he put it, 'devoid of any patriotic idea, imbued with religious traditions and absurdities, connected by no common tie', and sought to build up the army as an instrument of independent state power. The British responded by seeking to restrict the size of the army and building up the power of the tribal chiefs in order to weaken the embryonic nation state Faisal sought to build.[82] A similar process took place in the Arabian peninsula, where the Wahhabi zealots under Ibn Saud succeeded in the early 1920s in driving out Faisal's father, Hussein, the Sharif of Mecca. Ibn Saud was as much a British client as the Hashemites, only he was financed and armed by the India Office, and they by the Foreign Office. (Arnold Toynbee commented: 'It would be cheaper... and more manly of the civil servants in the two belligerent departments, if these had fought each other direct'.)[83] But even the state Ibn Saud created, Saudi Arabia, despite its dynastic politics and reactionary Islamic ideology, was able to use its oil revenues to generate substantial capitalist development.[84]

This process of state building took place, however, within definite limits. In part these were economic. The British ambassador to Iraq reported to the Foreign Office in 1934:

> The foreign commercial interests in Iraq are, owing to the existence of the British connection, predominantly British... The greater part of the country's foreign trade is carried in British ships. The foreign capital sunk in the country is almost exclusively British. Two out of three banks are entirely British ... All important insurance business is in the hands of British firms. In another sphere of activity, the Euphrates and Tigris Steam Navigation Co is a long established British company ... operating, with but one native competitor, rival transport on the Tigris between Basrah and Baghdad... In every direction, despite the intense Japanese competition, British commercial influence remains paramount.[85]

In addition to these ties of economic dependence, the Arab states were bound to the metropolitan power by formal political restrictions. Thus the Anglo-Iraqi Treaty of 1930, effectively renewed by the 1948 Portsmouth agreement, guaranteed Britain air bases and control over the country's foreign policy. Behind such formal ties lay the reality of imperial military power. When King Farouk of Egypt refused to appoint the Prime Minister proposed to him by the British ambassador, his palace was surrounded by tanks on 4 February 1942, until he gave way. States in this position, even though constitutionally independent, are effectively semi-colonies.[86]

Memories of such humiliating subordination to the imperialist powers survived long after the acquisition by these states of a much more effective degree of independence. They help to explain why anti-imperialist rhetoric continues to have a massive popular appeal in countries which can no longer in any sense be regarded as semi-colonies. What factors were involved in the emergence in the Third World of autonomous capitalist classes capable of aspiring to a sub-imperial role? First, decolonisation did play a part, because of what the dismantlement of the European colonial empires implied in economic terms. The exclusive control of colonial and semi-colonial economies by individual metropolitan powers was now replaced by a more fluid state of affairs in which multinational corporations from a variety of Western states invested in the same country, giving the local state room for manoeuvre between them and the tax revenues to promote the expansion of native capital. The transformation of the southern Irish economy over the past generation is a case in point: no longer an exporter of agricultural commodities to Britain, the southern state has become a major site of direct investment by US, West European and Japanese firms, especially in the chemicals and manufacturing industries which have now outstripped food, drink and tobacco as its main source of exports.[87]

This much more diversified relationship to Western capital has been accompanied, secondly, by the expansion of locally controlled industrial capitalism. One of the most careful discussions of this question is by two Argentine Marxists, Alexandro Dabat and Luis Lorenzano. Challenging the consensus on the Argentine left, including orthodox Trotskyist groups such as the MAS (Movement for Socialism), that Argentina is a Western 'semi-colony', they argue that the country experienced after 1945 'capitalist development on a state monopolist base' characterised by the stagnation of foreign investment from the late 1960s onwards and the growth, not merely of state intervention in the economy, but of state owned industries. Consequently, 'the bourgeoisie as a whole is the dominant class and... its most powerful fraction is now the modern monopolist-finance bourgeoisie (which articulates big agrarian, industrial and commercial capital) fused with state capital and the civil-military bureaucracy.'[88]

Dabat and Lorenzano therefore reject the view that Argentina is a 'dependent' capitalism, its bourgeoisie mere compradors:

> Argentina is a net importer of capital and of the goods (including technology) that it needs for expanded reproduction and intensive industrialisation. But from the 1960s onwards, as it increased its technological and financial independence, Argentinian capitalism began to develop an export industry and to strengthen its role as a regional exporter of capital. Since 1966, it has also managed to resume its role as a major grain exporter, while its powerful military state-machine has extended its sphere of operations into the Southern Cone, Central America and the South Atlantic. These active phenomena should be seen as expressing the 'external' interests of Argentinian capitalism—that is to say, a stage of externally oriented expansion in which commercial, financial and military factors are substantively unified. It is thus possible to characterise Argentina as an emerging regional capitalist power, combining financial, commercial and technological dependence with the development of a capitalist monopolist economy with regional imperialist features.[89]

On the basis of this analysis Dabat and Lorenzano attack the position taken by the bulk of the Argentine left during the Falklands/Malvinas War of 1982, when they supported the Galtieri regime against Britain on grounds well expressed by the MAS: 'Britain is an imperialist country, Argentina is a semicolonial country. We workers fight on the side of the colonised in any confrontation between an imperialist country and a semicolonial country'. Rejecting this left nationalism, Dabat and Lorenzano argue:

> The war... was a continuation of the Junta's anti-democratic internal policy and its expansionist external thrust. Although it was waged against British imperialism for a historically legitimate claim, it was neither an anti-colonial conflict nor a

struggle by an oppressed against an oppressor nation. The contending parties were an emergent capitalist country with regional and continental imperialist features, and a long-standing imperialist power which, though in marked decline, is still a powerful force. There was not a progressive and a reactionary camp... One reactionary side was bent on extending its influence, while the other was concerned to retain the last wisps of its former empire and to establish a pecking order among the national components of the capitalist bloc.[90]

Generalising from this broadly correct analysis of the Falklands War, we could then argue that the same process of capitalist development which gave rise to imperialism in the first place now produces sub-imperialism. As centres of capital accumulation crystallise outside the imperialist core of the system, the tendencies analysed by Lenin, Bukharin and Hilferding towards monopoly, finance and state capitalism take on an even more pronounced form, given the central role of state intervention in promoting Third World industrialisation. Inevitably, the expansion of industrial capitalism bursts out of national borders, giving rise to regional conflicts between rival sub-imperialisms—between Greece and Turkey, India and Pakistan, Iran and Iraq—and often, in the absence of such rivalries, to the growing regional dominance of a particular sub-imperialism (South Africa in southern Africa, Australia in the South Pacific).[91]

While this analysis has a large measure of truth, it is essential to qualify it. For the rise of the sub-imperialisms has not taken place in a vacuum. Nor has it created a world composed of capitalist states the differences between whose power are ones of degree rather than of kind. The bulk of the world's industrial production and military power is still concentrated in North America, Western Europe, Japan and the USSR: indeed, in 1984 the less developed countries' share of world industrial production was 13.9 percent, marginally less than the 14.0 percent share they had achieved by 1948 thanks to import-substitution during the Great Depression and the Second World War, but subsequently lost as a result of the long boom of the 1950s and 1960s.[92] This imbalance in economic power is reflected in the politico-military hierarchy which exists among the world's states, and in particular the dominant role of the Western imperialist powers. The emergence of regional powers in the Third World has altered but not abolished this hierarchy. Indeed—and this is the third factor at work in the rise of the sub-imperialisms—the policies of the superpowers have played a major part in permitting certain medium sized states to aspire to regional dominance.

Thus the very origins of the term 'sub-imperialism' can be traced to the strategy pursued by American capitalism as part of an attempt to extricate itself from the Vietnamese catastrophe. Called the Nixon Doctrine, after the President who first publicly announced the policy in July 1969, it envisaged part of the burden of defending Western interests in the Third World being taken on by regional powers which would receive in exchange military and economic aid. Iran under the Shah is a good example of the way in which industrialising Third World states sought to fill the vacuum left by a politically weakened imperialism— in this case, the Gulf after Britain's final withdrawal East of Suez in 1971.[93] More generally, sub-imperialisms have been able to aspire to a regional role not merely by virtue of a certain level of capitalist development, but thanks to the support of one or both of the superpowers.

Usually it has been the US, as the most powerful imperialist state in the world, which has acted as the patron of regional powers, but Russian aid to Vietnam allowed Hanoi to dominate Indochina despite an economy that was a basket case, and India has attained hegemony in South Asia thanks in large part to its ability to manoeuvre between the two superpowers, both of which were eager to cultivate good relations with it.

It does not follow that sub-imperialisms are mere puppets of their superpower sponsors. The arrangements which permit certain states to play regional roles typically rest on a convergence of interests between the two ruling classes concerned, rather than the control of patron over client. Interests that converge can also conflict. Thus, even the sub-imperialism most directly dependent on US military and economic aid, Israel (US aid at its peak of \$4.2 billion in 1986 amounted to 18 percent of Israeli gross national product) has been able often to defy Washington—the Shamir government's obduracy over the Palestinian question led US Secretary of State James Baker publicly to express his anger and frustration only weeks before the Iraqi invasion of Kuwait in 1991. Nevertheless, there are limits to the autonomy of any sub-imperialism which, if infringed, may lead to a direct confrontation with the Great Powers.

It is only in this context that events in the Gulf over the past decade become intelligible. The Iranian Revolution of 1978-9 removed the US's most powerful ally in the area. Willy nilly Washington began to tilt in the direction of the only state willing and able to take over the Shah's role, the Ba'athist regime in Iraq. The subsequent evolution of American policy gives the lie to those socialists who saw the first Gulf War of 1980-8 as a regional version of 1914-18, a struggle between two sub-imperialisms in which workers on each side should welcome their own government's defeat. Dilip Hiro summarises the US attitude:

> So long as stalemate prevailed on the front lines Washington was content to maintain a semblance of neutrality in the conflict. But as the scales began to tilt increasingly in Iran's favour in late 1983, the US changed its position and stated that Iraq's defeat would be against its interests.
> With every Iranian military success—from the Majnoon Islands in 1984 to Fao in 1986 and Shalamanche a year later—Washington increased its backing to Baghdad, culminating in an unprecedented naval build up in the Gulf and, for all practical purposes, the opening of a second front against the Islamic Republic.[94]

Iran's defeat in the first Gulf War was a brutal demonstration of US imperialism's ability to determine the outcome of regional conflicts. Soon, however, a much more savage display of American military power was mounted to crush the state which had won that war with Washington's support. The Iraqi invasion of Kuwait was a direct consequence of the first Gulf War, both because the Ba'athist regime sought to solve the economic crisis inherited from the war and to consolidate its regional hegemony by seizing Kuwait and its oil wealth, and because the good relations between Washington and Baghdad encouraged Saddam Hussein to misread the ambiguous signals coming from the State Department ('we have no opinion on the Arab-Arab conflicts, like your border disagreements with Kuwait,' the US ambassador to Iraq told him on 25 July 1990[95]) as a green light. The Bush administration decided, for reasons discussed above, to treat the invasion as sufficient cause for war. As a result, the difference between an imperialist and a sub-imperialist power was established beyond any serious dispute in the bombardment of Baghdad and the slaughter of fleeing Iraqi troops on the Basra highway.

3. A precarious balance between nation state and world market. The internationalisation of capital has, as we have seen, been a major factor in undermining the political and economic arrangements characteristic of post war imperialism. This tendency has, however, often been misinterpreted both by neo-liberals such as Tim Congdon and by some socialists as marking the effective obsolescence of the nation state.[96] Such arguments are mistaken. Although the pronounced tendency towards the global integration of capital over the past generation has severely reduced the ability of states to control economic activities within their borders, private capitals continue to rely on the nation state to which they are most closely attached to protect them against the competition of other capitals, the effects of economic crisis, and the resistance of those they exploit. This is obvious enough in the economic sphere. The long recovery of the Western economies from the 1979-82 recession would have been inconceivable without the spread of classical Keynesian policies of high state spending and easy credit from the US to Britain, Japan and, finally, Germany. More spectacularly, the collapse of the world financial system during the stockmarket crash of October 1987 was averted only thanks to the intervention of the US Federal Reserve Board and other Western central banks. The economic role of the state in Western capitalism may have been reduced and partially restructured, but it is the merest monetarist fantasy that it is being, or can be, abolished.[97]

The intensified competition made possible by the internationalisation of capital has if anything exacerbated the national antagonisms within the world's bourgeoisie. This is most evident in the tendency for the biggest economies in the world to form regional trade blocs around them. This process is most advanced in Europe; German trade and investment are heavily concentrated on the European continent. But there are striking similarities in the prodigious expansion of Japanese capital and commodities into East Asia over the past few years and in the conclusion in August 1992 of the North American Free Trade Agreement aimed at linking the US, Canada and Mexico in a common trading area.

The acute difficulties in concluding GATT's Uruguay Round, which was aimed at widening the free movement of capital and commodities underlined the danger that the world market might fragment into protectionist blocs as it did in the 1930s. However, a repetition of this process is unlikely because of the much greater degree of global economic integration: Japanese capital, for example, has not been concerned primarily with recreating the wartime Greater East Asia Co-prosperity Sphere by economic rather than military means but with expanding its direct investments in the US and Western Europe; equally, a full scale trade war with Japan would cut American industry from its main source of micro-electronic components.

Of the three main trading regions—North America, Western Europe, and Asia—trade within the region represented in 1990 72.2 percent of Western Europe's total trade, but only 29.4 percent of total Asian trade and 33.9 percent of North American trade. As the *Financial Times* commented, '[t]he only region of the world for which intra-regional trade has looked like a realistic strategy is western Europe, where a number of medium to small countries send almost three quarters of their exports to one another. For North America and Asia, however, markets outside the region account for two thirds of total exports.'[98]

Economies, however, move dynamically, and there is some evidence, especially in Asia, of trade and investment becoming more regionally concentrated. By the end of 1992, Asia represented 41 percent of Japan's total trade, and North America only 30 percent, while five years previously each region took 35 percent of Japan's exports; Japanese overseas direct investment collapsed during the recession of the early 1990s (by 27 percent in the 1991-2 fiscal year alone), but shot up in China, doubling in the 1992-3 fiscal year.[99] These crosscutting trends suggest, at the very minimum, growing trade tensions between the major Western economies (the early months of the Clinton administration saw running battles between Washington and Tokyo over Japan's rocketing trade surplus with the US). In these circumstances individual capitals would continue to look to their nation-state to defend their interests in a hostile world.

Prospects for imperialism

This analysis of imperialism in the post-Cold War era naturally raises the question of what implications it has for future developments. Although it would be hazardous to offer any too precise predictions, two issues are worth exploring.

The first concerns the nature of inter-imperialist competition. What, for example, is the future likely to hold for American capitalism? We have seen that its relative economic decline has played a decisive role in bringing about a return to an economically and politically multi-polar world. It would, however, be a mistake to exaggerate US weakness. In the late 1980s Paul Kennedy's claim in *The Rise and Fall of the Great Powers* that the US was now set on a downward path, like that of Britain before it, provoked a debate in American policy and academic circles. The critics of 'declinism' made some shrewd points. Robert Nye, for example, argued that prognoses of US decline relied on misleading historical analogies and an exaggerated picture of American 'hegemony' after 1945. Measuring power along four dimensions—basic resources (population and territory), economic resources, technological resources, and military resources, Nye concluded:

> the United States remains predominant in traditional power-resources at the end of the 1980s ... only one country ranks above the others on all four dimensions—the United States. Japan and Europe are not in the top rank in basic and military resources; China is not in the top rank in economic and technological resources; and the Soviet Union is a dubious contender in technological resources.[100]

Others concentrated on the thesis of US economic decline. Michael Boskin, chairman of the President's Council of Economic Advisers under George Bush, left office in 1993 aiming a Parthian shot at the 'declinists', whose 'allegations' he dismissed as 'nonsense':

> The US remains the world's largest, richest and most productive economy. With less than five percent of the world's population, it produces about a quarter of the world's total output of goods and services. The average standard of living—measured by the total value of output per person—exceeds that of any other industrialised country, being 20-30 percent higher than in Germany and Japan. Productivity is also higher, as is average private sector pay, than in those other countries.
> The fortunes of particular industries have ebbed and flowed,

but America is not de-industrialising.

Neither is it losing its competitive edge. The US is the world's leading exporter and, although many US manufacturers face stiff competition in markets with high volume and low profit margins, America has maintained its technological edge in areas such as microprocessors, advanced telecommunications, bio-technology, aerospace, chemicals, and pharmaceuticals.[101]

Naturally one needs to take with a pinch of salt arguments emanating from anyone associated with the economic debacle of the Bush years. Nevertheless, the 'revivalists' (as Kennedy dubbed critics such as Nye[102]) do provide a necessary corrective to some of the more exaggerated views of American decline. The pre-eminence of the US as an imperialist power can be plotted along several dimensions. In the first place, the competitive pressures American capitalism experienced during the 1980s did force a significant restructuring in many sectors. Thus the *Financial Times* commented at the end of 1992: 'while IBM is struggling, the US high technology sector in general is quietly prospering, and in some sectors winning back market share from international rivals.' Firms such as Intel, for example, were taking world leadership in the key semiconductor market from Japanese companies in what one Intel executive called the 'revenge of the dinosaurs'.[103] Even more remarkably 1993 saw the Big Three US carmakers—General Motors, Ford, and Chrysler—take advantage of the rise of the yen and the recession in Japan to wrest a larger share of the American domestic market from their hitherto apparently unbeatable Japanese rivals. The reorganisation required to make these gains was reflected in a more general increase in US manufacturing productivity, up by 55 percent between 1980 and 1991, compared to increases of less than 40 percent in Japan and Germany.[104]

To this evidence of economic revival must be added the sheer politico-military strength of US imperialism. The collapse of the Soviet Union left the US unmatched in its ability to project military power on a global scale. Not simply had its chief military rival imploded, but its two most important economic competitors, Japan and Germany, were a long way behind it militarily. Moreover, the end of the Cold War increased Washington's room for political manoeuvre. The transformation of the second superpower into a petitioner at Group of Seven meetings broke the logjam which had for long made the United Nations Security Council a talking shop. Instead it became a rubber stamp for American initiatives. Russia's and China's dependence on Western economic co-operation allowed what came to be known as 'the permanent three' on the Security Council—the US, France, and Britain—to call the shots. The deployment of Western military power in the Gulf, Somalia, and the Balkans was legitimised by the UN.

The recession of the early 1990s in some ways further increased US power. The slump hit America's two main economic rivals hard. The euphoria with which the German ruling class had greeted reunification soon dissolved when it became clear that the costs of absorbing the East German economy were helping to produce the biggest social and political crisis the country had seen since the 1930s. The second Gulf War highlighted the greater political weight still in some respects enjoyed by Britain and France, weaker capitalisms than Germany or Japan, but ones which had kept relatively large military establishments in order to preserve vestiges of a global imperial role. The Maastricht Treaty, whose signature in December 1991 reflected German and French ambitions to create a more politically and economically integrated EC, was soon in tatters. The economic strains caused by the German crisis wrecked the European Monetary System, and in the process threatened to break the Franco-German axis on which the EC had been built. And European political cooperation was discredited by the EC's inability to stop the Balkans descending into war.

But if the Balkan war underlined the weaknesses of the EC as a candidate superpower, it also exposed the limits of US power. The unwillingness of the same generals who had directed the destruction of Iraq to commit American ground troops to Bosnia reflected a perfectly rational fear of being bogged down in a potentially endless, unwinnable counter-insurgency war for unclear objectives. Behind this were the more profound difficulties facing the US, now genuinely, thanks to the USSR's collapse, the lone superpower. To some extent, these difficulties were technical, reflecting the inability of US ground troops, even when backed up by the 'force multipliers' of air and naval power, to police the vast Eurasian landmass so vital to American interests.[105] More fundamental, however, was the fact that the emergence, with the end of the Cold War, of a more unstable world—in which, for example, the collapse of Russian power had led to a flurry of wars in several ex-Soviet republics—had created disorder on a scale that the US, even if its resources were greater than the 'declinists' had claimed, would find it impossible to police.

Moreover, Washington would have to confront these challenges under the pressure of intense economic competition. Whatever restructuring of US industries may have taken place, the competition of other major economies, and new industrial powers such as China and South Korea, is likely to be unrelenting. The rulers of America's most important economic rival, Japan, have reacted to demands from the Clinton administration that they adopt specific numerical targets for American imports in key sectors in a much tougher and more politically assertive tone. Despite the travails of Maastricht, Germany and France are likely to continue to pursue closer European integration. The challenges to American political and economic leadership will, in other words, continue.

This raises a second crucial issue. Post-war imperialism was characterised, as we have seen, by a partial dissociation of economic and military competition: rivalries between American, Japanese and German firms over markets did not lead to wars between their respective states. Is the collapse of the superpower blocs likely to lead to a reintegration of economic and military competition, to Japan and Germany becoming military as well as economic superpowers? This is a particularly difficult question to address in the present state of flux internationally. All that can be safely said is the following. There are pointers which might suggest that the answer to this question should be a tentative 'Yes'.

Japan already has the third largest military budget in the world. One does not have to accept the alarmist prediction implicit in the title of a recent book by George Friedman and Meredith LeBard, *The Coming War with Japan*, to accept the nub of their analysis—that the end of the Cold War is likely to see a reassertion of long-standing conflicts of interest between the US and Japan, conflicts which concern not only trade but also control over the western Pacific, on whose sea-lanes Japan depends for its raw materials.[106]

The Balkan war has been notable for Germany's aggressive pursuit of its own policy. Bonn encouraged the Croat and Slovene regimes to sabotage Washington's efforts to hold Yugoslavia together, and declare independence. But the collapse of Yugoslavia also highlighted the distance Germany still had to travel as a Great Power: its rulers invoked constitutional restrictions and memories of the Second World War to avoid sending troops to the Balkans. Germany is likely to pursue greater military power under the aegis of the European Union, both because it is less likely to evoke fear of what Helmut Kohl calls 'the ugly German' and because it will provide access to the relatively formidable armed forces of France and Britain (plans for a joint Franco-German corps are well advanced).

The fact that 1993 saw the first real commitment of Japanese and German forces abroad since 1945—as part of UN operations in Cambodia and Somalia respectively—is a sign both of a tendency of these countries' ruling classes to translate their economic strength into politico-military power and of the truth that this tendency is still in its early stages. The development of this tendency is likely to be slow and uneven. After all, Japan's and Germany's success in capturing world markets has been in large part a consequence of their low rates of military spending, an advantage which their military expansion would undermine.

Whatever the pace at which inter-imperialist competition develops, and the forms it takes, Russia's implosion should not lead us to discount it as a major power. Russia is after all still the world's second military power. Its size, population, natural resources, and economic potential still make it formidable. Should a strong regime re-emerge in Moscow, it is likely to assert Russian interests in ways which will bring it into conflict with the Western powers. Indeed, late 1993 saw the Yeltsin government, beholden to the military and under pressure from the right, move to block Eastern European participation in NATO. No one should assume that Russia's eclipse is permanent.

One final point about the post Cold War world is in any case clear. The disintegration of the superpower blocs makes major wars more likely. The constraints which the Cold War imposed on individual states have been removed. It is unlikely that the second Gulf War could have taken place a decade earlier, when tensions between the superpowers were acute. Moscow, which then still counted Iraq among its closest allies in the Middle East, would in all probability have restrained Saddam Hussein from seizing Kuwait, while Washington would have been more cautious in its response to the invasion, had it occurred, for fear of precipitating another eyeball to eyeball confrontation with the USSR like the Cuban missile crisis of October 1962.

In the more fluid world which is emerging, regional powers are more likely to take risks which may in turn evoke a more savage reaction from a US no longer restrained by the USSR's presence in Eastern Europe and the Third World. Even if, unlike the second Gulf War, Western imperialism does not become directly involved in all the resulting conflicts, instead leaving it to existing and would be sub-imperialisms to slug it out, the portents for humankind are grim. Though the shadow of a general war between the superpowers has receded, the proliferation of nuclear arms in the Third World (Israel, South Africa, India and Pakistan are among the states known to possess such weapons) means that the first regional nuclear war may not be far off. After all, the collapse of the USSR produced three new nuclear powers—Ukraine, Belarus and Kazakhstan—in a region seething with national discontent and local wars. So long as a world system that consists of capitals competing economically and integrated into rival nation states continues to exist, war will remain the final arbiter of conflicts.

Conclusion

AT THE beginning of the present century Lenin, Luxemburg, Bukharin, Hilferding and others developed an analysis of imperialism as that stage of capitalist development in which the concentration and centralisation of capital led to a world dominated by the rivalries of a handful of military and economic Great Powers. Despite the transformations which the world system has undergone in the past 100 years, this theory still identifies some of the main characteristics of contemporary capitalism. Indeed we are now entering a period of more ferocious, and more unstable inter-imperialist competition.

The significance of these facts is very far from being primarily theoretical. Despite the weaknesses of his version of the theory, Lenin remains *the* theorist of imperialism for two reasons. Firstly, he grasped more clearly than anyone else that imperialism is not a mere policy, but a stage, indeed the highest stage, of capitalist development. Thus he attacked Kautsky for arguing that 'imperialism is not present-day capitalism; it is only one of the forms of present-day capitalism'.[107] The implication of Kautsky's argument was that military conflict and war could be eliminated within the framework of capitalism, to which Lenin replied that only socialist revolution could put an end to imperialism and its destructive tendencies. Lenin's political understanding of imperialism is indeed where his second main contribution lies. He grasped that the political and economic hierarchy which imperialism imposed on the world would give rise to struggles developing under the banner, not of revolutionary socialism, but of revolutionary nationalism, struggles therefore which would challenge imperialism in order to realise the aspiration for an independent capitalist state.

Lenin understood that, despite the political distance between these movements and international socialism, they could give rise to wars and revolutions which would weaken imperialism, and therefore the hold of the world's ruling classes. He expressed this insight most clearly when defending the Dublin rising of Easter 1916 against Bolsheviks who wished to dismiss it as a petty bourgeois 'putsch':

> To imagine that social revolution is *conceivable* without revolts by small nations in the colonies and in Europe, without revolutionary outbursts by a section of the petty bourgeoisie *with all its prejudices*, without a movement of the politically non-conscious proletarian and semi-proletarian masses against oppression by the landowners, the church, and the monarchy, against national oppression, etc—to imagine all this is to *repudiate social revolution*.[108]

So it is not merely that imperialism can be removed only through the overthrow of capitalism, but imperialism will provoke movements which, despite their bourgeois interests and ideology, in Lenin's words, '*objectively... attack capital*':

> The dialectics of history are such that small nations, powerless as an *independent* factor in the struggle against imperialism, play a part as one of the ferments, one of the bacilli, which help the real anti-imperialist force, the socialist proletariat, to make its appearance on the scene... We would be very poor revolutionaries if, in the proletariat's great war of liberation for socialism, we did not know how to utilise every popular movement against every single disaster imperialism brings in order to intensify and extend the crisis.[109]

The experience of the past 30 years has amply confirmed Lenin's analysis. The Vietnam War, though fought to establish an independent state capitalist regime, inflicted a serious defeat on American imperialism, and stimulated the growth of authentically anti-capitalist movements throughout the Western world. Since then even stranger forces than Vietnamese Stalinism have become the focus of confrontations with imperialism— the fundamentalist mullahs of Iran and of Lebanon and even the Iraqi Ba'athist regime, despite its miserable history of collaboration with the US. In such confrontations revolutionary socialists hope for the defeat of the imperialist power. Such a position in no sense involves revolutionaries giving political support to the regime fighting imperialism. Trotsky brought this out in his response to the Japanese invasion of China in 1937:

> In a war between two *imperialist* countries, it is a question neither of democracy nor of national independence, but of the oppression of backward non-imperialist peoples. In such a war the two countries find themselves on the same historical plane. The revolutionaries in both armies are defeatists. But Japan and China are not on the same historical plane. The victory of Japan will signify the enslavement of China, the end of her economic and social development, and the terrible strengthening of Japanese imperialism. The victory of China will signify, on the contrary, the social revolution in Japan and the free development, that is to say unhindered by external oppression, of the class struggle in China.
>
> But can Chiang Kai-shek assure the victory? I do not believe so. It is he, however, who began the war and who today directs it. To be able to replace him it is necessary to gain decisive influence among the proletariat and the army, and to do this it is necessary not to remain suspended in the air but to place oneself in the midst of the struggle. We must win influence and prestige in the *military* struggle against the foreign invasion and in the *political* struggle against the weaknesses, the deficiencies, and the internal betrayal. At a certain point, which we cannot fix in advance, this political opposition can and must be transformed into armed conflict, since the civil war, like war generally, is nothing more than the continuation of the political struggle... the working class, while remaining in the front lines

of the military struggle, prepare[s] the *political* overthrow of the bourgeoisie.[110]

It is necessary, therefore, in a confrontation such as the second Gulf War, to advocate the defeat of the imperialist side while continuing the political struggle against the bourgeois regime leading the anti-imperialist side. Underlying this stance is Trotsky's theory of permanent revolution. In its general form this asserts that no capitalist class can consistently fight imperialism. Even the most militant nationalist movement aspires essentially to its own independent capitalist state. It seeks, therefore, not to destroy the imperialist world system but to win a larger stake in that system. If it is forced to fight imperialism to achieve this objective, the ensuing struggle may weaken the entire system. But eventually the nationalist movement will come to terms with imperialism, as Sinn Fein did at the end of the War of Independence, the Vietnamese Communist Party after both Indochina wars, the Islamic Republic of Iran following its defeat in the first Gulf War. The aim of revolutionary socialists is therefore primarily, as Lenin puts it, to 'utilise' the crisis created by the confrontation between imperialism and its nationalist opponents to 'help the real anti-imperialist force, the socialist proletariat, to make its appearance on the scene'. But the working class can only settle accounts with imperialism by overthrowing, not merely the ruling classes of the advanced capitalist countries, but those bourgeois regimes which may temporarily challenge Western domination.

The importance of this analysis cannot be stressed sufficiently. One of the most notable features of the second Gulf War was the phenomenon of the 'B-52 liberals' — intellectuals often with a radical past who supported the West against Iraq: for example, Hans Magnus Enzensburger, Wolf Bierman, Neil Ascherson, and Michael Ignatieff. It was, however, Fred Halliday and Norman Geras, former members of the editorial committee of *New Left Review*, who sought to give this position a 'Marxist' veneer. Notoriously at the end of the war Halliday declared: 'if I have to make a choice between imperialism and fascism, I choose imperialism.'[111] More recently, he has explicitly linked this position to Bill Warren's 'critique of the Marxist view of imperialism', praising him for asking: 'Is everything imperialism does negative?', and attacking 'the moralistic post-Leninist position which has dominated over the latest 20 or 30 years', according to which 'because US imperialism is doing it [ie attacking Iraq], therefore it must be bad.'[112]

The implication is that imperialism can, in certain circumstances, play a progressive role. Thus Halliday and Geras denounced one of their critics, Alexander Cockburn:

> if Cockburn listened to what people in the third world say, he would hear that, in many cases, they are appealing for another, equally active, US policy. This is what the Eritreans, the PLO, the ANC, the human rights activists in China have called for. The alternative to imperialist intervention is not non-intervention, but, rather, action in support of democratic change.[113]

This argument rests on the fallacious assumption that the imperialist powers have a general interest in promoting 'democratic change' in the Third World. Rejecting this assumption doesn't require one to accept the kind of vulgar anti-imperialism which sees the machinations of the CIA behind everything that happens in the Third World. This essay has tried to show at some length how twentieth century imperialism has permitted considerable capitalist development outside the Western metropolis. And the strategy outlined by Trotsky above treats the struggle against 'anti-imperialist' nationalist regimes as inseparable from an effective fight against imperialism itself. But the rationale for this strategy derives from the links which bind *all* bourgeois regimes in the Third World to imperialism.

The end of the second Gulf War shows this very clearly. Halliday has echoed the complaint made by countless right wing politicians that, when in March 1991 the Ba'athist regime was reeling under the impact of military defeat, popular insurrection in the south, and advancing Kurdish forces in the north, 'the US did not go in to finish Saddam off'.[114] Washington's failure to do so did not reflect some intellectual mistake, or lack of willpower, but its calculation—and that of its chief Arab allies in Cairo, Riyadh, and Damascus—that their interests were better served by the survival of a weakened Ba'athist regime than by its replacement by a radical Islamic government or even Iraq's disintegration (which would leave Iran the major local power in the Gulf). Saddam's conquerers thus became his saviours. Rather than, as Halliday and Geras naively believed, being in fundamental conflict with each other, imperialism and 'fascism' were bound together by links of common interest.

The disastrous consequences of believing that imperialism can play a progressive role can be seen in the wholesale collapse of much of the Western left (including many who opposed the Gulf War) into support for UN intervention in the Balkans.[115] This collapse has taken place despite the lesson offered by the UN intervention in Somalia, where the US-controlled operation rapidly degenerated into an army of occupation at war with the local population. In a world still to a large extent dominated by a handful of Great Powers it is a dangerous fantasy to believe that these powers can be relied on to protect the interests of the exploited majority. Humanity will not be at peace till this majority takes control of the world, which they will do in the teeth of bitter opposition from the imperialist states. Classical Marxism contains, in the writings of Lenin and Trotsky, an analysis of imperialism and a strategy for fighting it which are indispensable to the success of this struggle.

The new imperialism

JOHN REES

THE COLD WAR is over, but what will replace it? For the leaders of the world's great powers that question used to be easily answered. All agreed, at least in public, that a new era of peace and security had dawned. The media were happy to repeat a message so obviously confirmed by summits and arms deals, aid packages and gestures of goodwill. The pictures of tanks and troops heading for home, of arms production lines turned over to civilian goods and the talk of a peace dividend soon to be in our pockets seemed all pervasive. Then suddenly Iraq's invasion of Kuwait, war in the Balkans, civil war in Somalia and Rwanda, to mention only the most widely reported conflicts, proved that the world could still threaten wars of mass destruction.

So which way is the world going? Toward peace or toward greater imperialist conflict? To throw light on this question it is first necessary to uncover the true situation that faces us in the last decade of the twentieth century—the extent of the superpowers' decline, the current levels of arms expenditure, the extent of the global arms industry. The second part of this chapter attempts an explanation of the imperialist order that has emerged from the Cold War.

Part I: Fact, fiction and the end of the Cold War

The power of the United States, 1945-1990

OUR WORLD was created by the settlement that ended the Second World War. That settlement, and indeed the outcome of the war itself, rested on the economic power of the Allies. This economic strength explains the emergence from the victorious states of the two political and military super-powers, the US and the USSR, capable of dividing Europe between them. This division was the basis of the world imperialist order for more than 40 years. The victors, however, were far from equal. The war cost Britain and France dear. Britain was severely weakened, France even more so. Even the two superpowers were unevenly matched, the US being very much the stronger.

The US ended the war in a position of unparalleled economic superiority. Its economic growth during the war years had been phenomenal. In 1945 the US economy's industrial production was more than double its annual production between 1935 and 1939. The US economy was producing half the world's coal, two thirds of the world's oil and over half the world's electricity,[1] and more steel than Britain and Russia combined.[2] It was this economic superiority which was vital in delivering Allied victory. US aircraft production rose from nearly 6,000 in 1939 to over 96,000 in 1944, more than Germany and Japan to-gether—*and* more than USSR and Britain's combined aircraft production. It was the same story with shipping. By mid-1942 US shipyards were already launching merchant ships more quickly than German submarines could sink them. Small wonder that it was only the US that had the economic power to fight both a European and a Pacific war *and* spend some \$2 billion on developing the atomic bomb.[3]

In other countries, whether they were among the victors or the vanquished, war production damaged the civilian economy. But in the US economic growth had been so great, over 15 percent a year, that the arms economy and the civilian economy expanded.[4] Even in 1952 nearly 60 percent of the total production of the top seven capitalist countries took place in the US. In 1953 the US was exporting five times as many manufactured goods as Germany and 17 times as many as Japan.[5]

The US ruling class used this enormous power to shape the world in its own image. The US had already moved to make the dollar the keystone of the world financial order. The 1944 Bretton Woods agreement fixed currency exchange rates in relation to gold. Since the US held 80 percent of world gold reserves this made the dollar 'as good as gold'.[6] This ensured that the dollar, and to a lesser extent sterling, were the international means of payment, forcing other countries to hold dollars in their reserves. So 'every dollar or pound held abroad... means that a similar amount of imports need not be met by exports—the rest of the world simply finance [the US and British] trade gap.' It also meant that other countries financed the erosion of their markets by more advanced US products.[7]

But at the end of the war US exports were still restricted from getting into Europe and Japan by trade and monetary laws. US policy, enshrined in the International Monetary Fund and the General Agreement on Tariffs and Trade, aimed to push these barriers aside.[8] The European powers had to allow their currencies to be devalued and their markets to be taken over if they wanted to grasp the economic lifeline which the US threw to them—the European Recovery Programme, or Marshall Aid.

The European economies were devastated. There was famine in parts of Germany, bread rationing in France and a tightening of rationing in Britain. The European powers' imperial pretensions had largely been reduced to rubble alongside many of their cities. Economic aid was dependent on political docility. As General George Marshall himself put it, 'Benefits under the European Recovery Programme will come to an abrupt end in any country that votes Communism to power.' Looking at Europe, one US Congressman put it even more succinctly: 'Too damned much socialism at home, and too damned much imperialism abroad.'[9] The US was now in a position to use its economic might to oblige the European powers to get rid of socialism at home—the Communist Parties were mostly marginalised in the late 1940s—and to use its military might to take over the imperial duties that Britain, Germany and France were no longer in a position to perform.

US military might was as great as its economic power. In 1949, even after demobilisation had begun, US forces were stationed in 56 countries and had the use of 400 bases worldwide. But perhaps the clearest demonstration of the US's growing imperial reach is the list of military alliances and treaties it agreed in the decade after the war. The most important of these was NATO. Ernest Bevin, Labour's foreign secretary and NATO's initiator, called the day in 1949 when the pact was signed 'the finest in my life'. A year earlier Stafford Cripps had told the US Secretary of Defense, 'Britain must be regarded as the main base for the deployment of American power.'[10] NATO was consciously designed to counter internal as well as external threats to its member states. As the US Secretary of State, Dean Acheson, put it, 'Revolutionary activity in a member country inspired and assisted from outside as in Greece would be considered an armed attack.'[11]

But it was not only in Europe that the US had military interests. The Rio Pact and the special defence arrangements with Canada meant that the US was militarily committed to the 'defence' of the entire western hemisphere. The ANZUS treaty added military commitments in the south western Pacific. The 1950s saw the addition of bilateral treaties with Japan, South Korea, Taiwan and the Philippines. In 1954 the US, Britain, France and Australia joined the Philippines, Thailand and Pakistan to form the South-East Asia Treaty Organisation (SEATO). The Middle East was given its version, the Central Treaty Organisation (CENTO, originally the 1955 Baghdad Pact), in which Britain, Turkey, Iraq, Iran and Pakistan stood against 'subversion and attack'. Dean Rusk was speaking for the US ruling class when, in 1965, he said, 'This has become a very small planet and we have to be concerned with all of it—with all its land, waters, atmosphere, and with surrounding space.'[12] But, even as Rusk spoke, the US was losing that economic predominance on which the post-war political and military order was founded. To see why, we have to look at the development of the world economy in the post-war period.

The period 1945-70 is, of course, the story of the greatest boom in capitalism's history—world manufacturing production grew threefold in the 20 years after 1953.[13] But within that boom some economies grew faster than others. In the race for growth the US was one of the losers. From 1955 to 1970 capital stock in the US grew by 57 percent, but in the major European countries it grew by 116 percent and in Japan by 500 percent.[14] West Germany's industrial output grew fivefold and Japan's grew thirteenfold between 1949 and 1970. Even in the years 1965-80, which include the slump of the 1970s, the US Gross Domestic Product grew by only 2.7 percent per year, while West Germany's grew by 3.3 percent, France's by 4.3 percent and Japan's by 6.3 percent. The figures for manufacturing industry, generally the most dynamic part of the industrial sector, are even starker— US 2.5 percent, West Germany 3.3 percent, France 5.2 percent and Japan 9.4 percent.[15] In 1957, 74 of the top 100 firms were American. In 1972 the figure was 53.[16]

Overall the US share of world manufacturing production sank from over 50 percent in 1945 to 31 percent in 1980 and it is still falling.[17] Car production typifies the problem. In 1962 the US accounted for 52 percent of world production, by 1983 that figure was 23 percent, overtaken by both Japan (24 percent) and joint European car production (34 percent). Even in high technology goods, where the US has long been a leader, she is heading toward a trading deficit.[18] The dollar has long since ceased to be as good as gold—Europe is now the major holder of both currency reserves and gold.[19] It is ultimately this economic decline which underlies the US's dramatic slide from being the world's largest creditor nation to being the world's greatest debtor nation over just a few years.

Along with this relative economic decline the US has also lost some of its military hegemony. Rows in NATO have shown the limits to US power even in this, its most integrated military alliance. Elsewhere weakness is more obvious. SEATO ceased to exist in 1977 in the wake of challenges to US power and the ANZUS alliance has come badly unstuck.[20] Vietnam was the obvious turning point, a defeat from which, even now, the US ruling class has barely recovered.

The US is, of course, still the world's largest economy. And the US has an important advantage over both Russia, in its present state, and the European Community (EC) which is often portrayed as an economic rival: the US is a single integrated state relatively free of centrifugal forces and capable of both international and domestic, economic and military control over its destiny. In addition, the US ruling class has developed an important economic advantage in recent years. It has cut workers' real wages and reduced the percentage of US workers in unions to below 20 percent.

So the decline the US has suffered is serious, but relative. The point is, however, that it is on just such relative decline that the fate of empires turn. Moreover the world order established after 1945 was predicated on the existence of *overwhelming* US economic and military predominance. The history of the Cold War and of detente, from the shock of discovering that the USSR possessed the atom bomb through defeat in Vietnam to the current international instability, cannot be understood without acknowledging US economic decline.

The decline of the USSR and the Eastern European revolutions

THE COLD WAR and the accompanying decades of talk about superpower rivalry have taught us to think that the USSR and the US were symmetrical. But, while it is true that they were both imperialist states, it was never true that they were imperialist states of equal power.

The USSR underwent barbaric but successful industrialisation during the 1930s, hauling itself from being an impoverished, broken and largely agricultural society in the late 1920s to the rank of a major industrial and military power. During the Second World War the USSR bore the brunt of the Nazi war machine, suffering invasion, massive war damage and some 20 million dead.

The USSR's power at the end of the Second World War rested less on economic strength and more on its military and strategic position. Where the US used its economic strength to bring Western Europe under its leadership, the USSR had no such means and was therefore dependent on the power of its army. Where the US used its economic predominance to insist on military and strategic subservience from the West Europeans, the USSR used its military dominance to strip industrial assets from the East European economies. Where the US projected its economic and military might to every corner of the globe, the USSR's empire remained a cohesive, geographical and military bloc in Eastern Europe.

Even so, the USSR emerged from the war as the third most powerful economy after the US and Britain. And, much as this runs against the currently fashionable view which sees centrally planned economies as incapable of growth, the USSR continued to grow during the long post-war boom, passing Britain on the escalators in the 1950s. In the late 1940s the USSR's rulers drew up a 15 year plan. When, in 1965, Brezhnev looked back to compare the plan with what had been achieved, he found that overall production exceeded the plan by 30 percent. But this had been achieved by massive growth in some areas, like oil and gas production, and underfulfilment in others, such as agriculture.[21] Planning had failed, but growth had been achieved. The USSR's industrial output per head was 25 percent of the European average in 1929, 40 percent in 1938, 63 percent in 1953,

84 percent in 1963 and 90 percent in 1980.[22] As Mike Haynes has explained:

> The Second World War disrupted most of the European economy and the Soviet Union in particular, but [the period]... from 1945 to the end of the 1960s was one of recovery and sustained growth. During this period the Soviet economy largely shared in this wider dynamism and therefore pulled even closer to the average European level of development... The CIA estimates that by 1950 Soviet output had risen to 33 percent of the American level and it continued to grow relatively until the mid-1970s when it reached a peak of just under 60 percent.[23]

We can agree both that the CIA is prone to exaggeration and that the gap has widened again since the 1970s without harming the conclusion that the USSR grew more rapidly than the US during the long boom. Indeed it was during this period of economic development that the USSR achieved its greatest strategic power. From Cuba to Angola, from Mozambique to Syria, from Egypt to India, from Central America to South East Asia the USSR began, however temporarily in some cases, to fill the gaps left by Western imperialism as it retreated before the flood-tide of anti-colonialism.

A similar story can be seen in the development of nuclear missile technology. In the early years of the space race it was the USSR's unmanned Sputnik and manned space flights which set the goals that the US then had to match. When Nikita Khrushchev banged his shoe on the table at the UN and shouted, 'We will bury you!' nobody in the Pentagon laughed. By the 1970s the USSR's naval power was growing and it had achieved nuclear parity with the US.

The USSR never did build an economy the size of the US, neither did it achieve an imperial reach to equal that of the US, but the competition between the superpowers undermined the USSR, as it did the US, just at the moment of its greatest success. The USSR's rate of growth began to slow dramatically in the late 1960s. In *The Challenge: Economics of Perestroika* Abel Aganbegyan, former President Gorbachev's chief economic adviser, gives both the official figures for the decline in growth rates of national income and his own calculations, which take account of hidden price rises and deterioration in the quality of goods. This later index shows growth declining from over 30 percent between 1966 and 1970 to zero between 1981 and 1985.

National income growth over 5 year periods[24]

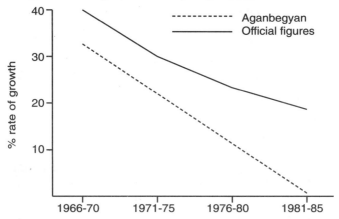

Even if we agree that Aganbegyan was exaggerating in order to make a point against the Brezhnevites, there is plenty of other evidence which points to the same conclusions. Both the USSR's official figures and CIA estimates, although they differ over the level of growth, show the same trend.

Average annual rate of growth of the USSR's economy (%)[25]

	1966-70	1971-75	1976-80	1981-85
CIA	5.3	3.3	2.3	1.9
USSR	7.7	5.7	4.3	3.6

For a Western economy these might look like respectable rates of growth. But no Western economy was directly pitted in military and economic competition with an economy twice its size. No other economy had, therefore, to commit twice as much of its resources as the US economy to military production. No other economy of comparable size had to bear the burden of a military alliance, like the Warsaw Pact, the other members of which contributed far less to its upkeep than the European members did to the upkeep of NATO. And, while US spheres of influence included some of the fastest growing economies in the world, the USSR's allies of the 1960s and 1970s had less to offer economically.

By the 1980s the economic decline of the USSR was threatening to undermine its ability to hold down its empire and compete with the US militarily. The USSR's military must have seen the writing on the wall when they eventually put their new Sukhoi SU 27 fighter into operation in the late 1980s after nine years of test flights. The comparable US fighter, the F-15, had already been in service for 12 years. They must have been even more distraught to hear Ronald Reagan say in 1985, 'We want to develop as complex a weapon as necessary to force the Soviet Union into bankruptcy if it should want to find a defence mechanism against it,' or to learn that Reagan's defence secretary, Casper Weinberger, had written, 'To fight stealth bombers the USSR will have to make enormous investments over many years into new anti-aircraft defences, while investment already made will very rapidly depreciate in value.'[26]

And so the New Cold War of the 1980s found the two superpowers on the point of exhaustion. The US brought the USSR to its knees, but it was a pyrrhic victory which left the US too debilitated to effectively control the unstable world it had inherited. Against this background Mikhail Gorbachev's strategy, despite its ultimate failure, was at least understandable. When he first came to power Gorbachev did not use the terms *perestroika* or *glasnost*. Instead he talked of the need for the acceleration (*uskoreniye*) of economic development. We have seen that he had a pressing need for such acceleration.

One of Gorbachev's first acts was to ensure that the military were behind him. His first move was to address a meeting of very senior officers in Minsk in May 1985. We do not know what Gorbachev said. But he was clear enough the previous year that 'only an intensive, highly developed economy can safeguard a reinforcement of our country's position on the international stage and allow her to enter the next millennium with dignity as a great and flourishing power.'[27] He soon moved to overhaul the party apparatus concerned with the military. In mid-1985 the ageing head of the armed forces' Main Political Directorate was replaced with a younger officer. This was swiftly followed by a shake up of the political directorates of all the main headquarters and commands.[28] It is clear, though less easily demonstrable, that Gorbachev had also secured a base in the KGB. Only after he had secured this base in the state apparatus did Gorbachev move to deal with what he called the 'human factor', that is resistance among the wider party bureaucracy and, for different reasons, among the working class.

The central component of Gorbachev's plans for economic acceleration was to try and open the USSR's economy to the world economy, hoping to drive up productivity under the direct threat of economic competition and to attract Western investment. In return for Western goodwill and in an attempt to cut the costs of arms production Gorbachev utilised his considerable diplomatic skills to try to force the Western powers into curtailing the arms race. He hoped to abandon the goal of nuclear parity in favour of a doctrine of 'reasonable sufficiency'. This assumed that so long as the USSR had an effective nuclear second strike capacity it did not need to match the US weapon for weapon. Gorbachev also tried to extricate the USSR from continued commitments to its Third World allies, most notably by co-operating with the US on peace plans for Central America and Southern Africa, and in the Gulf War.

All this was difficult and dangerous but still manageable until the masses of Eastern Europe intervened. Gorbachev was in favour of liberalisation and of developing economic links between Eastern Europe and the West. All this was necessary to try and revitalise the East European economies, including the USSR's. Gorbachev envisaged a gradual Polish or Hungarian style development towards integration with the world economy. In this aim he clearly had the support of considerable sections of the East European ruling classes. This is an unpalatable fact for the new democratic governments of Eastern Europe and the Western bourgeoisie, both of whom wish to disguise the continuity that exists between the old state capitalist regimes and the new regimes which combine state and multinational capital. Yet the desire of significant sections of old regimes to make this transition is obvious enough. Poland's ruling class clearly saw that manoeuvering Solidarity into government was the only possibility they had of getting workers to accept the cost of opening the economy to the world market. Hungary's move to the market and limited democracy predated the East European revolutions by 12 months. Both countries' strategies clearly enjoyed the support of the Kremlin bureaucracy.

In East Germany, Czechoslovakia and Romania, hardliners presided over a ruling class many of whom wanted change, but had no means to force their old leaders to start the ball rolling.

In East Germany the combination of mass pressure from below, both in the form of demonstrations and refugees leaving through Hungary, helped widen splits in the regime. During his 1989 visit to East Germany in the midst of this crisis Gorbachev made it clear, at a special meeting of the East German SED's (Communist Party) leadership, that any use of force would endanger his whole international policy. It is at this meeting that hardline Stalinist Erich Honecker is reported to have said that he would leave the room and that if no one followed him he would accept that he no longer had the support of the leadership. He left alone. So, between them, Gorbachev and Honecker propelled the East German ruling class down the path to reform. The final blow, indeed the constant pressure behind these events, were the hundreds of thousands of demonstrators on the streets. These pushed the SED leaders beyond the point at which either they, or indeed Gorbachev, were willing to go. Eventually, of course, they pushed the SED aside and opened the way for unification, fundamentally altering the balance of power in Europe and leaving Gorbachev a spectator, shocked at the implications of his earlier actions.

Events in Czechoslovakia and Romania also showed the degree to which sections of the state apparatus were looking for an opportunity to oust the old hardline leaders. In Czechoslovakia there is clear evidence that the secret service, the StB, contrived to get the students to begin demonstrating. In Romania it is clear that the National Salvation Front had some prior organisation within the ruling class for some months before Ceausescu fell. In all these cases Gorbachev, it seems, had been told by the KGB and his generals that any attempt at suppression was bound to fail in anything but the short term.[29] He also knew that Western reaction would hurl the USSR back into economic isolation and possibly a new Cold War.

None of this is to belittle the heroism of the demonstrators. Nor is it to claim that the revolutions would have taken place, let alone had the outcome they did, without the risings from below. It is simply to show that faltering economic growth and increasing economic contact with the West (or the desire for such contact by sections of the ruling class) had already hollowed out the East European regimes from the inside. That is why they could be pushed over with so little bloodshed, Romania excepted. It is also to make clear the political, rather than social, nature of the revolutions. One method of capital accumulation, the autarchic state capitalist method, was decreasingly effective. The ruling classes were already looking for an alternative method which combined elements of the old system with increased integration with the multinational capital of the world market.[30] The revolutions have forced them to face that transition much more sharply and much more quickly than they wished. Their economic problems have been exacerbated by the revolutions, not solved by them.

The Eastern European revolutions rebounded on Gorbachev with terrific force. His empire truly struck back. The example of the revolutions gave renewed heart to the oppressed nations of the inner empire everywhere from Baku, through Moldavia to Vilnius. And the popular, democratic movements and the workers movements all drew inspiration from the defeat Gorbachev suffered in Eastern Europe. On the other hand, Gorbachev's carefully constructed alliance with the armed forces began to fracture as a result of the revolutions. The military balance has swung heavily against them as a result of withdrawals from Eastern Europe.

Gorbachev's successors probably find little immediate consolation in the fact that whatever happens, short of a seizure of power by the working class or the complete dismemberment of Russia by the West, Russia will remain the most powerful military force and one of the most powerful economic forces on the Eurasian land mass. Yet this is the case. Any analysis of the world after the Cold War has to be clear that Russia will continue to exercise a major influence in every aspect of international relations and particularly on some of its former satellites in Eastern Europe.

Is arms expenditure falling?

THE AMOUNT the major powers spend on defence, compared with the total amount of goods and services produced by their economies, is falling. But this not because a new era of peace and stability has broken out since the fall of the Berlin Wall. Arms expenditure was falling long before the revolutions in Eastern Europe.

In the US arms expenditure has fallen, if unevenly, since the height of the first Cold War and the Korean War in the mid-1950s. Then US defence expenditure stood at 15 percent of Gross

National Product (GNP), a level unprecedented outside conditions of world war. Since then the declining trend has been in-
terrupted by the Vietnam War (when it reached about 10 percent)
and by the Reagan arms boom (7 percent).[31] The overall fall,
however, was dramatic. Reagan himself was already cutting
back in the last years of his presidency and US defence expenditure is projected to drop to around 3 percent of Gross Domestic Product by 1998.[32] This will be just 1 percent above the level
in 1947 when post-war demobilisation was complete and Cold
War levels of expenditure were not yet under way.

US arms spending (% of GNP)

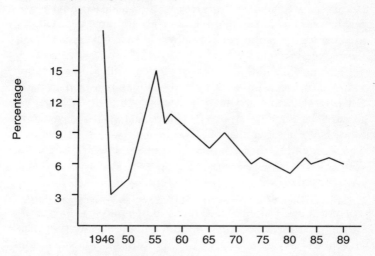

Britain's defence expenditure has followed a similar pattern.[33] Other NATO countries were much less willing to follow
Reagan up the hill, although they have followed Bush and Clinton on the way down, reducing their collective arms bill from 3.5
percent in 1985 to a projected 2.2 percent of GDP in 1995.[34]

Assessing the arms spending of the USSR was always more
difficult. Estimates of arms spending as a percentage of GNP
vary wildly. The CIA estimated expenditure at 15 to 18 percent
of GNP (up from 13 percent in 1970).[35] Andrew Kelly's excellent independent report, *The Myth of Soviet Superiority*, uses
figures from 1983 which show military expenditure as 14 percent of GNP (compared with 6.6 percent for America).[36]

Part of the problem is that it was only in May 1989 that

Gorbachev gave the first ever realistic figure for the USSR's arms budget, some 77.3 billion roubles or 15.6 percent of the total budget. This figure, much greater than the previous official figure of 20 billion roubles, was in line with the lower end of NATO estimates.[37] In his speech to the United Nations in December 1988 Gorbachev promised a 14 percent reduction in the arms budget, although subsequent events overtook those estimates.[38]

Whatever the precise figures, two vital facts can be asserted with some confidence. Firstly, at the time of its collapse, the arms burden was about twice as great for the economy of the USSR as it is for the US economy. Secondly, a drastic reduction of the proportion of economic resources directed to military production has now taken place. Even if these cutbacks are not as great as we are led to believe, they are somewhat greater than those undertaken in the US.

Arms expenditure is not, of course, limited to the major industrial powers. But the rapid growth in Third World arms expenditures does not outweigh the decline of military spending by the advanced industrial powers. United States arms expenditure alone is greater than that of all the other NATO countries plus Japan added together. And the US, Russia, the NATO and the former Warsaw Pact countries and Japan together account for the overwhelming bulk of the world's military spending.

Finally, some words of caution about the above figures. All reductions, proposed or actual, are from the very high levels of Reagan's massive arms build up. In the US, after five years in which arms expenditure fell as a percentage of GNP, in 1990 it was still 30 percent higher in real terms than it was in 1980. US arms expenditure is projected to be 19 percent higher in 1995 than it was in 1980. In Britain projected arms expenditure is still higher than in Germany, Italy or Spain. Most of the figures given above refer to the proportion of total production consumed by the arms industry. Thus, so long as the economy grows, the percentage of GNP consumed by the military can fall while the actual amount of guns, bombs and warships goes on rising. Indeed, a very powerful economy like Japan's can spend as little as 1 percent of GNP on arms and still maintain, according to some estimates, the world's third largest defence budget in absolute terms. In 1989-90 the Japanese defence budget rose by 5.9 percent without increasing its proportion of GNP.[39]

The upshot is this: the world's ruling classes can *decrease* the proportion of their total wealth spent on weapons and still *increase* the total destructive force at their disposal. This was roughly the situation until a two pronged crisis befell the superpowers in the final years of the 1980s. The first prong of the crisis was economic. The US budget deficit and the USSR's economic crisis, both of which were fuelled by previous arms spending, encouraged both to look again at the question of defence. But they made little real progress until, quite unexpectedly, the uprisings in Eastern Europe forced both superpowers into a global reconsideration of their defence commitments.

Economic and political necessity is driving Russia and America to rethink their military strategy much more quickly and much more fully than either of them had expected. Neither Russia nor the US are willing to part with those elements of its armoury they regard as vital, especially the most advanced nuclear weapons.

Are the US and Russia disarming?

THE MEDIA commonly give the impression that the 'historic' superpower summits of the late 1980s and early 1990s have made the world a safer place. The most famous treaty is the first of those which marked the beginning of the end of the Cold War, the 1987 Intermediate Nuclear Forces treaty designed to eliminate cruise missiles. Its failure, and it has been a failure, is an object lesson in the ways of the arms race.

The INF treaty covers a very narrow range of weapons—nuclear missiles launched from the ground and with a range of between 300 and 3,000 miles. It therefore did not even attempt to limit some 96 percent of America and Russia's nuclear weapons. But even these narrow provisions proved too wide for the NATO planners. A month before the treaty was signed they met to decide on 'compensatory measures'. These involved increasing the number of weapons which fell below the 300 mile limit and replacing ground launched cruise missiles with air and sea launched cruise missiles.[40]

Some 450 tactical air to surface missiles (TASM, also known as SRAM-T) were planned for Europe. The new missiles will be given the targets previously covered by ground launched cruise missiles like those which left Greenham Common amidst much publicity. There were only 106 cruise missiles at Greenham, but there are to be a minimum of 160 air launched cruise missiles deployed in Britain. The new missiles have also been upgraded. The original cruise missile flew at the speed of an airliner—the new rocket powered version flies at three times the speed of sound.[41]

NATO ministers have also agreed to deploy Tomahawk cruise missiles on submarines and surface ships.[42] By the end of the decade as many as 200 Tomahawk missiles could be handed over to NATO commanders in an emergency. NATO ministers have requested that the Supreme Allied Commander Europe (always a US officer) should 'consider the availability of the whole spectrum of nuclear weapons' as part of 'post INF restructuring'.[43] 'NATO's new nuclear arsenal' noted the *Independent* in a masterpiece of understatement, 'has been interpreted by some observers as a circumvention of the 1987 INF treaty.'[44] The *Observer*'s Nigel Hawkes caught the essence of the situation rather more accurately in an article headlined 'Sword grinding that sours NATO's sweet lullaby':

> What NATO appears to be doing behind all the protestations of peace and brotherhood is preparing a new generation of American air-launched nuclear missiles for Europe...
> The same ambiguity surrounds the sea-launched Tomahawk cruise missile—the same missile which in its ground based mode was 'eliminated' by the INF treaty—that the US intends should form part of NATO's strike force in a European crisis.[45]

So the US and its NATO allies are not just circumventing the INF treaty, they are already planning to circumvent the next treaty but two!

The INF treaty is going the same way as the Strategic Arms Limitation Talks (SALT) and the Anti Ballistic Missile (ABM) treaties of the 1970s. Neither of these stopped, or were intended to stop, an increase in nuclear weapons.[46] Arms experts agree, among themselves at least, that summits and agreements are about arms *control* not arms *limitation*. They are about laying down the rules of arms competition, not about abolishing that competition. Michael Sheehan, then of the International Institute of Strategic Studies (IISS) says:

> During the 1970s arms control was successfully achieved but it was done by mutual build-ups rather than by reductions

leaving the public feeling that its wishes were being ignored—
as indeed they were...

The object of arms negotiations is not so much to reach an
agreement as to be seen by the public as trying to do so and
to pin the blame for failure on the other side. It is a mechanism
for tranquillising anxieties...[47]

When then Presidents Gorbachev and Bush met in Washington in May 1990 they set in motion just such a 'mechanism
for tranquillising anxieties'—the START agreement on intercontinental nuclear missiles. Bush and Gorbachev signed a piece
of paper at the end of their summit, but it wasn't a treaty. Martin
Walker correctly described it as 'a solemn promise to reach a
framework agreement to agree a treaty on reducing their strategic arsenals'. Gorbachev and Reagan had made a similar statement at their first American summit in 1987. The declaration
had been repeated at the Moscow summit and repeated again at
the Bush-Gorbachev summit in Malta.[48]

Bush and Gorbachev eventually managed to sign a treaty,
but it fared little better than its predecessors—it certainly hasn't
slashed nuclear arsenals in half, as Gorbachev and Reagan originally predicted. When the START treaty was first proposed it
was primarily concerned with the huge intercontinental missiles
aimed at hardened silos and large cities. But now technology
has moved on and the new cruise missiles, stealth bombers and
low trajectory (short flight time) ballistic missiles are a major and
increasing concern.

True to form, the START agreement cut the number of
older weapons but allowed for a massive increase in the new
weapons. So under START the US and the USSR were to cut
their total of intercontinental missiles by 4,476 and their sub-
marine launched ballistic missiles by a similar number. But they
planned to increase the numbers of more accurate air launched
cruise missiles and short range attack missiles by 2,990.[49] The
US Navy's nuclear capable aircraft are not included at all. Even
after the treaty was signed the US still had the same number of
strategic nuclear warheads as it did before. The nations of the
former USSR, although taking a cut, still inherited more nuclear
weapons than the USSR had a decade ago.[50]

One academic study claims that START 'will probably do
little more than remove large numbers of obsolete systems,
while leaving in place around 17,000 modern strategic

weapons.'[51] In fact, neither START, nor the subsequent START II have been formally implemented, although some missiles have already been destroyed. In 1993 the II SS reported 'the failure of Ukraine to ratify the START I treaty. As a result, START I implementation cannot begin nor can START II be considered for ratification.'[52]

Neither treaty covers British or French nuclear missiles. In fact the Tories are, as usual, following the US lead. Whatever else is going to be cut from the defence budget, it will not be the Trident II missile which will double the number of nuclear warheads on British submarines.

One final proof that the US ruling class are desperate to maintain their nuclear strategy is the 'Defence Planning Guidance', the key White House guidelines to the armed forces for their planning, budgeting and weapons procurement.The first post-Cold War version was issued in January 1990 and covers the years 1992-97. Its language is less bellicose than that of the Reagan years, but it still insists that 'should the war become global, the United States must be prepared for an extended conflict' and to 'prevail in a nuclear conflict and to dominate a post-nuclear world.' Although it admits that the Russian threat has diminished, the document urges an acceleration in the technological revolution in modern weaponry. There is however a shift away from defending Iran from invasion by Russia to a broader policy of defending oil interests in the whole Middle East, which 'ranks above South America and Africa in global wartime priorities.' For this reason the US is planning to develop more 'multi-purpose and reprogrammable weapons' that can be used against other adversaries.[53] It was, of course, precisely this scenario which was acted out with such brutality by the US and its allies in the 1991 Gulf War.

A similar pattern can be seen with regard to conventional weapons. An early response to critics' accusations that President Bush lacked what he himself described as 'this vision thing' was a speech in May 1989, in which he suggested troop reductions as part of the Conventional Forces in Europe (CFE) negotiations in Vienna.

Unfortunately for Bush, by Christmas 1989 the Eastern European uprisings were making his initial proposal look mealy mouthed, the budget deficit was intractable and Congress was smacking its lips at the thought of the peace dividend. So in his

State of the Union speech in January 1990 Bush tried to adjust the horizontal hold and get back in the picture. His second proposal suggested the US would trim its troops from 305,000 to 225,000 while the USSR would slash its troops from over 575,000 to 195,000 at the same time as the Warsaw Pact began to crumble.[54]

These proposals were designed to forestall calls for larger cuts in the future by making smaller cuts in the present. On the evening of Bush's State of the Union speech the White House announced that 'the United States does not envisage a further reduction of its forces in Europe below this new level.'[55] The *Financial Times* commented:

> His fear is that, without such an accord [CFE], Congress will simply go on a 'chopping spree' in search of defence cuts to pay for domestic programmes. Mr Bush's proposed troop cut is an attempt to head off such a stampede...
> But the President... seems also to be trying to put a floor under future force cuts in the next round of conventional arms talks—CFE 2.[56]

So, officially, the series of treaties begun by President Reagan and Gorbachev are leading to a reduction of nuclear and conventional forces. In reality something very much more dangerous has been happening in the 1990s—the new world order has led to an international arms bazaar of military hardware.

The Conventional Forces in Europe Treaty was meant to reduce the risk of war by limiting the amount of non-nuclear weapons that each country could hold. But the vast majority of weapons have not been destroyed. NATO has followed a policy of 'cascading' weapons from the countries that are above the CFE limits to those of is allies that are below the CFE limits. So, although the US army has lost some equipment, this is 'mainly through the "cascading" to European allies of tanks, APC (armoured personnel carriers) and artillery in excess of the CFE Treaty limits', according to the IISS.

The process has led, for instance, to the Greek army receiving 590 American M60 tanks and another 170 German Leopard tanks plus 70 self propelled 203mm guns. The Greek navy has benefitted to the tune of three US destroyers, one German frigate, three frigates from the Netherlands and three German corvettes. Under the same scheme the hardware of the Turkish army has 'risen drastically' according to the IISS. Some 700 M60 tanks, 20 Leopard tanks, 60 APCs and 70 artillery pieces have found their way to a country close to two of the hottest spots in the world—the Balkans and Iraq. Hundreds of tanks, artillery pieces and APCs have also 'cascaded' into the armouries of Spain and Portugal.

But although the cuts in conventional forces are not benign, they are real. Moreover, they are happening throughout the US forces and not just among those in Europe. This is because the uprisings in Eastern Europe hammered home a point that some defence experts have been making for some time: the Second World War is over. US and NATO strategy, particularly in Europe, has been based on the expectation that a future war would repeat the pattern of 1940; mass tank formations, this time Russian rather than German, would sweep across Europe. The major powers now find themselves with the wrong sort of army deployed in the wrong sort of numbers in some of the wrong sort of places. The US and Britain, harried by economic difficulties, are using the opportunity to restructure their armed forces. If they can, at the same time, save some money that is all to the good. If, moreover, they can sell this to the public as a step toward peace, so much the better.

So what sort of armed forces is the US after? It certainly doesn't want to give up the development of technologically sophisticated weapons. New conventional weapons are now being deployed which are as lethal as small nuclear devices and are subject to no existing arms control. They can destroy a small town in one minute. One arms expert says, 'This level of firepower means a single conventionally armed missile launcher could be as effective as a small tactical nuclear artillery shell and represents an immense increase in firepower compared with traditional conventional artillery.'[57]

However, the US has cut the number of troops operating such weapons, particularly in Europe where 60 percent of its entire defence budget is spent. But even here the US is being careful not to cut back to the point where it endangers the 'New Atlanticism'— the ability to play a leading role in the politics of the continent. Most of all the US wants to reduce the tanks and infantry army in favour of a more mobile, more technologically equipped force capable of fighting 'low intensity warfare' of the sort practiced against Grenada, Panama, Nicaragua, Libya and in the Gulf War.

The US army chief of staff has drawn up a plan which 'would transform the army from a service with its primary focus on defending Western Europe with tanks and other heavy equipment into a lighter, more flexible force that could be deployed rapidly in trouble spots around the world.' This 'worldwide contingency force, with more emphasis on airborne, air assault and light infantry' is necessary 'because regional instability, terrorism and drug trafficking present new challenges to the army'.[58] Since the global communist menace has ceased to be an effective bogeyman, 'terrorism' and 'drug traffickers' have taken its place in the Pentagon's lexicon of excuses for bashing anyone who gets in its way.

Similar plans are being canvassed in Britain as the government reviews its defence commitments. Again, it would be wrong to overestimate the amount of real arms cuts that are taking place, although the government's dire economic situation has helped to ensure that the cuts have been bigger than originally planned. But the main purpose of government policy, as in the US, is to ensure that the end of the Warsaw Pact gives the armed forces the excuse to carry out a much needed remodelling of their strategy. The *Financial Times* outlined three dangers which such remodelled forces would have to face—'resurgent Russian military ambitions', 'flare ups in remote places' and 'civil violence at home'.[59]

Meanwhile, beneath it all the economic certainties guaranteed by the high arms spending of the Cold War are disappearing faster than ever.

In summary, there are some cuts in conventional weapons, though as in the nuclear sphere they are not as great as we are led to believe. Neither are they 'honest responses to a decreasing threat', but attempts to gain new advantage from changed circumstances. Furthermore they disguise a far more important process of restructuring designed to make the armed forces more deadly and more effective in this changed environment.

For both Russia and America the revolt in Eastern Europe has transformed the arms negotiating process. Before 1989 they were trying to make some essentially marginal changes, the better to manage their relative economic decline. After 1989 arms negotiations became, in addition, a question of damage limitation. Both these factors weighed most heavily on Russia, which is why the INF treaty, the START treaty and the Conventional Force Reduction agreements require that Russia make the biggest cuts. But the Russian military, even though they are playing the weaker hand, are just as capable of presenting the appearance of cutting more military hardware than they actually are.

For instance, the unilateral cuts of 10,000 tanks and 500,000 troops announced by Gorbachev in 1988 were not the great step towards world peace predicted by the media. Closer examination revealed that the packaging is more attractive than the product.

Firstly, only 5,000 tanks were to be 'physically destroyed'. But since the USSR had some 20,000 old T-54 and T-55 tanks, many of them already in storage, scrapping 5,000 of these would be no great sacrifice. Some of the other 5,000 were supposed to be converted to civilian use, although it is hard to see what use civilians will find for 38 to 42 ton main battle tanks. So the overwhelming majority of these 5,000 tanks are likely to be redeployed in the already established army practice of using old tanks to train tank crews.[60] The cut of 500,000 troops represented about 10 percent of the USSR's army, but again things weren't as good as they looked. During Gorbachev's crackdown on the risings in Armenia and Azerbaijan in early 1990 it became clear that soldiers 'cut' from the regular army were simply being transferred to security and Interior Ministry forces. Apparently this involved some 300,000 troops, which, although not equal to the numbers being withdrawn from Eastern Europe, were still a very large addition to interior security forces.

Some of the restructuring of Russia's army is similar to that in the West. The military want to move away from a conscript army towards a more professional force, but conscripts are cheaper — 'a mercenary army would involve a sharp increase (at least six or sevenfold) in the expenditures needed to maintain it.'[61] Like many institutions in Russia, the army seems caught between, on the one hand, the need to adopt similar structures to Western capitalism in order to compete more effectively and, on the other hand, the cost of making such a transformation.

Close examination of Russia's 1989 commitment to stop producing weapons grade uranium and to close two plutonium manufacturing reactors shows that it means little. The uranium used in nuclear missile warheads is virtually indestructible and so can be endlessly recycled from old to new warheads. The US stopped producing weapons grade uranium in 1964 for the simple reason that it already had enough, either in current warheads or in stock, to meet its needs. The announcement simply means that Russia is now in the same position. The uranium it keeps after the destruction of 1,700 missiles under the INF treaty will help ensure plentiful stocks. As one commentator notes, 'the only surprise is that it took the USSR so long to reach this point.'[62]

The announcement that two plutonium plants would be shut down was also disingenuous. It omitted to say that the former USSR will still have between seven and 11 facilities, each of which will probably have several reactors, continuing to produce plutonium. US sources estimate that the former USSR has a stockpile of 115 tonnes of plutonium compared to 93 tonnes in the US in 1987.[63]

So the various unilateral cuts and summit agreements are as much to do with restructuring the armed forces as they are to do with disarmament. Many will feel, however, that the Eastern European revolutions have carried this process far beyond the point where Russian and US leaders would like to have called a halt. In particular, the argument goes, the destruction of the Warsaw Pact is a step toward peace irrespective of the superpowers' plans.

The collapse of the Warsaw Pact

A FULL SCALE invasion of Western Europe by Russia is now impossible to imagine. As a result both Russia and, to a lesser extent, the US now have to countenance much bigger reductions in their European armies than they might otherwise have done. Yet even here, where change is real and not merely cosmetic, some close analysis is necessary to determine exactly what is changing and why.

How deep are the Eastern European arms cuts? The published figures have been eye-catching: Bulgaria announced defence spending cuts of 12 percent, Czechoslovakia 15 percent, Hungary 17 percent and Poland 4 percent.[64] Two points need to be made about these figures: i) they were all announced *before* the uprisings of 1989 and ii) the figures are unreliable. The first point is important because it sheds light on the motivation for the cuts. The fact that they were made by the old regimes as a counterpart to Gorbachev's troop withdrawals announced at the UN in 1988 shows that the motivation was primarily economic, rather than the result of a new peaceful atmosphere born of the West's triumph in the Cold War. And, if they are economic in origin, they are more likely to be reversed if the economic situation recovers or if alternative cuts can reap the same dividend. It is noticeable that Romania, with no foreign debt, and Poland, with its new security worries, are making few cuts.

The figures need to be treated with caution, since it is often unclear to what the percentages refer. We are not told, for instance, whether Poland's and Hungary's double digit inflation has been discounted. In addition, different government figures sometimes contradict each other—at the same time that Hungary announced its cuts the Hungarian government's budget details showed an increase in military spending for 1989.[65]

It is also worth noting that, in part at least, the collapse of the Warsaw Pact makes the world look a safer place than it actually is because the West has always exaggerated the Pact's level of cohesion. Certainly, the Pact offered the USSR a useful figleaf with which to cover its imperial policing operations in Hungary in 1956 and Czechoslovakia in 1968, although they did not risk the same operation against Solidarity in 1981, preferring to let the Polish ruling class solve its own problem. But the thought that there would ever be a united Warsaw Pact invasion of Western Europe was always more fiction than fact. Not only were the Warsaw Pact countries always inferior in wealth, population and arms, they also lacked cohesiveness. Before the Eastern European revolutions Andrew Kelly wrote in *The Myth of Soviet Superiority* that in any East-West conflict:

> It might be regarded as doubtful that East German troops would wish to fight West Germans, and Romania would almost certainly attempt to continue her policy of independence throughout the conflict. Even with other allies the Soviet Union could not be too confident of support: both Hungary and Czechoslovakia have been invaded by the Soviet Union over the past 30 years and considerable anti-Soviet sentiment remains. Finally, Poland has friendly relations with a number of Western countries although its traditional enemy is Germany.[66]

Now, however, the countries of Eastern Europe are much more likely to resort to the use of arms to settle internal problems or conflicts with neighbours while the spectre of the Balkan War is haunting many parts of the former Soviet empire.

In 1994 the IISS reported that the Hungarian ruling class, worried by the war in the neighbouring Balkan states and mindful of nationalism directed against Hungarian minorities in Slovakia and Romania, have been buying arms from Russia. Yeltsin has been happy to do the deals in return for the cancellation of rouble debts. So $800 million worth of modern Mig-29 fighters are now on their way to Hungary. A further deal to supply new surface to air missiles is now likely. Both bits of equipment are likely to be aimed at Serbian aircraft which overfly Hungarian airspace en route to Croatia.

Germany, not to be left out, has given Hungary spare parts and equipment from the vast stockpiles of the old East German army. Indeed, much East German military equipment has turned up in the Baltic port of Kaliningrad, making it 'one of the great arms bazaars in a region awash with military equipment and demoralised soldiers', according to the *Financial Times*. Slovakia, unnerved by the Hungarian deal, has now made a similar debt-for-Migs arrangement with Russia. Poland, meanwhile, like the Czech Republic and Slovakia, is rebuilding its arms industries, partly by close links with foreign, including Israeli, companies.

There is one final irony which should help to put the collapse of the Warsaw Pact in perspective: many of the problems that have afflicted the Warsaw Pact are increasingly becoming problems for NATO. Just as it is inconceivable that the Warsaw Pact would attack Western Europe, it is equally inconceivable that NATO would attack that nice President Vaclav Havel and the other Eastern European democrats. And what is the rationale for the continued existence of NATO or for US troops to remain in Europe?

Even before the crisis in Eastern Europe reached its climax, NATO was developing more cracks than at any time since France left the integrated military structure in 1966. The mass movements in Europe against the deployment of Cruise and Pershing missiles produced strains, particularly between the US and Germany. Spain and Greece both made threatening noises about throwing US bases out. Then many European countries showed themselves reluctant to follow Reagan's massive arms build up, particularly his pursuit of the Star Wars and neutron bomb projects.

These strains have been exacerbated, not lessened, by the end of the Cold War. Germany was reluctant to have a modernised short range nuclear missile on its soil in the first place.

In May 1989 Chancellor Kohl managed, against US and British wishes, to get the decision on replacing the existing Lance missile delayed until 1992, after the German general election. But since the fall of the Berlin Wall the project has been a non-starter. The US and Britain kept up the pressure the longest, but eventually gave way, realising that there was little they could do to persuade the Germans. Kohl's decision to bolt for unification immediately the Wall came down had already been a salutary lesson to the US that the days of unquestioned US leadership of NATO were all but over, at least as far as the Germans were concerned.

No sooner was the Lance issue out of the way than the question of siting air launched Cruise missiles in Germany arose. Again Britain and the US would have preferred that some of the weapons go to Germany. Margaret Thatcher took special care to lecture Chancellor Kohl and the then Foreign Minister Hans Dietrich Genscher on this issue at the NATO summit in Turnberry, Scotland, in June 1990. German officials immediately let it be known that they weren't taking the slightest notice and that the chances of the weapons making their way to Germany were minimal. In response the US tried to convince François Mitterrand to accept the missiles in France and generally to draw France back into the NATO military structure. The US has been unsuccessful.

Cracks are also appearing elsewhere. Belgium has, without consulting any of its NATO allies, announced plans to unilaterally withdraw its troops from Germany. These troops represent a third of Belgium's army. The Dutch have now made a similar announcement and in February 1990 they doubled the defence cuts that they had announced only a month before. A senior NATO official in Rome reports, 'Now that the US itself is cutting back, Rome is out with the hatchet.'[67]

Business Week describes the situation emerging in the following terms:

> Already, gaps in the policy among NATO's 14 member nations are widening as small countries such as the Netherlands opt for speedy unilateral reductions in military spending—despite pleas for unity from NATO Secretary General Manfred Wörner. Other small countries are likely to grab defence money back as fast as they can. The result is that two tiers of NATO Europe are emerging: one—including nations such as France, Britain and Germany—

dedicated to maintaining genuine military capabilities and another engaged in a dash for demobilisation.[68]

Mitterrand has subsequently announced French plans to unilaterally withdraw her 50,000 troops from Germany. The IISS notes,

> NATO's security concepts have developed only slowly, fitfully and at times fractiously... The CFE process has produced its own strains; between France and the US over co-ordinating the NATO line with the avoidance of direct bloc-to-bloc negotiation; between Turkey and Greece over the geographical definition of the zone; between flank countries and those of the Central Region over the key targets for reductions and over zonal schemes which might increase threats to Norway and Turkey; between the major European countries and the US over constraints on armaments production...

The study went on to mention the difficulties over Lance and German unification, and concluded that 'at the extreme, these could call into question the continued viability of NATO.'[69]

The likelihood of the 'New Atlanticism' (that is US hegemony in partnership with Germany rather than Britain) surviving all this is not particularly high. After all, the 'New Atlanticism', according to Secretary of State James Baker's keynote speech to the Berlin Press Club in December 1989, is about 'forming common Western approaches' to 'regional conflicts, along with the proliferation of missiles and nuclear, chemical and biological weapons.'[70] Yet these are precisely the issues—from Lance to the Libya raid, from Nicaragua to the Balkan war—where NATO co-operation is at its most elusive.

That is why President Clinton spent so much time promising money to Russia and gradual inclusion in the Western club to former members of the Warsaw Pact. But NATO itself is still not free of strains. Clinton wants to shape the future of Europe, but he no longer has the money to pay for the privilege. That's why US troop numbers in Europe are down to 100,000, a third of their Cold War numbers. It's also why, for all the talk of NATO solidarity, the 1994 summit declaration insisted that the 'European pillar' of NATO must be strengthened. The US military is already reshaping itself for this new system. Equipment and rapid force deployment spending has hardly fallen, neither has spending on nuclear weapons, but savings have been made in the unworkable Star Wars programme and in cutting nearly 100,000 personnel from the armed forces.

These cuts will reduce US defence spending to a post-war low of just 3 percent of GNP by 1998. In the last three years some 400,000 workers in the US defence industry have lost their jobs. Similar numbers have been made redundant in the former USSR. The same pattern is observable in every arms industry. The result will be smaller, more 'professional' armies equipped with the most destructive weapons money can buy — 'more bangs per buck' as the military like to put it. And their cast off weapons circulate in the biggest and most dangerous tank boot sale the world has ever seen.

In short, the troop reductions in former Warsaw Pact countries and the diminished 'threat' that this entails are real, although not as great as those who fail to see the inherent instability of the Eastern European economies believe. Finally, NATO is undergoing a similar, if less severe, crisis in which the US's ability to dictate policy is weakened. The question that must now be answered is whether the decline of the two great superpower dominated alliances necessarily means a more peaceful world.

Part II: After the Cold War

The end of the Cold War and the permanent arms economy

WE HAVE seen a decline in the relative power of Russia and the United States, that arms expenditure — while still high in absolute terms — is, as a proportion of GNP, rapidly heading towards a post-war low and that the great alliances of the Cold War are breaking up. But why has arms expenditure fallen? Why has the power of Russia and America declined?

There is one commonplace explanation, perhaps most famously advanced in Paul Kennedy's *The Rise and Fall of Great Powers*, which says simply that arms expenditure ate away at the ability of the United States and Russia to compete on the world market, that economic decline is the result of 'imperial overstretch'. This is now the common cry of embattled senators looking for the peace dividend, Federal budget managers and White House officials urging 'burden sharing' on their allies. Much the same explanation used to be advanced for Mikhail Gorbachev's peace initiatives. Gorbachev, it was argued, inherited an economy hobbled by its commitment to an arms race with a much more powerful competitor. Now, it is said, if Russia is to re-integrate its economy with the world economy it must transfer resources from military production to civilian industry.

There is nothing wrong with these explanations, as far as they go. But if we try to apply the argument that high arms spending leads to industrial decline to the whole post-war period then it no longer seems to fit the facts. For instance, in the 1950s and 1960s, when arms expenditure as a percentage of GNP was considerably higher than it is today, the United States economy, the USSR's economy and indeed the world economy grew as fast as at any time in its history. Yet for most of the 1970s and 1980s, when arms expenditure has been much lower, the economies of the superpowers and the world economy have been increasingly beset with stagnation and economic crisis.

To understand why arms expenditure can at first produce a long boom which then suddenly turns into its opposite, stagnation and great power decline, we have to look beneath the most superficial relationships between arms expenditure and economic growth. There is a theory which has attempted to do this—the theory of the permanent arms economy. This analysis was pioneered by American Marxist WT Oakes (who also wrote as TN Vance) between the end of the Second World War and the 1950s. It was developed in the late 1950s by Tony Cliff, in the 1960s and 1970s by Mike Kidron and latterly by Chris Harman.[71]

The theory of the permanent arms economy is rooted in Marx's labour theory of value. For those not familiar with Marx's argument, a summary is provided in the footnotes.[72] The central consequence of Marx's theory is that there is a long term tendency for the rate of profit to fall. The only way in which the capitalist class can restore the rate of profit is to increase the rate of exploitation (lengthen hours, lower wages and welfare spending or raise productivity) or to destroy capital. The latter is the historic effect of slumps and wars. Both destroy capital and so offset the rising organic composition of capital. A third, historically insignificant, method of reducing the capital stock is the luxury consumption of the capitalist class. To the extent that capitalists buy Rolls Royces or caviar they are destroying the surplus which could otherwise be used to expand production by investing in labour or machines. Since the luxury consumption of the capitalist never re-enters the productive process, either as sustenance for labour or as means of production, it is a leak from the system.

The insight of the first theorists of the permanent arms economy, particularly Mike Kidron, was to see that arms expenditure functioned in the same way as the luxury consumption of the capitalist class, but on a historically significant scale. Arms production set masses of capital to work producing goods which would never re-enter the system either as commodities for consumption or as means of production. Huge amounts of capital that would otherwise have produced machine tools or cars or TVs were set to work producing satellites or missiles or tanks which simply stood around until they rusted or became obsolete. In the case of the arms-related space race some of the most technologically advanced capital in the world was, literally, jettisoned from the system. The effect was therefore the same as destroying capital in a slump or a war—it reduced the ratio of dead labour to living labour and so stopped the rate of profit from declining.

The end of the Second World War provided unique circumstances for such a permanent arms economy to emerge. All but two of the major imperialist powers were militarily and economically exhausted. And of those two powers, the US and the USSR, neither had the power to overrun the other. The United States might talk about 'rolling back' the USSR's forces in Eastern Europe, and Stalin might dream of an empire beyond Eastern Europe, but neither seriously attempted to match words with deeds. Conflict was banished to the periphery of the system, while at its core the arms race remained a 'cold' war.

And during the Second World War the two superpowers had developed social and industrial structures which not only had important elements in common, but were also tailored neatly to the mobilisation of resources for an arms economy. The structure of the USSR was obviously autarchic and state capitalist and its economic development had always been closely tied to the arms sector of the economy. But the 1930s and the war had also, though less obviously, bequeathed the United States an isolationist, state directed economy. Being more powerful and less war damaged, the US quickly overcame its isolationism. But a core of state directed industry remained, the arms industry. For instance, even by 1974, the funding of the US Defense Department, the Atomic Energy Commission and the space agencies was greater than the national product of every country in the world bar the USSR, Japan, West Germany, France, Britain, China, Italy and the US itself.[73]

The unintended consequence of military and economic competition between the superpowers was unprecedented levels of arms spending. This spending prevented the return of a slump for 30 years. The system might not be growing as rapidly as it would have done if all the surplus was productively invested, but at least the economies of the major powers were not periodically sucked into the whirlpool of recession. Year after year, decade upon decade the system grew.

But the permanent arms economy contained the seeds of its own destruction, as its original theorists had recognised. The burden of destroying productive capital was not borne equally by all the major capitalist powers, although they all benefited from the long boom. In particular Japan and West Germany spent something like 1 percent and 3 percent of GNP respectively on arms, while the amounts for the USSR and the United States were, as we have seen, in double figures. Or, as S Melman says:

> For 1967-69 we know that for every dollar of gross domestic fixed equipment (all investment in factories, equipment, buildings and homes) the United States spent 52 cents on the military. In Germany 14 cents were spent for the military, while in Japan the figure was two cents.[74]

While the superpowers produced tanks and missiles, the West German and Japanese ruling classes produced cars and TVs. The effect on the competitiveness of United States industry can be seen by the growth of imports:

US imports of 'high technology' goods 1960-82 ($m)[75]

	1960	1982	increase (%)
Chemicals	807	9,493	1,076
Non-electrical machines	438	9,620	2,096
Electrical apparatus	286	16,122	5,537
Transport equipment	742	33,635	4,433

Such a situation inevitably meant that those countries where the ruling class was not bearing the same arms burden as the superpowers began to encroach on US supremacy:

Military spending, productivity and growth (%) 1960-73[76]

| | ratio to real output | | | |
	military spending	invest- ment (a)	productivity growth rate (b)	output growth rate
US	8.1	13.6	3.3	4.1
UK	5.6	15.2	4.0	2.9
France	4.8	18.2	6.0	5.9
W Germany	3.9	20.0	5.8	5.5
Italy	3.1	14.4	6.4	5.2
Canada	2.8	17.4	4.3	5.4
Japan	0.9	29.0	10.5	10.8

(a) non-residential fixed investment
(b) manufacturing output per man hour

Share of combined advanced countries' GNP (%)[77]

	1953	1977
US	69.0	48.0
Japan	3.6	17.7
W Germany	6.5	13.2
France	8.0	9.7
Italy	3.8	5.0
Britain	8.9	6.3

As the superpowers' share of world production declined, their arms spending began to have progressively less effect in preventing a return of economic crises. The lower arms spenders were now investing in productive capital and therefore renewing the old tendency of the organic composition of capital to rise and the rate of profit to fall. Even if the superpowers had been able to return to the post-war levels of arms expenditure, it would no longer have been enough to do the trick. As Japan and West Germany piled on productive investment, the US and the USSR would have had to destroy ever greater amounts of capital in the arms race just to allow the system to stand still. In any case, the fact that the Japanese and West German capitalists were eating away at US markets and, in West Germany's case, exercising a magnetic pull on the USSR's Eastern European satellites, meant that the superpowers were increasingly unwilling to meet even the reduced levels of arms spending which prevailed at the start of the 1970s.

Cold War gave way to detente, as the superpowers tried to cut their losses. There could be no return to the high post-war levels of arms spending. Even Reagan's attempt to lift arms spending to 7 percent of GNP (nowhere near the 15 percent of the 1950s) sent the US economy spiralling into debt, financial crash and much more serious recession. The smaller economy of the USSR was sent into a terminal crisis, partly by its attempt to match the Reagan arms boom. And so long as the superpowers are threatened by capitalist powers who do not have any intention of matching their levels of arms spending it is difficult to see how a permanent arms economy can be reimposed on a world of competing great powers.

A second aspect of the arms spending long boom which threatened the superpowers, especially the USSR, was that, as the world economy grew, so did the capacity of multinational firms to produce by combining labour and means of production from across the globe. Thus, any state capitalism with a more limited access to the world market is at a competitive disadvantage. This was, of course, most true of those societies in which state capitalism has developed a more completely autarchic structure for the longest time—the USSR and the states of Eastern Europe. As Mike Haynes and Pete Binns wrote in *International Socialism 7*:

> To understand the crisis of autarchy it is important to remember that Marx saw two important tendencies inherent in capitalist development: a) the increase in the size of capitals as the result of the concentration and centralisation of capital and b) the increasing division of labour on a world scale, this resulting from the increasing complexity of production plus reducing the costs due to returns of scale, long production runs etc. State capitalism solves the first problem by fusing all the nation's capital resources into one unit. But if it does so by the autarchic method—removing the home economy from exchange with the rest of the world—then it has to replicate the machinery to make all the things that a modern economy needs entirely from its own resources, thus incurring enormous costs...[78]

That was written in 1980. Compare it with Gorbachev's 1988 speech to the UN:

> The retention of some kind of 'closed' societies is hardly possible today... The world economy is becoming a single organism outside of which no state can develop normally, no matter what social system it belongs to or what economic level it is on.
>
> This puts on the agenda the working out of a fundamentally

new mechanism for the functioning of the world economy and a new structure for the international division of labour. At the same time, the growth of the world economy is laying bare the contradictions and limits of the traditional type of industrialisation.[79]

The rapid decline of the Eastern European and USSR economies, the entire secret of their 'backwardness' and 'inefficiency', was a result of the way in which they emerged in military competition with the West at the end of the Second World War. They were forced, because of their historic weakness, to maintain a state capitalist arms economy at a higher pitch, for a longer time and on a narrower base than their Western rivals. The USSR's subordinate position and the nature of its empire always made it more dependent on purely military power than the US, preventing it from reducing the percentage of GNP spent on the arms economy, as did the US. One detailed study notes the USSR's 'defence burden increased from 14.4 percent in 1970 to 15.1 percent in 1972 to 15.3 percent during 1980-84'.[80] For these reasons the fall was all the more dramatic when it came. Even the difficulties with the extended empire that it gained in the 1960s and 1970s can be traced to their root in the USSR's isolation from the world economy. Looking at the expansion of the USSR's influence in the 1970s one observer has noted:

> Attempts to win influence and support in the post-colonial countries, whether through aid, trade or arms sales, not only proved immensely costly but produced little in return. The lack of Soviet integration into world financial markets and its lack of access to such instruments of 'Northern' control as the World Bank and International Monetary Fund, proved a particular source of weakness, because it meant that, unlike the USA, the USSR had no effective control over its debtors.[81]

Russia's leaders are still trying to extricate themselves from the nutcracker crisis of, on the one hand, the legacy of high arms spending and, on the other, the gale of international economic competition. But if this contradiction is most characteristic of the former state capitalisms of the East, it is also partly characteristic of Western states which have a large military state capitalist kernel hidden in a private capitalist shell. Just as Russia's leaders have tried, largely without success, to use the arms sector—

necessarily the most competitive and efficient sector of the former USSR's economy—to take over the production of civilian goods, so Western arms firms are busy dumping their arms dominated portfolios and seeking to diversify. Just as Gorbachev was handing 260 enterprises from the Ministry for machine building for the Light and Food Industries over to the military sector, so General Electric, Boeing and United Technologies were transferring resources, not particularly successfully, to civilian production.[82] If the bell of multinational competition tolled for the Kremlin bureaucracy, it also tolls, if not so loudly, for the Pentagon bureaucracy. This, of course, raises a vital question. How will the modern state respond to the contradiction between the need for economic power and the necessity of military power?

The new imperialism

THE WORLD after the Cold War is less stable economically. Indeed the turning point in this respect was not 1989, but 1973. The decline of the arms economy was a major contributor to the slump and stagnation that gripped the world economy in the 1970s and early 1980s. Even before oil prices began rising, both the US and the British economy were sliding into recession. Now the grand folly of the Reagan arms boom has been so cruelly exposed, and as arms expenditure makes another qualitative decrease, the tendencies towards economic crisis are likely to be more marked.

Secondly, the dog days of the arms economy are producing a dangerous paradox. A world economy more integrated than ever before—at the level of production as well as trade— is also being pulled apart by the emergence of blocs of capital forming around the most economically powerful nations. A senior official in the Japanese Foreign Ministry has observed that, on the one hand:

> In the capitalist economic system, the trend towards economic deregulation, together with the modernisation of telecommunications, has diminished the significance of borders between states; the 'borderless economy' is gradually emerging in the shape of free capital flows, international co-operation among large enterprises and international mergers and acquisitions.

On the other hand, this prospect is contradicted by the fact that:

> The United States no longer dominates international economics... Consequently, to prevent any major economic disruption, co-ordination of economic policy among the industrialised nations of the West is now indispensable. Furthermore, increasing divergence of productivity rates among industrialised countries has encouraged some of them to form economic blocs, thereby accelerating the disintegration of the established order. As a result of these recent developments the international economy now finds itself at a crossroads.[83]

It doesn't look as if we should hold out too much hope of 'international co-ordination' if recent trade disputes are anything to go by. But, whatever the prospects, the current 'disintegration of the established order' owes a lot to the decline of the arms economy. Even its initial phase of decline produced a simultaneous period of stagnation, in the advanced countries at least. The further diminution in its importance leaves behind a world unevenly integrated in production and trade within which states have to battle to protect their industries, markets and spheres of influence.

During its heyday the arms economy, East and West, served both industrial and military development well. Now the contradiction between military and industrial needs is massive. To weaken arms production in the name of international competition is to run the risk of being pushed to the sidelines of great power politics. This, in turn, risks the very economic weakness the state had hoped to avoid. But to maintain an arms industry is to risk further economic decline, which in turn threatens to further undermine an effective arms industry.

Trying to understand this paradox has sometimes led Marxists to stress one side of the contradiction at the expense of the other. Mike Kidron, for instance, finally abandoned the theory of the permanent arms economy because he thought the tendency towards state control of society had become so great that it could override the contradictions of the international system of production.[84] We need not spend a great deal of time disproving this approach, since history has achieved much of the work. The former heads of the Eastern European states, their new governments, the leaders of the movements which overthrew them and most observers concur on one point, even if they evaluate it differently: the pressure of international competition and the class struggles that it engendered broke open the autarchic state capitalisms of the East. Many will even agree that the same pressure is transforming the state capitalist elements of the Western economies. Whatever else it demonstrated, 1989 proved that the world of Orwell's *1984* is not round the corner.

But if the myth of an all powerful state capable of subduing the waves of competition and suppressing the class struggle has receded, a new variant of an old myth has taken its place. The Second International's Edouard Bernstein argued that the world economic system had become so integrated that there could no longer be wars between capitalist states.

> The economic development of nations will intensify their enmity: what nonsense! As if nations were petty shop-keepers competing for a limited clientele such that a gain for one necessarily represented a loss for the others. A mere glance at the development of the commercial relations among the advanced countries demonstrates the fallacious character of these ideas. The most industrially developed countries are simultaneously competitors and customers of one another; likewise their trade relations expand simultaneously with their mutual competition... the era in which peoples attempted to subjugate one another is finished in Europe and the same will more and more tend to be true in Asia. We have entered a new epoch, an epoch in which international law will prevail.[85]

Only a few years later the First World War bloodily refuted Bernstein's argument that increasing world trade and the exhaustion of territories that could be colonised would result in world peace. Today the modern form of the same argument is that the rise of the multinational corporation and international *production* makes armed conflicts between the major powers impossible. As the Japanese government official quoted earlier puts it, 'Wars fought to win new markets are a thing of the past; the balance of power is no longer determined by military force but by economic strength.'[86]

But the relationship between the state and multinational capital is not so simple, nor is the outcome likely to be peaceful.

Capital, even multinational capital, needs the state. It needs it to police the working class and to provide welfare for the working class. Even the Thatcherite state was never in favour of 'deregulating' the former and, much as it would have liked to, it was unable to do very much about reducing the latter. Indeed the complaint frequently made by some capitalists in Britain and the US is that the workforce is insufficiently educated and badly served by public transport.

Even where the state has retreated from a direct role in production, and this retreat is less marked than Tory propaganda would have us believe, it remains the ultimate guarantor even for multinational capital. It was only the Federal Reserve System that prevented the 1987 stock market crash turning immediately to slump. Only the US government could stop the failure of the saving and loans banks from dragging substantial sections of capital into the abyss. In Britain, British Steel and the privatised parts of the car industry were made profitable by state instigated austerity programmes *before* privatisation. Their profitability depends on continued state protected monopolies, favourable trade regulations and so on.

Since capital can only exist as many competing capitals, it still needs a state that can try to stand above the fray and attempt to regulate the competition. The move to international capital does not dispense with this requirement, but raises it to the level of conflicts between states and trading blocs. The conflicts between the US and Japan and between the US and the European Community over tariffs, production quotas, imports and indeed over the states' macroeconomic policy are an example of this process. It is a process which can, of course, spill over into the threat or use of force.

Indeed, as Iraq's invasion of Kuwait, and America and her allies' massive response to that invasion, so clearly demonstrated the armed power of the state is vital in protecting the ability of multinational capital to make profits. A more unstable world and more global production intensify the need for such protection—they do not diminish it. That is why an already successful capitalist economy, if it is to continue to be successful internationally, must seek to develop a political, diplomatic and military profile commensurate with its economic power. Such states must try to woo multinationals, defend 'their' multinationals and repel 'foreign' multinationals, and ensure a supply of raw materials. Any particular state is bound to clash with others as it seeks to attain these goals. The less political and military weight a state possesses, the less successful it will be. This is why every major capitalist state must also attempt to become a successful imperialist state. It is why, just as one imperialist world order breaks down, a new imperialist order is being born.

Not every powerful economic bloc of capital will be able to project its power in an imperialist manner or to the same degree. Japan and Germany are starting down this road, but there is no guarantee that they can reach their destination. Other states may frustrate them, or their internal weaknesses may cripple them. Nevertheless, they must try. Far from increased global production leading to peace, it intensifies the contradictions between states and between the international productive forces of society and its state dominated superstructure.

So the instability of the world economy has neither been controlled by the state, as Kidron implied, nor has it abolished the role of state capitalism and the drive to war. It has raised the contradictions in the system to a new level and it has ensured that they cannot be resolved by the peaceable functioning of the market. The end of the Cold War has allowed these contradictions to burst over the world with renewed force. Once again we face the prospect of emerging great power rivalry. Germany and Japan are now demonstrating a desire to exercise a political and diplomatic power more appropriate to their economic power.

i) The German question and the stability of Eastern Europe.
The Eastern European revolutions introduced instability into the heart of the capitalist system to a degree not seen since the early days of the Cold War. There are two closely connected aspects of this instability. One is the internal political and economic instability of the Eastern European regimes as they open their economies to the forces of the world market. The second is the state of flux that has been introduced into international relations by the demise of the USSR.

A united Germany is the hinge on which many future events in Europe will turn and it reflects both these conflicts. Even before the fall of the Berlin Wall Germany had begun to add some political muscle to its economic strength. The IISS has noted, 'The emergence of the German question in 1989 should have been no surprise to NATO. West Germany had long been the Alliance's [NATO] key front-line state... without its voice being given proportional weight in Alliance counsels.'[87] In this West Germany was a special case of a more general condition: the relative economic strengths of Europe, the US and Russia and their relation to the world economy were vastly different in 1989 than in the aftermath of the war, yet the political and military structures had remained virtually unchanged. As the IISS goes on to note, there were increasing signs that change was on its way.

> The harsh pressure exerted on Chancellor Kohl during INF Treaty negotiations in 1987 over the Pershing-1A based in West Germany and Mrs Thatcher's sudden abandonment of support for his position in the run up to the UK general election of that year may well have constituted 'last straws'. West German insistence in 1988 on NATO's development of a *Gesamtkonzept* [total concept] linking its conventional nuclear and arms control strategy signalled a new level of German assertiveness. The tough fight to postpone decisions on a follow on to the Lance missile and to keep SNF [Short Range Nuclear Forces] negotiation options open was another sign.[88]

Even before the Berlin Wall was breached, the question of unification had begun to take on a new prominence. In West Germany the subject used to be the sole province of right wing nationalists and fascists, like the Republican Party. But, as soon as tremors began to shake the East German regime, Kohl felt confident enough to make a speech claiming the German question was back on the agenda.[89] Even as early as East German leader Erich Honecker's 1987 visit to West Germany Kohl issued a communiqué which stressed his 'commitment' to 'the unity and freedom of Germany in free self-determination'.[90] And in September 1989 Kohl was arguing, much to the annoyance of the USSR, that the West German government had found the key to 'changing the status quo and overcoming the post war division of Europe'.[91] In a speech to his Christian Democratic Party convention Kohl explicitly stated that his government had gone beyond the traditional West German policy of *Ostpolitik*—the gradual process of normalising relations between the two German states by extending economic aid.[92]

But all this was merely a prelude to the kind of influence which Kohl was to wield once the Wall fell. Kohl has used Germany's unique position as an economically powerful nation at the heart of the transformed Europe to leap into the first rank of world powers. In every phase of the process of unification he left the US chasing his coat tails. The very decision to go for unity, announced to the West German parliament in November 1989, was taken without consulting the US or any other NATO member. Kohl's electorally motivated refusal to give guarantees about the Polish border, until unification was assured, was carried through in the face of unanimous international condemnation. His opposition to the replacement for the Lance missile buried the issue in the face of opposition from the US and Britain. Kohl, needing to buy the USSR's acquiescence in the unification process and then to position German business in the new Russian market, has also been in the forefront of urging economic aid to Russia.

This impressive record has forced the other capitalist powers to dramatically revise their attitudes to Germany. Soon after the fall of the Berlin Wall President Bush, seemingly without a second thought for the sensibilities of the British ruling class or the proprieties of the 'special relationship', was quick to describe the US and Germany as 'partners in leadership'. Certainly the declaration of the London NATO summit July 1990 was agreed in advance by Washington and Bonn. But events at the summit and since seem to have left the US government wondering whether it is the senior or the junior partner in leadership. After the summit the *Financial Times*' Ian Davidson noted, 'All NATO governments say that they want the Americans to stay in NATO and in Europe; but everybody knows that the decision will be up to the Germans.'[93] Democrat Lee Hamilton, a key House of Representatives foreign affairs spokesman, clearly expressed US concerns:

> This makes it clearer than ever that the Germans are leading Western policy toward the Soviet Union. I'm not saying that it's George Bush's fault. I'm not saying that we've become a non-power, but this is an example of the multipolar world that's going to make us learn a new meaning to the word 'consult'. These days it doesn't just mean us going to Europe and telling them what to do.[94]

These are just the worries that the US is willing to admit to in public. Its unstated worry is far more serious: the possibility of Germany dominating the West's policy toward Russia and

Eastern Europe. It is this worry, and concerns over trade, which lie behind the US's policy reversal on European integration. While being in principle in favour of the EC, the US could be heard to complain bitterly about 'Fortress Europe', about barriers to trade and so on. As soon as the prospect of a resurgent Germany emerged, such complaints were less strident as the US sought to encourage the EC to anchor Germany in Western Europe.

Similar concerns were obvious in France and Britain. The IISS reports, 'Fears of a possible diminution of the US commitment to Europe, and of the West Germany's *Drang nach Osten* [push to the East], drove France and the UK to some enhanced measures of defence co-operation.'[95]

In Britain the anti-European feeling in sections of the Tory Party reveal the fear with which an important section of the ruling class looks on a united Germany which can both dominate a more closely integrated EC and act as a bridge to the economies of Russia and Eastern Europe. A leaked Cabinet memorandum argued :

> It is likely that Germany would indeed dominate Eastern and Central Europe economically... the fact was, the pressure for German economic presence came from the East Europeans themselves as much as from the Germans. They wanted and needed German help and German investment; indeed it was probably the only way to restore and revive Eastern Europe... it might indeed be ironic that after 1945 Eastern Europe had set out to avoid ever again being dependent on Germany, but after 45 years of communism was more dependent than ever. But it was nonetheless a fact. The East Europeans might prefer British or French presence. But neither was prepared to commit adequate resources.[96]

What this memorandum shows—if we discount the smug assertions that the Eastern Europeans 'want' to be dominated by the Germans, let alone the British or the French—is the dramatic shift in the post-war balance of power. The US is not mentioned, the second rate status of Britain and France is admitted and the emerging power of Germany, half jealously, half fearfully, allowed. The solutions, beside 'being nice to the Germans', are even more striking. The memorandum continues:

To an extent Soviet and East European interests paralleled those of Western Europe. We wanted Germany to be constrained within a security framework which had the best chance of avoiding a resurgence of German militarism. We wanted a continuing American military presence in Europe as a balance to Germany's power. We would want to see limits, preferably self-imposed through a further CFE agreement, on the size of Germany's armed forces. We would want a renewed self-denying ordinance on acquisition by Germany of nuclear and chemical weapons. We would want to involve the Soviet Union institutionally in discussions of Europe's future security... not least because in the long term (and assuming continued development in the direction of democracy) the Soviet Union would be the only power capable of balancing Germany.[97]

So Russia, for all its problems, is being courted not just by the US and the Germans, but by the West Europeans as well—and each carefully watches the manoeuvres of their erstwhile friends and allies in case some alignment emerges from which they will suffer. In its fluidity and duplicity this situation more closely resembles the internecine rivalries of nineteenth century balance of power politics than it does the relatively simple bipolarity of the Cold War.

This shift in the international balance of power would be dramatic enough even if a united Germany could replicate the economic stability and political quietism that characterised most of West Germany's history. This assumption has been, however, proven false. And if the new Germany proves even less stable economically and more volatile politically than it has already become, then the careful plans to domesticate Germany in a broader united Europe may turn to dust.

There are reasons to expect a high degree of economic instability. Unification led to an unparalelled industrial collapse in East Germany. Industrial output fell by 65 percent in 1990-91. Despite some recovery, open unemployment remains at 17.6 percent and hidden unemployment at 30-35 percent in 1994. The social dislocation can be judged by the 60 percent fall in the birth rate and the 65 percent fall in marriages. In the west, taxes are already some of the highest in the world as debt interest payment incurred by unification is the biggest single item of public spending. A new emergency income surcharge will be added in

1995, bringing Germans to 'the upper tolerable limit of taxation' at a time when the welfare state is being cut.[98]

Wages have also taken a battering. The initial increase in money wages was nowhere near enough to cover the hike from East German to West German prices. Essential items doubled, trebled and sometimes quadrupled in price.[99] On top of this East German workers were asked to pay some 17 percent of their wages in social security deductions and up to another 10 percent in taxes, where previously almost no tax was deducted. By 1994 wages in western Germany were rising at less than 1 percent while prices were increasing at nearly 5 percent.[100]

It is little surprise then, that German unions have been engaged in battles of unprecedented scale for the post-war era. Metal workers, steel workers and miners have all contributed to an industrial scene which makes the previous quietude of West Germany's industrial relations look like a distant dream.

To survive this kind of resistance the German ruling class may have to dig far deeper into its reserves than it imagines. Forcing higher taxes on an unwilling population has been one strategy to pay for heavy state investment in building new roads, railways and telecommunications systems in east Germany.[101] Private business has not met the massive rise in social security payments and subsidies to ailing industry. So the final irony is that unification has called forth a massive growth in 'state capitalist' economic intervention.

East Germany was the Eastern European economy with the best chance of successfully integrating itself with the world market. Elsewhere, except possibly in Czechoslovakia, prospects were always considerably worse. The depth of the crisis in Russia speaks for itself and there is simply no prospect of Western aid on a level sufficient to make any real difference. America and Britain are against giving much aid, even supposing they could afford it. Even those who wish to provide aid, like Chancellor Kohl, do so because they wish to gain political advantage, not because they think it will really be able to solve Russia's economic crisis.

No one really knows what reconstruction in Eastern Europe will cost. The Credit Suisse First Boston international investment bank estimated that it would take $16 billion a year merely to offset the effect of Russia demanding hard currency for oil and gas supplies. The UN Economic Commission for

Europe estimates that in order to mount a Marshall Aid type operation for Russia and Eastern Europe it would take nearly $17 billion every year for four years.[102] Actually, the relatively small amounts of aid given to Europe under the original Marshall Aid plan would never have lifted the devastated economies out of disaster had it not been for the functioning of the permanent arms economy. But, even leaving this primary objection aside, the amounts of aid initially on offer came nowhere near meeting the UN's $17 billion a year figure. When President Bush made his original offer of $380 *million* aid for the whole of Eastern Europe in March 1990, one US Senator commented that it was 'barely enough to bail out a failed savings and loan institution, much less to jump start national economies that have been dead for decades'.[103] Since then the cost of the whole savings and loan rescue has rocketed to $500 *billion*, making large scale US aid to Eastern Europe impossible. If Kohl was to offer Russia the same level of assistance he has given East Germany it would cost DM 2 *trillion*, 50 times what was sent by the West in 1993.[104] There has been more money from the new European Bank of Reconstruction and Development, the EC and some bilateral aid packages, but they have been insufficient to haul the East European economies out of a pit that they have spent 20 years getting into. In any case much of this 'aid' will be loans, running the danger of deepening the crisis of the Eastern European economies in the way that Poland's economic crisis was worsened by Western loans in the 1970s.

Private investment by Western firms looks even less likely to deliver the resources the Eastern European economies need. Wage rates, infrastructure and the prospects of political stability all look more attractive elsewhere. In particular the world economy's current trend for most investment to take place between the advanced economies is unlikely to be altered by an area in which included Poland, Romania, Bulgaria, Czechoslovakia, East Germany, Yugoslavia and Hungary who together accounted for less than 10 percent of the output of the EC.[105] Of course there will be some investment, but this is likely to take the form of what the *Financial Times* calls 'cherry picking'. A less euphemistic term would be asset stripping or, at best, absorbing the profitable and letting the rest rot. The OECD has warned banks against lending to Eastern Europe, while the *Economist*'s 26 nation 'country risk' investment chart has Russia second with a 90 percent risk factor, just behind Iraq's 100 percent. Poland is sixth, Hungary twelfth and the Czech Republic twentieth.[106] The *Economist* concludes:

> Direct investments... could double or triple the GNPs of the ex-communist countries in just 10 years. The era calls for courage and vision from Western business leaders. The early birds will get the choicest worms.
>
> A mouthful of worms may be all they ever get. Investing in ex-communist countries is fraught with risk. Unless, or until, they establish all the paraphernalia of capitalism to go with their new found enthusiasm for free markets, the risks to foreign investors are likely to grow, not shrink... Completing such tasks will embroil the region in all the wrangles about wealth distribution and the size and role of the state which Western countries have spent generations trying to solve.[107]

So the new Eastern European governments look as if they are largely being left to their own devices, trying to make good a massive productivity and growth gap with the world market into which they have been thrust, at the same time as they try to construct stable parliamentary democracies.

As a result of these competing forces there has been instability at every level. Many Eastern European societies are riven with ethnic rivalries, plagued by the growth of fascist and right wing nationalist political movements and, in Lithuania, Poland and Hungary, a resurgence of parties representing the Stalinist old guard. Former Yugoslavia has become a by-word for the chaos into which, in the worst case, these societies can descend.

Long suppressed ethnic conflicts are reappearing now that the lid has blown off the Stalinist pressure cooker: in Bulgaria, between Bulgarians and the Turkish minority—threatening relations with the Turkish government; in Romania, between Romanians and Hungarians, threatening relations with Hungary. And to these we have to add the already numerous nationalist conflicts flaming on the borders of Russia and its former 'inner-empire'.

How these tensions work themselves out depends a great deal on the kind of resistance the working class mounts to the attempts to make it pay the price of reintegration into the world market. The relative lack of bloodshed so far over the persecution of the Turks in Bulgaria is a product of the opposition's determination, especially among the independent trade unions, not to allow the government to divide and rule. In the early days after the fall of Ceausescu the weakness of the Romanian opposition in Tigues Mures meant that it failed to prevent ethnic conflict, while the integrated nature of the opposition in the Romanian revolution's birthplace, Timisoara, managed to direct the anger and frustration at the National Salvation Front.

More generally, the point of light in the gathering darkness is that these revolutions have bequeathed the reconstituted ruling classes a working class that has won some measure of political freedom through its own actions, even if it did not transform one mode of production, state capitalism, into another based on its own power, socialism. In this sense the greatest gain of the revolutions is the experience of revolution itself, not the often fragile and limited democratic structures on which the West places so much emphasis. Certainly there is no gain for the working class in the renewed, harsher exploitation now being inflicted on them by the 'market' or, more accurately, by monopolies and oligopolies often staffed by the very same bureaucrats who ran the old regimes. It is this contradiction which makes the Eastern European revolutions the opening, not the close, of a period of social upheaval. We cannot, of course, predict the time scale or intensity, let alone the outcome, of these class and ethnic struggles in Eastern Europe. What we can assert is that the end of the Stalinist empire is not leading to a period of stability. Here, right in the heart of the system, is the prospect of renewed struggles and renewed imperialist conflict on a greater scale than we have seen since the 1930s.

ii) The rise of Japan. In the Second World War the United States used just 10 percent of its GNP to defeat Japan. In the 1950s US GNP was 25 times bigger than that of Japan. Today the US government would grind to a halt without Japanese purchases of US treasury bills. Perhaps nothing illustrates this economic transformation so clearly as the weakening of the US semi-conductor industry in the face of Japanese competitors. Here is a spin off from the space race, essential to the military, undermined by the effects of the very permanent arms economy which gave it life.

This difference in economic fortunes has long niggled at the sensibilities of the US ruling class, but the end of the Cold War has allowed tensions between the two countries to reach new levels. As one commentator put it, 'There is little question that the improvement in US-Soviet ties has had a strong impetus on the deterioration of the Tokyo-Washington relationship.'[108] While the 'Russian threat' hung over both Europe and the Pacific no disparity in economic growth rates could disrupt the military and political alliance between Japan and the US. The US bases in northern Japan were vital for spying on Siberia and without naval facilities in Japan the US Seventh Fleet would have been useless. Equally, Japan needed US military protection from both the USSR and, for at least some of the Cold War period, China. Now that both threats are receding, economic tensions have gained new prominence. Opinion polls now show that a majority in the US see Japanese economic power as a bigger threat than Russia's military machine.

As the US economy struggles with the legacy of the permanent arms economy, it has attempted to shift the terms of competition with Japan in its favour. Increasingly bitter rows have broken out between the two countries over trade restrictions. These go well beyond the normal issues of tariff barriers and import quotas and touch on issues that concern the management and direction of national resources. For instance, during the 1990 negotiations a kind of hostile, competitive Keynesianism emerged. The US tried to reduce the competitive advantage of the Japanese economy by insisting that they invest more in parks and sewers (only about a third of Japanese houses are connected to sewers). In response the Japanese told the US to increase investment in education and to reduce the demand for imports by increasing savings. Such wrangles, heightened by the symbolically important purchase of Columbia Pictures by Sony and the Rockefeller Centre by Mitsubishi, are constantly on the verge of tipping over into a trade war.

The end of the Cold War has also meant a change in political and military relations. This has two aspects: the US's attempt to cut back its military commitments in the Pacific, in part trying to shift some of the burden onto Japan, and Japan's partial re-emergence onto the stage of world politics after 40 years of US tutelage.

In the first instance the military relationship is the extension of trade wars by other means. In February 1990 US defence secretary Dick Cheney raised an issue that has been dead for 40 years: that US willingness to defend Japan militarily might be linked to progress in trade talks.[109] Meanwhile some US Congressmen are demanding that the Japanese government pays the full cost of maintaining US troops in Japan, rather than the 40 percent which it meets at present. Similar conflicts can be seen in the history of the joint US-Japanese fighter project, the FS-X, based on the US's F-16. The company agreements were in place in 1988, but the project was held up, as President Bush and Congress objected that the US share of production was too low and Japanese access to new computer technology too great.[110] Japan, for its part, has not been slow to respond, as the IISS notes: 'It was no doubt symptomatic of Japanese disillusionment with US attitudes that, in the summer of 1989, the Air Self-Defence Forces placed their first order for non-US aircraft (the British BAe 125, a navigational and calibration aircraft) and began serious discussions over the purchase of the British Harrier VTOL fighter.'[111]

But the US's direct military relationship with Japan is only one aspect of its role in the Pacific which is now under review. The familiar equation of economic problems at home and better relations with the USSR (and China) meant that the US began to cut back on its commitments in the area. Dick Cheney toured the area in 1990 telling allies that the US remained committed to the region but that forces were to be reduced by 10 percent. The US can hardly withdraw from a region which is vital economically, because of its links with Japan, and unstable politically, containing the Philippines, North Korea, Cambodia, Vietnam and China. On the other hand, economic pressure is squeezing military spending. This contradiction is dramatised in the case of the US bases in the Philippines. The US would like to maintain its Subic Bay naval base, but it is unwilling to do so at any cost. So for the first time in nearly 100 years the US and Philippine governments are sitting down to talk about US withdrawal. An internal memo by a senior US official in the Agency for International Development spells out various negotiating options:

> It ruled out 'near term [US] departure' as unacceptable and 'long term status quo' as politically impossible, opting for 'medium term phase out'. Let's assume that we hit them with a big stick and dangle that fat debt-reduction carrot and they sign, we will still be out by 1999'.[112]

Japan, and indeed Taiwan, now have a bigger economic stake in the Philippines than does the US. The same memo continues:

> I see no reason why we shouldn't get the Japanese in on this deal. In strategic terms Japan is probably more vulnerable to disruptions in the sea lanes running by the Philippines than any other single factor save a nuclear war.[113]

The US's planned withdrawal from the Philippines also highlights the changing nature of imperialism. With the US presence diminishing, the emergence of regional imperialist conflict grows more likely. As the *Far Eastern Economic Review* notes:

> As superpower rivalry wanes, fears of regional middle power rivalries grow... to see the back of the Americans (and Soviets) is one thing. To leave the region's waters to be patrolled by China, India and Japan is quite another... Indeed, there is clearly a danger that without some outside hegemonistic influence the region could become rent with nation state rivalries or its members go separate ways and establish their own 'special relationships' with one of the regional powers—as some say Thailand has already done with China.[114]

Some commentators see Japan as the natural successor to the US as the guarantor of capitalist stability in the area. Certainly Japan has recently begun to demonstrate its independence on strategic questions. Japan's massive economic growth has allowed its defence budget to grow by 5 percent a year in real terms for the last 15 years while still taking no more than 1 percent of GNP.[115] Such spending has given Japan the third largest arms budget in the world. This year the Japanese government officially participated in a NATO meeting for the first time and discussed security concerns in the Asia-Pacific region. 'The Japanese delegation said there was growing support at home for a more vigorous military policy, so long as it was co-ordinated with national allies.'[116]

In diplomatic areas too Japan 'has been adopting stances that would earlier have made it blush.'[117] Japan has now surpassed the US as the biggest donor of foreign aid. Its aid to Eastern Europe is now in the same league as the US, although that doesn't amount to much. Japan is also increasingly independent in choosing to whom it gives its aid.

All this is important in seeing the direction of events, but it is too soon to see Japan 'replacing' the US, even as the dominant power in the Pacific. In any case, the emerging imperialist rivalries do not simply repeat the pattern of the old superpower rivalry, but with different countries taking the lead. Now the competing major powers have disproportionate strengths. Some are primarily economic, like Japan and Germany. Some, like China, have a military capacity out of proportion to their economic strength. Others, like both Russia and US to different degrees, still retain great, though declining, economic power *and* massive military capacity. The United States obviously remains the world's greatest economic and military power, but it no longer has the hegemony in the West or the power to control events on a global scale that it once did. More controversially, it is important to assert that Russia is still a great power, and not just militarily. Russian diplomacy and the deployment of Russian troops were crucial to lifting the siege of Sarajevo in 1994. As the *Economist* noted: 'Russia's involvement sent new signals to the outside world...The message is clear: for all its problems, Russia still matters.'[118] And Germany still has a long road to travel before it has the capability to intervene militarily, even within the confines of Eastern Europe. Japan, like Germany in Europe, has to overcome the historic distrust of other Pacific countries before it can even play the role of an effective regional military power.

So the central feature of the new imperialism is that even the greatest of the great powers is no longer *so* great that it has the same capacity to structure the world, or even particular regions of the world, that two superpowers had at the height of the Cold War. They now try to control a less stable world while still competing with each other. Sometimes they will achieve this through mutual but unstable agreement, sometimes through economic competition, sometimes by war or the threat of war and most often through a combination of all these. In this limited sense the competition between the major powers is beginning to resemble that between the wars or even before the First World War. Then Germany, France, Russia, Britain and the US battled for supremacy. They were not equal militarily or economically. Some were declining and others rising. Yet it was precisely in the combined and uneven competition that the instability of the system rested. Nevertheless, there are strict limits to this parallel. Most importantly, the whole economic structure surrounding this competition has been transformed. So, as a result, has the situation in what used to be these imperialist powers' colonies.

iii) The Third World. The new struggle between the major powers takes place in a world which the arms economy has left more highly militarised than ever before. And, especially for the superpowers in economic decline, their absolute military superiority is increasingly the one decisive advantage that they have over their rivals. The temptation to use that power is heightened, not lowered, by the decline of the arms economy and the end of the Cold War. The Cold War was always a method of disciplining those in 'your camp', as well as threatening those in the 'enemy camp'. Now such Cold War discipline has been partially removed, the discipline of hot war may be its replacement. And this takes place in a world where weapons of mass destruction have proliferated to Third World countries whose possibility of independent economic development is increasingly curtailed. Third World arms spending quadrupled between 1960 and 1980. Since 1984, the year when Third World arms imports exceeded their imports of grain, the arms spending of the less developed countries has increased twice as fast as that in the rest of the world.'[119]

Geographical distribution of world military spending (in 1973$)[120]

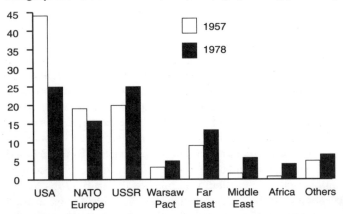

This growth in Third World arms spending is the result of changes in political structure which have swept the Third World in the post-war years. This period has seen the end of formal empires and the coming to power of indigenous ruling classes in much of the Third World. Many are heavily armed in order to fill the space left by departing great powers. These regimes are willing to make and break alliances both with their neighbours and with the major powers as they squirm under the twin pressures of unrest at home and great power economic and political pressure internationally .

The Iraqi invasion of Kuwait in August 1990 demonstrated this process. It also highlighted many of the themes outlined earlier. Firstly, the situation in the Gulf showed the changes that have overtaken the Third World in the post-war period. Neither Iraq nor Iran are colonies of great powers. They are independent states in which nationalist regimes, albeit of very different ideological colouring, replaced colonial control or subservient client regimes of the major powers. Both have created formidable military machines which they have used to try and gain regional dominance in the post-colonial world. This was the origin of the Iran-Iraq war.

But, even in a world where direct colonial rule is mostly a thing of the past. the major powers cannot simply stand aside from such conflicts, especially in an area which supplies so much of their most vital raw material, oil. The US and most Western powers watched with malevolent neutrality as Iraq tried to invade Iran in 1980. The US hoped Iraq would tame the regime which issued from the Iranian Revolution the previous year. It even tried to repair its relations with the Iranian regime. Frustrated in this by the Irangate scandal, and with Iran on the verge of winning the war, the US backed Iraq. It was US support in the Gulf tanker war which gave Iraq victory. Yet within a few years the US found itself at war with its erstwhile ally.

The Gulf crisis also showed that Germany and Japan still have a long way to travel before they are any match for the US militarily. Neither has anything like the capability to sustain the kind of operation that the US mounted in the Gulf. Indeed Israel, France and Britain had a far more important military capacity as far as operations in the Gulf was concerned, hence Bush's sudden rediscovery of the 'special relationship' with Britain and renewed warmth toward the Israelis after a period of worsening US-Israeli relations. Yet even here, where old patterns seemed to be reasserting themselves, some changes are observable. It was at the time of the Gulf War that some German politicians, encouraged by Kohl, began talking of abandoning the constitutional commitment only to deploy their forces defensively and the customary practice of not straying outside Europe. In this respect the pressure to involve Germany and Japan in military affairs outside their normal sphere of influence may be to the US's short term advantage, but it may also be a precedent which the US will later regret having encouraged its competitors to set.

The Gulf War demonstrated the continuing strengths and the emerging weaknesses of the great powers. Russia's weakness was demonstrated. It needed to enter the world economy and was therefore obliged to follow the US's lead. But that phase is already ending under the twin impact of nationalist resurgence in Russia and instability internationally, particularly in the Balkans and Russia's 'inner empire', leading Russia's 'nationality adviser' to talk of his country's need to develop a 'fragmented imperialism'. And it is not true that the Gulf crisis showed the US to be as powerful as it has always been. Firstly, the US could do little to stop Iraq seizing Kuwait. Secondly, to achieve its aims the US had to rely primarily on force and the threat of force—the one overwhelming advantage that it still has over its competitors. Thirdly, even though the US's massive military force did get Iraq out of Kuwait it could only do so at enormous cost. Even the initial troop build up was costing the US $10 million a day. US appeals for Japanese financial aid for the task force illustrate precisely the dilemma outlined earlier. Military power gives the US the capability to punish enemies and discipline 'allies'—but at the risk of weakening its economic position.

It is precisely the intractability of these problems which forced the US to try and involve other countries. The *Financial Times*, having observed that 'at first sight' the Gulf crisis looks like 'an old-fashioned demonstration of raw American power', went on to conclude:

> In fact, the presidential order [to send troops to Saudi Arabia] caps several days of intensive US diplomacy aimed at 'internationalising' the Persian Gulf crisis. Mr Bush has broken with the unilateral action favoured by some of his post-war predecessors, particularly former President Ronald Reagan...
> Ever since the crisis broke last week he has dialed a dozen world leaders: President Francois Mitterrand of France; Chancellor Helmut Kohl of West Germany; Mr Giulio Andreotti; current president of the EC Council of Ministers:

and Prime Minister Toshi Kaifu.[121]

Such international co-ordination is not just a question of cloaking US power in multilateral clothes. The US found such co-ordination *necessary* as well as *desirable*. Unilateral military action against Iraq was too dangerous and unilateral economic action was impossible. So the need for international action speaks of US weakness, not strength. That such action was forthcoming speaks of the unique importance of oil to world capitalism. These conditions cannot be expected to last or, necessarily, to exist in other cases. After all, the invasion of Grenada, the bombing of Libya and the initial deployment of ships in the Gulf during the Iran-Iraq war were all much smaller problems—luckily so for the US, since its allies often refused it assistance. And since the Gulf War, despite US claims that its victory had banished the Vietnam syndrome, American might met humiliation in Somalia and has been too nervous to even consider serious action in the Balkan wars or the civil war in Rwanda.

Such are the shifting sands of the new imperialism. All the talk of a more peaceful and stable world suddenly seems a faint echo from another time, drowned by the sound of fighter engines.

Class and crisis: the transition in Eastern Europe

MIKE HAYNES

POPULAR power in Eastern Europe in 1989 lasted no longer than the length of a smile, according to the Czech president, Vaclav Havel. For the length of that smile everything seemed to be possible. Speaking to an audience of American bankers in the autumn of 1989 Lech Walesa told them, 'There will not be any unemployment because there is so much to do'.[1] The picture is very different today. The smile has now gone as crisis has intensified throughout the region. Where austerity programmes have been put in place, standards of living have fallen and unemployment has risen. But in countries like Romania, Bulgaria and Albania, where change has been more halting, the development of the crisis has been no less intense—undercutting the idea that there was any salvation in the old ways.

As the pain has intensified enthusiasm has melted away. In Poland and Hungary in particular the result has been astonishing levels of apathy and alienation from the political systems. Elsewhere the main beneficiary has been nationalism. The Yugoslav example is a dreadful warning of what might lie down that road. For Haval now 'the happiness is gone. The second act is called crisis. The crisis will be chronic and then the catastrophe will happen. Finally the catharsis will come and after that everything will go well'.[2] He may be right, but a look at the real conditions in Eastern Europe suggests that his hope is based rather more on a literary model of life than on a cool assessment of the objective possibilities in the foreseeable future.

The aim of this article is to try to make such an assessment. It is an urgent task because the disorientation produced by the collapse of Eastern Europe has affected the left across the world. At the same time the ideologists of the right are trying to maintain the initiative by presenting bullishly optimistic accounts of the change. But their promises of brighter tomorrows and visions of newly liberated peoples advancing towards the rising sun, after the temporary difficulties of transition, have as much basis in reality as some of the worst excesses of Stalin's propaganda about the promised land.

The events of 1989 in East Germany, Poland, Hungary and Czechoslovakia and the ongoing pressures for change in the former Soviet Union, Romania, Bulgaria and Albania reflect the coming together of two distinct movements. At one level they have been an expression of popular pressure from below and they could not have developed without this. But, as in any revolutionary crisis, there was a second movement, this time at the top of the system. The existing ruling classes, in order to maintain the core of their power shifted their ground, accommodated to the popular mood, sacrificed their most hated representatives and recomposed themselves so as to be better able to maintain themselves in the future. They were able to do this the more easily in this case because the demonstrating crowds and striking workers in Eastern Europe posed primarily political demands. They left the question of the social base of power of those who ruled them largely untouched except insofar as it was partially expressed through the role of the Communist Parties. It is this that accounts for the apparent paradox of the 'revolutions' in these societies.

The state is being dismantled to some degree, planning is giving way to more market control but the same social group, shorn of its figureheads and old secret police, is still in control. What it has succeeded in doing has been to partly shift the institutional base of its power out of a 'state pocket' and into a 'private pocket'. In the process there has been some upward mobility within the ruling class and the occasional new entrant. There has also been a change in the balance of power within the ruling class between its sections. But, contrary to those who claim that what was at stake was the substitution of a socialist mode of production or a new form of class society by a capitalist society, there is no evidence that a fundamental change has taken place in the nature of the ruling class. What is striking is how little change has actually occurred. To sack a general and promote a colonel hardly constitutes a social revolution any more than selling off a state enterprise to its managers does or renationalising it with a similar group of people in control. Rather it suggests that what is at stake is an internal transformation within a mode of production, in this instance a shift in the form of capitalism from one of a strong state capitalism to more mixed state and market forms.

There will be many people who will try to resist this conclusion, so in order to support our argument we will later explore in more detail how the ruling class in Eastern Europe has shifted the base of its power. But a full understanding of how and why this has happened requires us first to explore how the Eastern European crisis developed and then to tie down the real possibilities of a market transition in the 1990s. We will then be better able to see what has been at stake socially and how this relates to the internal class character of these societies.

Rationality and irrationality under the old regime

IN THE wake of the collapse in Eastern Europe and the revelations of corruption, waste and inefficiency many commentators have marvelled that these regimes could have survived so long. But the fact that they did points to an important issue — for a long period these systems were both dynamic and viable. Their dynamism was frequently overestimated but it was nevertheless real. Just as it makes no sense to judge a bankrupt company's past performance on the basis of its final winding up balance sheet of devalued stocks and assets, so in Eastern Europe and the former Soviet Union the enormous scale of the collapse should not blind us to past achievements. The fears of the Cold War, for all their exaggerations, were based on the threat of something real.

This reality did not lie in the achievements of 'socialism', for these societies were based on the enormous exploitation and oppression of the working class which led to periodic revolt. Rather the reality lay in a period of successful state directed competitive industrialisation which lasted in the Soviet Union from 1928-29 to the 1970s and in Eastern Europe from 1948 to the 1970s. What lay behind this was the attempt of the different ruling groups in these societies to break out of their relative economic backwardness so as to be better able to cope with the military and economic pressures of the world economy.

Past reliance on the market to achieve this had proved spectacularly unsuccessful. For Eastern Europe (excluding the former East Germany and the Soviet Union after 1917) the most recent calculations show that the economies of the area were failing to make any significant impression on the gap that had developed with advanced capitalism before 1945.[3] The region as a whole was especially badly hit by the inter-war economic crisis which led to a final collapse of faith in market forces. At the same time piecemeal and pragmatic state intervention, whose content was a prisoner of narrow vested interests within the existing ruling class, also proved unable to deal with the area's difficulties. Here was a section of world capitalism that was characterised by 'complete economic chaos, almost inextricable confusion and a state of utter hopelessness', say two of the area's leading historians. For an American commentator 'a gigantic backlog of backwardness, increasing demographic pressures, consistently erroneous economic policies, insuperable nationalistic barriers to fruitful cooperation in the area all but arrested the process of economic growth'.[4]

Thus although the particular forms of development after 1945 were not pre-determined, the history of past failures and the immediate post-1945 pressures within the world economy were pushing towards industrialisation drives involving substantial state elements irrespective of the precise political forms that developed. It is worth recalling, for example, that the original ideas in 'Third World' development economics that became so influential in the three decades after 1945 of state directed growth were actually formulated as a response to the inability of these Eastern European states to break out of the vicious circles of backwardness and stunted growth within the capitalist world economy.[5]

In the event the circumstances of war, Cold War and Stalinist control dictated that the ruling classes in these societies after 1948 would pursue policies of state directed industrialisation that paralleled those of the Soviet Union after 1928-29. The particular circumstances that led to the adoption of this pattern and the more detailed logic of these moves in terms of the pressures of the world economy and the needs of the Soviet ruling class and the recomposed Eastern European ruling classes have been discussed elsewhere and need not detain us here.[6] The important thing is that the new policies worked for a long period in terms of their own objectives. The costs were enormous, but the previous barriers were broken and these states did move forward at a pace that for a time gave rise to real concern amongst their competitors in the advanced West. The basis of this is shown in Table 1 below.

Table 1
Annual average per capita growth rates 1950-1980[7]

World average	2.7
Centrally planned economies	3.6
Industrialised economies	3.1
Middle income market economies	3.0
Low income group	1.5

As a result of these growth rates there was some closing of the gap with the advanced West as well as some convergence within the Eastern bloc itself as the weaker economies grew slightly faster.

This was what the ruling classes in Eastern Europe had hoped for. But over time growth slowed and by the late 1970s and early 1980s the Eastern European economies were stagnating and the gap between them and the advanced West was growing again. For our purposes what is important is the way in which this emerging crisis gradually exposed the limitations of the long run strategies that had been adopted in order to compete with the West.

The industrialisation drives (as with the earlier Soviet one) had been based upon attempts to compete in a world dominated by the imperatives of accumulation and commodity production. To compete here economies had to be built whose structures were in direct competition (both militarily and economically) with the states of the advanced West. Army was set against army, nuclear missile against nuclear missile, steel industry against steel industry and so on. In the Soviet Union in the 1930s the impact of the world crisis forced the economy to turn inward, reducing the importance of foreign trade and therefore of direct commodity competition. The main competitive drive came indirectly through the military sector. This continued to be a major axis of competition forcing the process of accumulation ever onward, but over time it was supplemented more and more by the direct pressure of competition through trade. In the case of Eastern Europe this latter form of competition has always been more important. But in both instances trade relations were controlled to some degree in order to be better able to build the economic base in the face of superior Western competition. In other words, in order to better compete with the most advanced military and economic powers in the world economy the integration of these weaker economies into the world market had to be limited.

Over time this pattern began to break down under the pressure of growth and integration tendencies in the world economy. But integration and specialisation remained weak compared to what existed elsewhere. In particular there was relatively less movement of labour as the migration of both skilled and unskilled workers was restricted. Without these restrictions Eastern Europe would have been a major exporter of migrant labour in the post-war world, as indeed Yugoslavia became. Secondly, there was also relatively little movement of capital with limited direct investment and penetration by Western multinationals. Thirdly, trade, the international exchange of commodities and services, was much less integrated. Trade shares rose substantially over time, but production specialisation and integration was limited.[8] The Eastern European bloc and the states within it tried instead to duplicate the structures that they were competing with, but they lacked the levels of development and the market sizes to do this successfully and this became especially so as the pace of integration in the rest of the world economy intensified in the most recent decades. Since an understanding of this is important for any appreciation of the impact of transition it is worth exploring the dimensions of these structures more precisely.

The first was that these economies developed over-large industrial sectors which gave them the base for military and great power competition but which made little sense from the view of the world market as a whole. This contradiction between the global logic of capitalism and its particular national form in Eastern Europe meant that industries could only be kept going by large subsidies which imposed considerable strains on these economies. The problem became even more evident in the 1970s and 1980s when the pressure of competition forced a shift towards more high technology industries such as computers. The result was a series of weak 'low tech-high tech' industries reflected best perhaps in the East German computer industry—advanced in bloc terms but nowhere in world terms.

Within these industrial sectors, because of the smaller markets, it was impossible to develop full economies of scale or to have the level of diversification and product competition apparent in the West. Although these features were accentuated by planning decisions and preferences, the relative weaknesses of the Eastern European economies dictated that if they were to have a whole range of industries within their borders then this would have to be on the basis of higher levels of vertical integration, a smaller number of producers and higher levels of plant size than in the West. Table 2 shows one aspect of this, the large size of plant in Eastern Europe as production concentration developed to a much higher degree than in the West.

Table 2
Percentage concentration of the labour force by plant size in the 1980s[9]

No of workers in plant	West*	West Ger.	East Ger.	Poland (total)	(state)	(co-ops)
100 or less	35	17	10	2	6	42
101—500	33	30	25	13	21	54
501—1000	13	13	15	12	16	4
1000 or more	19	40	51	73	58	1

* average for Austria, Belgium, France, Italy, Japan and Sweden

The other side of this concentration was that most of these large plants were in effect monopoly producers of their products within these economies (and sometimes the bloc at large). In the former USSR, for example, an examination of production by industry has shown that of nearly 6,000 separate items produced in the engineering industry 87 percent were produced by single firms with an absolute internal monopoly—over a further 8 percent of the product range only two to three firms were involved in the production of each item. This reliance on the concentration of the production of individual products in individual plants was extreme in this industry but reflected the basic pattern across the Soviet and Eastern European economies. In Soviet metal production, for example, 28 percent of the product range was made in firms with an absolute monopoly but for a further 49 percent of the range there were only 2 to 6 producers for each item. It was the same story for chemicals where 47 percent of the product range was made by single producers and a further 40 percent by 2 to 6 producers for each item.[10]

Opening these economies further to the world market has therefore led to the beginnings of a radical restructuring. In particular, the share of industry in output is being cut both relatively and (in the short term) absolutely. The relative cut reflects the expansion of the service sector which had been suppressed to encourage the competitive industrial base as well as some more minor swing back towards agriculture. The absolute cut reflects the inability of key sections of industry to withstand the world competition they are now being directly exposed to rather than in the more state mediated forms of the past. This is also producing a slimming down of plant size and a disintegration of production within the economies to allow more specialisation and integration with the world market. What it is not doing, however, is producing intensified internal market competition in the economic cores because over a wide range of industries there is no basis for such competition and, as the restructuring proceeds, the dependence on a limited number of producers is likely to be maintained because only a limited number will survive.[11]

The question that has to be posed, therefore, is why an attempt to shift to a more market based structure with a higher level of integration with the world market appealed to the Eastern European ruling classes at all?

Did they jump or were they pushed?

THE ANSWER to the question of whether the ruling classes jumped or were pushed is a little of both. They jumped in the sense that they made the first moves and established a basic momentum. They were pushed in the sense that pressure from below drove them to make their own great leap in the dark in 1989. There were a number of factors alongside the longer term economic contradictions that we have just noted that pushed key sections of the ruling class in this direction.

The first was the growing internal dissatisfaction of the ruling class with its own position. One aspect of this was that as the system stagnated so its ideological strength withered and with it the willingness to accept less than their counterparts in the West. Indeed as the crisis developed it even began to cut directly into the privileges of the ruling class itself. In Poland Adam Michnik has expressed this well in what has been called the 'doctrine of the radiators':

Ten years ago all the radiators stopped working... Shivering in his apartment ... [Michnik]... thought that at least the Party officials were warm in their dachas. Then he met the wife of the former Polish premier at a friend's wedding. She was shivering, 'Why are you so cold?', he asked. She said, 'My husband is sitting at home wearing the fur hat given to him by Kosygin'. The country's heaters were on a 'permanent strike'.[12]

A second element was the way in which the growing crisis of the 1980s intensified the short term contradictions of the bloc. One aspect of this was the growing debt burden which was built up as attempts were made to draw on Western capital to provide the means of rescue from falling rates of growth. This proved unsuccessful and by the late 1980s the bloc had some of the highest rates of capital accumulation in the world but negative or low rates of profit and growth. The result was that the chickens very quickly came home to roost. In particular the debt burden began to become critical. Table 3 sets out its basic dimensions.

Table 3
The growth of net debt in Eastern Europe ($bn)[13]

	1985	1986	1987	1988	1989	1990
Bulgaria	1.6	3.6	5.1	6.1	8.0	9.8
Czechoslovakia	3.6	4.3	5.1	5.6	5.7	6.3
Hungary	11.5	14.7	18.1	18.2	19.4	20.3
Poland	28.2	31.9	35.8	34.1	37.5	41.8
Romania	6.5	6.3	5.1	2.0	-1.3	1.3
USSR	15.8	16.6	25.1	27.7	39.3	43.4
Total	67.3	77.5	94.3	93.8	108.9	122.9

It became increasingly difficult to penetrate Western markets to generate the foreign exchange needed to maintain the debt burden and to take advantage of the growth that did exist in the world economy. In the case of Poland, for example, between 1978 and 1989 exports to the West rose by only 19 percent while world trade as a whole expanded by 60 percent and exports in Western Europe by 50 percent.[14] The paradoxical result was that as a growing recognition dawned of the importance of integration with the world economy what was taking place in practice was a forced and unwanted inward retreat in the pattern of trade of these countries. This is reflected in Table 4. Although some conservatives took satisfaction in this in the mid-1980s they were a minority and for reformers the need to halt the trend only became more evident.

Table 4
The changing regional structure of Eastern European trade in the 1980s crisis[15]

	1980	1985	1988
Exports to			
Eastern Europe	42.1	46.8	49.0
Developed Countries	32.0	25.6	21.9
Developing World	13.8	13.2	14.3
Other 'Socialist'	12.1	14.4	14.8
Imports from			
Eastern Europe	42.9	47.6	54.0
Developed Countries	35.4	27.8	25.1
Developing World	11.5	11.0	8.2
Other 'Socialist'	10.2	13.6	12.7

The third element was that the ruling class itself began to adjust its social position before 1989 (and especially in Poland and Hungary) so as to place one foot in the new emerging order. In the case of Hungary the process was trenchantly observed by the sociologist Elemer Hankiss:

it is not unusual today [1988] to meet a family belonging to the Kadariste oligarchy where the father is a high ranking party or state official, the daughter owns a town centre clothes shop, the eldest son represents a Western company in Hungary, the son in law is the chairman of a recently created company or a Western bank and a grandmother owns a family hotel on the edge of Lake Balaton.[16]

For Hankiss what was happening was the 'migration of the bureaucracy' into new positions of power. We would rather describe this as a partial shift in the social base of the ruling class, but its political implications were the same either way. Even before 1989 there was already a movement towards a new system which prepared the way for the rapid acceptance of change under popular pressure in 1989.

This is not to say that the final destination was clearly understood. Instead Hankiss calls the process only 'semi-conscious'. Most people's assumption was that moderate levels of reorganisation would be capable of producing the desired result and in some states reorganisation could probably be avoided completely. Early in the process of restructuring in the Soviet Union, Gorbachev's then adviser Abel Aganbegyan was promising that with perestroika 'the Soviet national income by 2000 would closely approach that of the United States'.[17] But once embarked on this road, the pre-1989 subterranean social and ideological shift of the base of the ruling class strengthened its ability to make its eventual jump from the middle of 1989 as pressure mounted. At the start of that year the then Hungarian Communist Party reformer Imre Pozsgay expressed the situation in the following terms,

> I think that we have got to a river, a very steep and very quick river, that you can only cross by stepping from one stone to another and you need a certain speed, because if you stop on one stone you will lose your balance and fall into the river. And this is the state of affairs in Hungary. But a quick run through the river might be successful.[18]

In the event the run was even quicker than Pozsgay imagined, but the analogy is a useful one. What happened is that the ruling class had already achieved enough momentum so that, when it realised that it could not turn back and there was safe ground on the other side, it could continue its run across the stones.

What caused them to speed up their run was the pressure from below that erupted in the autumn of 1989. The history of the Eastern European societies had been punctuated by major and minor revolts from below. Now, in the autumn of 1989, as the grip of the ruling groups weakened, people began to first vote with their feet by trying to migrate from East Germany and then, as confidence grew, to demonstrate, protest and strike. The whole process began spilling over national borders, as it had done before in the great revolutionary turning points in the history of capitalism.

Faced with this situation the ruling groups within the ruling class wobbled visibly. Some looked to repression, others to compromise and their indecision—sometimes forced, sometimes deliberate, paralysed the police and the army in the face of the swelling clamour for change. The scale of the protests and the obvious weakness of the state machine stiffened the resolve of those at the top looking for compromise and change. The ruling class as a whole began to run to keep up with the pressure from below.

Once again it was Hankiss who captured the essence of the situation. In the midst of the turmoil of the autumn of 1989 he wrote an article posing the question, 'Why did they not shoot?'. Earlier that year in China the rulers had suppressed a popular revolt by force, but this had not happened in Eastern Europe. Hankiss's answer remains at the core of any understanding of the transition:

> A section of the elite in power recognised that it could quite easily, and without losing anything, transform its authority from the bureaucratic party where it was founded on compulsion into a political and economic power capable of functioning in a new system which integrates both the market economy and democracy. The party-state could then sink peacefully beneath the waves of history.[19]

In the light of our own insistence that we are dealing with a ruling class we might prefer a slightly different terminology but it would be hard to better this as a contemporaneous insight into what was at stake in 1989. And, as we shall see later, by one of those ironical tricks that history often plays, Hankiss was to come to embody a part of the process he was describing.

Eastern Europe and the general crisis of the weak state economies

MOST ACCOUNTS of the transition in Eastern Europe have been written as if the process of crisis there is specific to the area—a part of the collapse of some supposed 'socialist' mode of production. There are, of course, specific elements in any situation but in the case of Eastern Europe the specific problems of its crisis serve more to differentiate what has happened quantitatively rather than qualitatively from the crisis that hit much of the world economy in the 1980s. In fact unless an attempt is made to understand the tendencies of development in the world economy at large and the particular way in which problems have arisen in the recent past it becomes impossible to understand the particular manifestations of crisis in Eastern Europe.

Put at its crudest, any long run analysis of the development of the world economy shows two basic tendencies. One has been towards integration as trade and flows of capital and labour have tied the production process closer together on a world scale. The result has been the increasing multinationalisation or globalisation of the world economy. The second tendency has been towards an extension of state control which has varied in degree but been a universal long run tendency in world capitalism. Charting the scale of this is difficult because state ownership, regulation and control cannot easily be reduced to a common denominator and measured. But Table 5 shows one measure of this tendency—government expenditure growth which reflects both the way that the state produces itself and the way it draws in and redirects resources from the 'private sector'.

Table 5
Government expenditure as a percentage of GDP at current prices 1880-1986[20]

	1880*	1913	1929	1938	1950	1973	1986
USA	n.a.	8.0	10.0	19.8	21.4	30.7	37.1
UK	9.9	13.3	23.8	28.8	34.2	41.5	45.9
Germany	10.0	17.7	30.6	42.4	30.4	41.2	47.8
France	11.2	8.9	12.4	23.2	27.4	38.8	53.2
Holland	n.a.	8.2	11.2	21.7	26.8	49.1	58.0
Japan	9.0	14.2	18.8	30.3	19.8	22.9	35.5
Average	n.a.	11.7	17.8	27.7	26.7	37.4	46.3

* figure for Germany for 1881 and Japan for 1885

Depending on their form these two tendencies can contradict or complement one another and their precise relationship and balance have varied in the past in important ways.[21] Most recently the first impact of the growing difficulties in the world economy in the 1970s was to increase the level of state action especially, but not exclusively as is evident in Table 5, in the weaker parts of the world economy.

The pattern that emerged presented uncomfortable problems for those who wanted to draw a sharp distinction between capital and the state and to argue that state domination, as in Eastern Europe, in some way implied the negation of capitalism. Comparing the level of state control is notoriously difficult because competing measures give competing results. But on any measure it is certainly true that Eastern Europe has experienced some of the highest measures of *peacetime* state control anywhere in the world economy. What is often insufficiently appreciated, however, is that if we put all the world's economies on a scale of state control measuring from 0 percent to 100 percent then virtually all the economies would cluster in the middle to third quarter. Table 6, for example, shows one measure of state control in Eastern Europe in terms of the share of central government expenditure in output (net material product). The unwary should be warned that Table 6 cannot simply be compared with Table 5 as a measure of state control. But the tables well illustrate our main point which is that the gaps between the two blocs have frequently been overstated because of an under-appreciation of the role of the state in the advanced West and an overestimation of its role in the former Eastern bloc.

Table 6
Central government expenditures in Eastern Europe and the USSR as a percentage of output.[22]

	1982	1985	1989
Bulgaria	54.7	55.2	61.9
Czechoslovakia	67.0	69.8	76.6
Hungary	61.2	61.1	59.0
Poland	52.2	48.2	48.1
USSR	49.3	49.8	51.4

Under the impact of crisis in the world economy that gap has frequently diminished still further. Take the way in which the crisis at the turn of the 1980s affected Latin America. In Peru there was an increase of public expenditure from 24 percent to 60 percent of GDP from 1970 to 1982; in Mexico the increase was from 22 percent to 46 percent in the same period; in Argentina and Venezuela by 1980 public expenditure had risen to more than half of GDP and so on.[23]

With the expansion of state control also came an intensification in the West of features normally associated with the Eastern European system. Consider, for example, a set of economies characterised by

> massive centralisation of decisions on the mobilisation and use of resources, on pricing, investments, and on the relationship between management and labour ... Public agencies and enterprises ... hosts to inefficiency, waste and vested interests.

Eastern Europe? No. This is a World Bank Vice President for Latin America writing on the region in 1989.[24] Of course, he was writing to highlight what the World Bank believes needs changing but even allowing for an element of exaggeration the question remains of whether we are really dealing with qualitatively different forms to those which existed in Eastern Europe. And exactly the same question must be posed about the nature of the crisis. As the general difficulties of the world economy continued and the build up of state measures grew, often financed by foreign debt, the differential impact of the crisis began to increasingly expose some of the weaknesses of state driven attempts at salvation.

Overall the crisis caused the whole rate of expansion in the world economy to slow (subject to the ups and downs of the economic cycle). But the sharpest impact was perhaps felt in terms of a growing differentiation of performance. If the world economy on average grew more slowly, its weakest and most exposed parts grew not at all or fell back. In the 1960s only 15 countries had experienced such economic difficulties that over the decade their per capita income fell. In the 1970s the figure was 27, and 62 in the 1980s. Table 7 shows what this meant if we look not at states but the shares of the world's population experiencing the problems of the world economy living in states.

Table 7
Proportion of the world population living in states by type of economic performance[25]

	percentage of world population living:			
	in advanced states	in states closing gap	in states falling behind relatively	in states with falling output per head
1960s	28.5	25.2	43.3	3.0
1980s	22.6	2.6	51.1	23.7

The result of this was the development of external pressures on the weaker countries to restructure and these were given shape by institutions like the IMF and the World Bank as well as in the foreign policies of advanced capitalist states. These policies found uneven acceptance within many of the ruling classes and the result was the implementation of a whole series of IMF backed austerity programmes in Latin America, Africa and Asia. These programmes were direct forerunners of what is now being constructed in Eastern Europe:

> a typical programme in Latin America embodies a variety of policies—devaluation, limits on banking credit and public borrowing, removal of price subsidies, reduction of tariffs and elimination of some import controls, encouragement of foreign investment, and financial resistance to nominal wage increases.[26]

The logic underlying these programmes has been to restore the rate of profit and the ability of these countries to repay their debt. The general impact on inflation before 1981 was limited, although policy has been more successful since then. Austerity programmes have also had a variable impact on growth, weakening it in some cases but not in others. Their two unambiguous achievements have been 'improvements in balance of payments' and 'the strongest and most consistent effect of Fund programmes: absolute and relative reductions in [the] labour force share of income'.[27] What this means is that such austerity programmes have been designed to achieve particular ends at the cost of growing poverty on a scale that even the IMF and World Bank economists have not been able to ignore.[28]

What is now happening in Eastern Europe is a particular development of this whole logic of crisis and austerity response. Indeed in the IMF and World Bank community it is often the same people who are constructing programmes for Eastern Europe who in the mid and late 1980s cut their teeth on Latin America. The most notorious example of this has been Jeffrey Sachs who has been called 'the Indiana Jones of economics'.[29] Sachs was the architect of the 'Bolivian miracle' who became an adviser to Solidarity and the Solidarity government and who then worked on some of the many reform programmes for the USSR and Russia.

It is therefore instructive to see what happened in Bolivia itself and how this relates to the Latin Americanisation of Poland and Eastern Europe more generally.

The Bolivian model and the logic of austerity

LANDLOCKED Bolivia with a population of only 6.4 million is the poorest Latin American country. But in the late 1980s it replaced Chile as the model testing ground for the 'free market'.[30] Bolivia's past history had been built around the mining of silver, antimony, copper, wolfram and especially tin. Despite its small size and general backwardness the development of mining in Bolivia welded together a labour force of miners and peasants partly engaged in both mining and agriculture who in 1952 helped to create the basis of one of the three great revolutions of modern Latin American history alongside those of Mexico and Cuba.[31] Despite its failure this revolution left Bolivia with one of the strongest trade union organisations in Latin America, the Central Obrera Boliviania, as well as helping to consolidate a tradition of state capitalism that meant that by 1985 *some 70 percent of the economy was in state hands*. Bolivia, however, remained trapped in its backwardness and a prisoner of tendencies in the world economy despite a series of swings from left to right in the decades after the 1952 revolution.

For the Bolivian economy the growing crisis in the world economy in the first half of the 1980s culminated in 1985 when the tin market crashed and hyperinflation hit 25,000 percent. Backed by the IMF, a section of the ruling class seized the opportunity to impose a vicious austerity package designed by Jeffrey Sachs. The core of this programme was financial discipline, massive state cutbacks and the abandonment of much of the regulatory role of the state.

Sachs was disconcertingly frank about what this strategy would achieve: 'What you have is a miserable, poor economy with hyperinflation, if you are brave, if you are gutsy, if you do everything right, you will end up with a miserable, poor economy with stable prices'.[32] In the long run, however, he insisted that such a strategy would be the basis for sustained growth. This is what the IMF, Sachs and the World Bank claim has now been achieved and it has been these claims that have helped to sustain the credentials of Sachs and his acolytes as gurus of Poland's market strategy and now more widely that of the former Soviet Union and Eastern Europe. It is important, therefore, to understand what has really happened in Bolivia.

As an anti-inflationary strategy Sachs' plan was spectacularly successful. By 1987 inflation had come down to 15 percent and it was still only 18 percent in 1990—an outstanding record in Latin American terms. But Sachs had been rather immodest in his prediction, for what the plan had achieved was not 'a miserable, poor economy with stable prices' but 'a miserably poorer economy with almost stable prices'. It is true that once the austerity programme was introduced there was some growth in the economy in the late 1980s but the standard of living had been falling before 1985 and on one estimate it fell a further 60 percent in 1985.[33] Thus for all of the propaganda of success the key issue for ordinary Bolivians would be when their standard of living would return to 1978 levels. On the basis of the growth rates after 1985 the answer would appear to be that it will take up to 40 years! Moreover, much of the growth that was achieved after 1985 has been based on something that Sachs did not anticipate—cocaine. Coca production is now estimated to directly employ 75,000 people and creates some 10 percent of Bolivian GNP, providing between a third and a half of its export earnings—a testament to the virtues of profit and the logic of the free market.

Prior to 1985, Bolivian state policy had been directed towards subsidised development of modern sectors and exports. As in Chile in the 1970s, the removal of protection and wholesale liberalisation combined with tight financial discipline and a reduction in state expenditure all led to a sharp restructuring of the economy in line with the logic of the world market. Much of the small industrial sector, although relatively modern in Latin American terms, could not survive. But agriculture also suffered because imports at world market prices frequently undercut peasant production. Mining also contracted as world market prices remained low.

The economy therefore experienced not only a fall in output per head but a degree of deindustrialisation leading to a distorted swing to the primary sector and services. The losers in this were the core modern sectors. But the peasants also began to increasingly turn to coca production and the continued development of the drugs trade was also assisted by the financial liberalisation which made it easier to hide drug profits. At the same time the urban population had to turn more and more to the informal sector which rapidly increased in size, sucking in not only men but large numbers of women and children desperate to survive by small scale production and trade.

The strategists had promised a private enterprise boom and saw the growth of the informal sector as evidence of the development of entrepreneurial virtues. To Sachs it was a demonstration of what could happen in Poland and Eastern Europe. If 'the peasant Indians in the Bolivian market' could operate this way what was to stop the 'cultured Poles' rapidly learning the logic of the market. This is, of course, a fairy tale. Even if it were true that the informal sector was a spawning ground for entrepreneurship and capital accumulation it would take decades for it to form the basis of anything substantial. In reality the standard of living in the informal sector fell too as the austerity programme hit, worsening the prospects of any serious capital accumulation there. The other part of the promised free enterprise boom was to come through privatisation. The objective was to sell off the 158 state companies to the private sector both nationally and internationally. But nothing has materialised. In fact by the start of the 1990s not a single one of these companies had been fully privatised.

This is the underside of the Bolivian miracle that is omitted from the glossy publicity. But the problems are not hard to find, and they raise an obvious question—if this is the cost of moving from one state of miserable poverty to another, what is the point? Are we not looking at a world where market zealots are imposing their ideas, blind to the reality of what is happening?

From the point of view of the economists themselves there is a considerable truth in this type of judgment. Market economic theory has a compelling simplicity which, if the falseness and restricted nature of its assumptions are ignored, is incapable of refutation because every practical refutation is explained away by the fact that some evil force—the state, monopoly, the left—is preventing the market from working as it should. For Sachs and his supporters, politics and economics are separate spheres in which there is always a danger that the political sphere will invade the economic one making 'smooth, professional solutions to problems... impossible'.[34] The remedy for this then becomes that of giving an even greater role to the market.

Market economists become like those Victorian doctors who believed in bleeding their patients with leeches and who, when the patient stubbornly refused to get better, drew the conclusion that even more bleeding was necessary. And, of course, those patients who had confidence in their doctors accepted the 'cure' even to their dying breaths. It was perhaps Keynes who best captured the 'irrational rationality' of the market theorists when he noted of a work by Friedrich Hayek, the grandfather of post Second World War free market economics, that it was an example 'of how, starting with a mistake, a remorseless logician can end up in Bedlam'.

But this is only a partial explanation. The market is such a powerful weapon not only because of its ideological content but because behind this other objectives are being secured which are partially recognised by some theorists but at a tangent to their general discussions, just as the real world of capitalism is at a tangent to their models.

What has been at stake in Bolivia has been a restoration of economic and political order. The benefits and gains have been made by those who try to control world capitalism and its Bolivian branch. The losses have been experienced by someone else—some sections of the ruling class in Bolivia have certainly suffered but in general it has been the working class and the peasantry that have been made to pay the price of order.

The first of these objectives is to discipline weak states financially and politically in the interests of advanced capitalism. What successful austerity programmes achieve in the first instance is confidence in the world financial community—'the IMF seal of approval'. This denotes that economies are being restructured so as to maintain their debt repayments through internal financial discipline and the turning round of balance of trade deficits. This is both an economic and a political task.

The political task is the most fundamental in as much as it is necessary to defeat those internal forces that might try to buck the interests of the world's financial markets. Once these have been brought into line it may then be possible for Western banks and states to be more generous in economic concessions, confident that advantage will not be taken of such 'generosity'. In addition such generosity, even though there is no chance of it being generalised, can help model economies (Bolivia, Poland) to succeed as an example for others to follow. Occasionally such programmes can have unintended consequences for advanced capital, as the expansion of cocaine in Bolivia shows. But even here it is possible to turn such consequences to advantage and to strengthen international discipline as the United States has done by effectively militarising the drugs war in this area of Latin America.

The second of these objectives relates particularly to the internal issue of state authority. The crises that preceded the introduction of IMF backed shock programmes have usually involved social disintegration. This has partly been reflected in the way that states have proved incapable of arbitrating between the demands of different groups and imposing order. The clearest expression of this is inflation being let rip in an attempt to satisfy everyone and, of course, no one. To eliminate this the internal authority of the state has to be recreated and imposed on the competing factions. This is how a Bolivian Finance Minister put it: 'rather than a strictly economic programme, the New Economic Policy is a political plan... The first political task consists of restoring the state's authority over society at large'.[35]

The third objective flows specifically from the second, for while the spiralling competition of warring groups in general is a threat, the underlying internal problem tends to be that of bringing the organised working class as a whole under control. Restructuring achieves this politically by forcing or winning working class leaderships over to the acceptance of austerity programmes and socially through the way that these programmes cut into the bases of the organised working class through industrial restructuring and unemployment. If the social process is sufficiently sharp this itself can be sufficient to achieve acquiescence even without the formal complicity of the old working class leadership. This is substantially what happened in Bolivia, where the combined effect of crisis and austerity ripped apart much of the tin industry, leading to the dismissal of 80 percent of its 75,000 workforce and so destroying one of the core groups of the COB.

The seductive appeal of the market model

It is not that we are unwilling to put our own house in order. It is that we want to keep our house and not let it go up in flames.

—Dominican Republic Planning Minister in the early 1980s after riots induced by IMF austerity plans.[36]

The degree of consensus in Eastern Europe in favour of establishing a Western style market economy exceeds the levels of consensus found in Latin America and other parts of the developing world.

—David Lipton and Jeffrey Saches, Solidarity's American Economic Advisers.[37]

As the Western advisers began to flood into Eastern Europe they were genuinely astonished at the lack of resistance to their ideas from people whom they had imagined to be

Marxists. Everywhere it seemed that the more right wing the idea the more approval with which it was met. This consensus had and has two aspects—one is suggested by the planning minister of the Dominican Republic—there was little or no resistance from below in Eastern Europe which was formulated either as resistance to the Stalinism of old or to the new style market reforms. This meant that it was easier for the ruling class to swing behind the market because it had only to worry about the diminishing opposition of its weaker and more bureaucratic sections. Unlike some Latin American countries there was less need to worry so much about the whole house going up in flames because of resistance from below.

The second aspect has been the widespread seduction of the larger part of the ruling class and most of the opposition by the market, as Lipton and Sachs suggest. The nature of this ideological volte face—the shift from a belief in the efficacy of the state to that of the market—can be traced especially sharply in the influential work of the Hungarian economist Janos Kornai. Kornai has deliberately avoided direct entanglement with the old or new regimes in Hungary and Eastern Europe but his work has provided much of the theoretical structure for orthodox accounts in both East and West of the way the old economies of Eastern Europe functioned and is now at the heart of discussions of the most brutal forms of 'shock therapy'.[38] Kornai originally tried to stand between what he once called holding 'a belief in the almightiness of planning' and 'trusting the perfection of the market'. So far as the former was concerned Kornai emphasised that in Eastern Europe enterprises necessarily performed badly because they had 'soft budget constraints'—essentially there was no fear of bankruptcy to discipline and encourage managers. This inefficiency was further accentuated by 'the shortage economy', 'a social relationship in which the buyer is at the mercy of the seller—and feels himself to be so'.[39] But at the same time Kornai also saw himself as a critic of the market and did indeed have penetrating insights into its tendency to unemployment and the unreality of theories that the market could produce balance and equilibrium.

In the light of this it might have been thought that Kornai was ideally placed intellectually to be the theorist of some middle way of a social democratic kind. Yet by the early 1990s even Alec Nove could condemn him as a supporter of 'capitalism with an inhuman face'. 'It is probably inevitable', wrote Kornai, 'that history moves not in a straight line, but like a pendulum... it is now time to take great steps in the direction of a minimal state'.[40]

The resonance of the phrase 'minimal state' is clearly intended by Kornai who has been a frequent visitor to the West. It reflects his own disillusion with previous attempts to reform the Eastern European economies and particularly that of Hungary where all that happened was (as he saw it) a shift from 'direct bureaucratic regulation' to 'indirect bureaucratic regulation', '20 years of muddling through with... partial changes'. Kornai now argues that there is no way in which the state can be made efficient and while this does not mean that mass privatisation could be undertaken tomorrow (quite the contrary, the continuing inefficiency of the state sector prevents this) it does mean that 'it is time to abandon hope that the budget constraint can be hardened'. State bureaucratic inefficiency is inevitable, 'there are certain problems that have no solution, one of them being the efficient operation of a large state owned sector'. As a result 'the basic idea of market socialism simply fizzled out'. For Kornai:

> bureaucratic subordination is as much the spontaneous effect and natural mode of state property's existence as market co-ordination is of private property. This is no longer a debating point, but simply a fact that must be accepted.[41]

Since our interest is to understand the evolution of Kornai's thinking as perhaps the single most influential Eastern European economist we will simply note our view that what Kornai asserts as 'fact' is far from that and both aspects of this statement are wrong. What is more interesting is how this argument simply echoes the conventional wisdom of the right. Its logic, however, has led Kornai to be a major influence on the 'shock therapy' imposed on Poland and to formulate plans for a similar dose of medicine in Hungary. The former Solidarity's two American economic advisers note that their conclusions 'run parallel to those of Janos Kornai... We have benefited enormously from detailed discussions with Professor Kornai' and Kornai has returned the compliment—'the policy proposals David Lipton and Jeffrey Sachs advance... will get no criticism here. Sachs and I discussed these issues several times, and we are in complete agreement on all basic principles'.[42]

So far as Hungary is concerned Kornai has argued in support

of his proposals that the Hungarian population is like a patient who in desperation is finally ready to risk an operation.

> I feel that the Hungarian population is approaching a point where it cannot tolerate further suffering... I believe they are ready to take the risks of a radical operation. And for all the temporary trauma troubles it would cause, the operation at least holds out the promise of genuine order and calm.[43]

What we see here is the comfortable ideology of the 'doctor's mandate'. Not only does the doctor not feel the pain but he deliberately blinds himself to what is at stake. For even if the operation is a success it can hardly lead to 'genuine order and calm', for that is not the way of the market. Moreover in the process of trying to achieve this illusory state of good health the suffering is likely to increase. But once arguments are developed in this way it is but a short step to blaming the patient for his lack of effort to assist any recovery. Thus for Kornai, 'if someone becomes unemployed, his first duty is to help himself'. Of course government assistance can help the unemployed to help themselves but in a phrase redolent with nineteenth century assumptions Kornai advises that 'a complete demoralisation of the able bodied and healthy unemployed' should be avoided through too much indiscriminate aid.[44]

For those who imagined that what existed in Eastern Europe was a non-capitalist society the alacrity with which such arguments have been taken up has come as an enormous shock. How has it come to be that the market exercises such a powerful sway on the minds of reformers in Eastern Europe? The most obvious explanation is that the West has had the power to enforce its ideological vision in Eastern Europe on such a scale that it has simply marginalised any alternative account from the Western or Eastern left who themselves have been disoriented by the last decade and even more by the rapidity of collapse in Eastern Europe.

In fact the Western left, although hampered by confusion in its analysis of the nature of Eastern European did not have a bad record in supporting dissent under the old regime.[45] No doubt more could and should have been done but real support on the basis of limited resources was forthcoming whereas the Western ruling classes, for all their rhetoric, preferred deals with the existing ruling classes of Eastern Europe. The notorious romance with the Ceausescu regime, despite its long history of internal repression, because it was apparently a thorn in the Soviet side was only the most visible and repulsive expression of this. But when the tactics of the Western states changed to encouraging a market transition their power swamped any past history of commitment except amongst a small honourable minority of socialist oppositionists.

The base of the advanced West's power here lay in the reality of its superior economic performance to that of Eastern Europe in the recent past. This superiority was attributed to the magic of the market in order to help sell it to the reformers in the East. 'Today leaders around the world are turning to market forces to meet the needs of their peoples... the jury is no longer out. History has decided', George Bush insisted on a number of occasions.[46] History, of course, demonstrates nothing of the sort. During the 1980s the importance of the state to Western capitalism has not generally diminished despite the claims of the right. This has been especially so in the United States where state intervention has kept crucial parts of the economy going. But such realities have not been allowed to disturb the mythologies of the marketeers. Their ideas, given the added authority of national governments, the IMF, the World Bank and the OECD and backed by assistance funds, have appeared to most commentators in Eastern Europe to contain the secret of the success.

But it is not enough to simply look to the power of the West to explain the attraction of these ideas. Two aspects of the ideological pattern in Eastern Europe and the former USSR predisposed their opinion makers and reformers, and the larger part of the opposition, to accept market economics as an explanation of their past failures and a mechanism of future successes. The first has been the widespread illusion that what has determined the way in which the Eastern European societies have developed has been a monstrous ideological imposition in the form of 'socialism'. So long as these economies seemed to work, 'socialism' was not seen as a problem. Once they faltered, the insistence that 'socialism' had been at the root of their successes was turned on its head and 'socialism' became the cause of their difficulties.

What socialism meant here was simply *state control*, but when economic reformers tried to vary the degree of state control and still failed to turn these economies around a degree of disillusion set in. The lurch to the market was under way. In fact, as with the stress on the market in the West, this whole conception was at a tangent to the real forces determining development in both parts of the advanced world. The problem was the same in both instances — a failure to understand the role of the state in capitalist competition, not only in indirectly supporting this competition but also directly acting as a state capitalist producer and competitor itself. The result of this failure has been a pre-disposition towards the market in both East and West that failed to appreciate the way in which expanded state action had emerged as a pragmatic response to past competitive pressures and structural constraints.

The consequence has been ideological programmes of rolling back the state which have floundered pragmatically wherever they have come up against the same constraints and pressures or new ones. This was the experience of Thatcherism and Reaganism in the 1980s and it is already evident that it is becoming the experience of Eastern Europe in the 1990s. The fundamental reason is that, irrespective of the political party in power, so long as Eastern Europe remains a weaker part of the world economy it will require a large state sector. It is possible to reduce its size, but it can only be abandoned at the expense of enormous deindustrialisation as state backed industries go under.

There is a second and more deeply rooted reason. This lies in the nature of the ideological structures that dominated Eastern Europe under Stalinism. Ideologies work in complex ways. At a casual glance, for example, Christianity, with its frequent positive comments on poverty, might be taken as an ideology of revolt. That indeed is how it began. But for the larger part of its history it has been an ideology of power, a means through which ruling classes have expressed their domination and articulated their interests and policies. The real content of Christianity was determined by the way that religious thinking developed as a total set of ideas with particular emphases and stress which marginalised and neutralised its origins. The relationship between class and ideology in Eastern Europe has been the same. Although some phrases and concepts were retained from its origins in 1917 these were 'iconised' — workers were turned into what one Russian writer has called 'poster heroes' while their real interests were trampled underfoot.

Behind this the inner content of socialist ideas that had

been there in 1917 were emasculated, their core ripped out and replaced with a new core whose values were those more associated with the modernising conservatisms of the West. Many orthodox commentators, trapped in the concepts of the Cold War, were incapable of recognising this because they looked only to the outer shell, at the posters and icons, the set phrases and invocations. But without an understanding of the fundamentally conservative character of ideas in Eastern Europe it is impossible to understand the past or the present ease with which it has been possible to sell the market idea.

The destruction of the revolution in the Soviet Union in the 1920s and 1930s also led to the death of the ideas that had informed early Bolshevik thinking.[47] But this did not simply leave an ideological vacuum or some confused and incoherent mix as some would have it. Instead a new and coherent ideology emerged which had two main components. At the most obvious and formal level Stalinism became a particular ideology of state capitalist development, of competitive modernisation stressing the need to remould society to meet the objectives of catching up and overtaking the West.[48] But at a deeper and more informal level this 'bourgeois' ideology was complimented by the proliferation of ideas and measures which expressed and reinforced the real class relations dominating the USSR and Eastern Europe. These attitudes affected every aspect of life, from an emphasis on the acquisition of material things (including money), to attitudes to women where, although they were expected to work to help the development effort, they were encouraged to adopt traditional feminine images, to attitudes to sex where a prudishness developed that would warm the heart of a good Catholic (and no doubt did comfort the future Pope in Poland), to a celebration of the virtues of the nuclear family and so on. The suspicion and repression of gays as 'diseased' threats to the family and social values was just one of the better known extreme examples of the fundamental conservatism of the underlying social values. The extent to which this small minded thinking permeated the whole social ethos can be seen in any examination of the structures of thought about everyday life as expressed, say, in popular literature or simply a discussion with most Eastern Europeans.[49]

Its most important expression, however, was a genuine hostility towards the real working class which resembles nothing so much as the class prejudices that George Orwell describes as being instilled into the middle class English child in the early twentieth century. The working classes were stupid, coarse, crude, violent, '... it is summed up in four frightful words which people nowadays are chary of uttering, but which were banded about quite freely in my childhood. The words were: *the lower classes smell*'.[50] Anyone familiar with the general attitudes of intellectuals and administrators in Eastern Europe to the working class will recognise the affinity of their views to those Orwell describes. It is a reaction that is often returned in kind by the workers. Consider again the resonance of the class prejudice in Kornai's comment about the need to avoid 'a complete demoralisation of the able-bodied and healthy unemployed'. Now listen to the Russian reformer Nikolai Shmelev oozing the same attitudes and arguing that 'the threat of losing your job is an excellent medicine against idleness, drunkenness and irresponsibility'.[51] What we see here is not merely a reform programme based upon the abstract principles of the market but one built upon the gut principles of class—where the class at the top is a conservative force concerned to maintain its real power and privilege and to make someone else pay the price of reform.

Perhaps the most striking demonstration of the truth of this argument lies in the way that the mass Communist Party memberships in some Eastern European countries have swung their electoral and political support to the new right wing parties. Unless we postulate an opportunism on an enormous scale the only explanation can be that once the need to pay homage to the old icons had disappeared these party members swung to their natural political homes. In the case of the former GDR, for example, it has been estimated that two thirds of the former SED membership—the old East German Communist Party—voted for the right wing Christian Democrats after the Berlin Wall fell.[52] No less tellingly in former Yugoslavia, Romania and the successor states to the USSR we have the wholesale adoption of traditional nationalist programmes by wide sections of former and current 'communists'.

In these terms the appeal of the market is that it appears to allow people to get their 'just deserts' and coarse, feckless, alcoholic workers can be brought into line. The tragedy is that on the left those who have not shared these assumptions and had fought against such attitudes in the past have now compounded the problem by their own view that the only choice was between Stalinist planning and the market.

The result has been a process of transition which is not creating the basis for overcoming the legacy of backwardness with which Stalinism could not deal. Instead these economies are being restructured to fit in more closely with the world economy, thus allowing the ruling class to perform its 'great escape trick' while throwing the costs of the transition and crisis onto the working class. The people who were the real victims of the old order are now also the real victims of the new.

Bitter realities—the East German example

IN THE TRANSITION the former economy of East Germany collapsed, it experienced what one group of economists has called 'a depression... virtually without historic precedent'.[53] The reason for the collapse is simple. After unification the economy was opened to the full blast of competition from the most powerful economy in Europe. Unprotected by tariffs or an ability to manipulate the value of its currency, the usual weapons used by capitalist states, the economy was forced to sink or swim. It promptly sank.

The underlying reason was that East German productivity levels, although the highest in Eastern Europe and high in world terms, were still low compared to the advanced economies that it now had to compete with. Here the logic of the market is clear. If you are less profitable, you go under. It does not matter whether you are 10 percent, 50 percent or 90 percent less efficient, your immediate competitors will still force you under. The alternative to this logic was a massive investment programme to renovate the old economies of East Germany and Eastern Europe and to bring them up to world standards. But the costs of such a programme would hardly make it attractive to Western capital. Nor could capital in the West be expected to look with favour upon the encouragement of a new group of direct competitors. Such a transition from Stalinism could only have been based upon a different kind of logic which contested the dynamics of the world economy. But to do this would mean to challenge the real social basis of power both East and West. Since that challenge has not been forthcoming it has been the logic of the world market that has set the form of the transition. What we have seen in East

Germany has been a microcosm of the way in which this logic operates.

In fact subsequently published East German data have allowed economists to measure much more precisely the real costs of East German industry and its ability to compete at the exchange rate fixed for the mark. On this basis only 8 percent of the former East German industry was viable in direct competition with the West. The sectors with the lowest relative costs (though still excessive) were energy, metallurgy and glass—those with the highest costs were electronics, chemicals and food. Left to its own devices, therefore, the market would destroy large swathes of the more advanced industries of East Germany and integrate it into the German and world economies as a depressed, less advanced area rather than upgrading its production in the short or medium term to West German levels.

The same study also estimated that to make the leading 88 *least bad* industrial units viable (the Kombinate) would require an effective wage subsidy of 75 percent.[54] This scale of subsidy had not been anticipated. Helmut Kohl, the West German Chancellor, had promised a relatively painless transition. In the event subsidies had to be increased to stop an even more spectacular collapse occurring. By the spring of 1991 it was estimated that 50 percent of the GDP of the five new East German Lander was made up of transfers from the West but such transfers were being spent to directly hold up consumption, not to prop up the industrial core of the old economy.[55]

The result was that the cumulative decline in industrial output was over 50 percent. As this economic collapse took place the labour force suffered an equally dramatic contraction. The unemployment figures measured only a part of this as the workforce haemorrhaged. Table 8 gives some of the basic data that must be added together to gain a measure of the full impact of the collapse. Some groups simply left the old GDR labour force altogether. Those easiest to estimate were migrants to West Germany and those who took advantage of early retirement provisions. Another component found new jobs in the west but commuted from the east. But there is yet another group, more difficult to estimate—who now began to drop out of the labour force as it was defined by the new system. This especially affected women who had a high participation rate in the old GDR due to the drive to expand production which sucked in a mass of labour. Here a more complex process of social redefinition of roles was and is taking place as the balance of the 'double burden' of home and work is shifted more to the home. Other groups remained in the measured labour force but were now categorised as registered unemployed. Other groups were put on short time working which bizarrely included being on nil hours but still being registered as on short time. The percentage of the labour force on short time peaked in the spring of 1991 at nearly 23 percent but then began to fall as more of these workers were shifted to the unemployed category. Another smaller group secured places on various job schemes and training programmes. Add all of these categories together and it is clear that between 40 and 50 percent of the jobs that existed in 1989 had disappeared by the end of 1991. Analysed by economic sector we find that over half of these job losses were concentrated in industry and nearly a further fifth in agriculture.

Table 8
Some elements of the contraction of the former East German labour force[56]

	,000s	% 1989 labour force
Emigration	509	5.2
Commuting	386	4.0
Early retirement	665	6.8
Registered unemployment	1,050	10.8
Short time	1,200	12.3
Programme work	360	3.7
Retraining	115	1.2
Total	4,285	43.9

There is still controversy over whether there was an economic alternative to this. But leaving aside the political constraints, accepting the logic of the market trapped policy makers between two unpalatable alternatives. Either they allowed wages in the former GDR to rise to West German levels, so further reducing competitiveness, or they maintained former GDR wages at less than one fifth or one sixth of West German levels but then risked an enormous labour migration to the west and massive conflict there as wages were pulled down. Although schemes were suggested to try to escape this dilemma, none could generate support quickly enough to limit the damage and, as is so often the case, the costs of the failure of the market—no less than the costs of the failure of the state—were picked up in an ad hoc and inadequate way.[57]

The decline in the standard of living for those eligible for benefits has been moderated because unification has involved the adoption of West German social security legislation. Workers in the rest of Eastern Europe have been less fortunate in as much as their social security systems have been designed to relate to their existing levels of low pay. But even in the old East Germany the wider costs of such a dramatic collapse could not be moderated. One year after the Berlin Wall fell a notice was pinned to the door of the church in Leipzig which had been at the centre of opposition which simply read, 'With 2,000,000 unemployed we see little cause for celebrating'. A year on, such a notice might have spoken of twice as many.

Bitter realities—the Eastern European case

Table 9
Percentage change in real GDP in Eastern Europe[58]

	1990	1991	1992	1993*e*	1994*p*	1995*p*
Bulgaria	-9.1	-12.0	-7.7	-4	-1	-2
Czechoslovakia	-1.6	-14.7	-7.2			
Czech Rep.			-7.1	0	+2	+5
Slovak Rep.			-7.5	-5	0	+2
Hungary	-3.3	-10.0	-5.0	-1	+2	+1
Poland	-11.6	-9.0	+1.0	+3	+4	+3
Romania	-5.6	-15.0	-15.4	-4	-3	0
USSR	-4.0	-17.0				
Russia			-19.0	-11	-9	+1
Ukraine			-14	-20	-10	0

(*e* indicates estimate, *p* indicates projection)

THE FALL in output in the rest of Eastern Europe is shown in Table 9. Unlike the East German case, the Eastern European states still have control over their own policies. No economy, not even Poland, has been completely opened up to the world market as was East Germany. In this sense the externally imposed crash was not as great. Nevertheless, the optimism of Western agencies like the OECD and the IMF (both of which have predicted small falls in output) was punctured by the real scale of the collapse. The breakdown of the old Comecon trade mechanism, the inconsistencies of reform programmes, the infighting at the top, the related impact of growing national tensions boiling over in some instances into civil war, the slow down in the world economy—all combined to have a dramatic effect on output in general and industrial output in particular. The consequence was to continually falsify the optimism of the OECD-IMF projections.

Against this logic the theorists of transition have held out hope along the lines that the quicker the transition, the sooner the recovery will start. But the conditions for success are hardly likely to be met in the foreseeable future. Consider, for example, the argument of Lipton and Sachs:

> In the case of Eastern Europe... one can identify the primary engine of growth in the coming years: economic integration with Western Europe... To achieve the full fruits of trade liberalisation, existing trade barriers should be removed. The Eastern European countries must negotiate a new association status with access to Western European markets... in the longer term, the European Community should be expanded to allow the actual membership of the East European countries.[59]

In fact, even if they are right about the primary engine of growth, the most optimistic scenarios of the future development of the world economy hardly suggest that it is likely to experience a sufficiently powerful boom to fuel such an engine.[60] As a result, while there will be much rhetoric about integration and some concessions from the EC, 'the full fruits of liberalisation' in these terms are unlikely to emerge. Moreover the situation is so unstable in Eastern Europe that even were such conditions met the chances of derailment would be high. The Gulf War and trade embargo posed major problems in Eastern Europe in the first half of 1991 through increased prices and trade losses. Hungary has been affected by an earthquake. The trade embargo against the warring groups in former Yugoslavia has hit some hard. Hanging over the whole of Eastern Europe is the threat of conflict which even if it is contained militarily, still threatens to spill over in the form of fleeing refugees as in the Yugoslavian case.

But, of course, such optimistic scenarios are unlikely to need such 'unplanned' developments to disrupt them because they are based on a false logic which obscures the real potential of closer integration into the world market. We can see this if we look at the realities of the changing patterns of trade and flows of capital and labour.

Trade and the logic of comparative disadvantage

BEFORE 1989 the pattern of trade in Eastern Europe reflected the attempt of the ruling classes to sponsor competitive processes of industrialisation. The trade pattern fell into three types. Because production was less developed than that in the advanced West, 'East-West' trade generally took the form of an exchange of raw materials and semi-manufactured goods for manufactured and high technology goods. Trade with the less developed part of the world had a different character. There the more advanced nature of the Eastern bloc did allow a higher export of manufactured goods but because these industrial exports were generally inferior to those available elsewhere in the world market it was necessary to boost this pattern by aid, subsidies, political leverage and a willingness to accept less competitive Third World goods in return. The third area of trade, the largest, was within Eastern Europe itself. Here a more complex pattern developed reflecting the uneven levels of development within the bloc. But in general intra-bloc trade took the form of the Eastern European countries importing raw materials and energy from the USSR and exporting their manufactured goods to it. Unlike trade with the West, which was carried out in hard currencies at world market prices, this trade was carried out in Eastern bloc currencies at prices which came closer to those of the world market over time but which all had a degree of deliberate insulation from it.

In particular because stronger trade barriers were put up against the world market to protect the process of competitive industrialisation, a double subsidy developed. The Soviet rulers sold their raw materials and oil to Eastern Europe at less than world market prices and accepted in return manufactured goods that were overpriced and poorer in quality than those available to it elsewhere. This trade pattern achieved two things. Economically it encouraged a higher level of industrialisation than would otherwise have occurred and so underpinned the attempt to compete with the West. Politically, the effective subsidy was part of the price the Soviet ruling class paid to hold the Eastern European bloc together in order to achieve its wider political and military objectives.[61]

Since 1989 this pattern has fallen apart. The result of opening up these economies to the world market and carrying out the larger part of trade at world market prices in hard currencies has been a major restructuring of trade which has effectively deindustrialised a significant part of the trade structure.

To see how this is taking place it is necessary to look at the change in the total pattern of trade. Once the Soviet ruling class relinquished its hold on Eastern Europe there was little incentive for either side to maintain the old trade pattern within the bloc and intra-bloc trade collapsed by 20-30 percent in 1990. This collapse continued through 1991. From January 1991 all intra-bloc trade is supposed to have been carried out in dollars at world market prices and the old Comecon structure through which trade had been organised was wound up. In particular Eastern European and Soviet importers of Eastern European manufactured goods stopped buying, either because they preferred to go elsewhere or they lacked the hard currencies to support their purchases as the Soviet Union began to charge dollars for exports of raw material and energy, especially oil.

At the same time trade with the less developed world also began to contract as hidden subsidies were removed and the Eastern European countries looked for more hard currency payments. The only positive area was in terms of trade with the advanced West. The Eastern European countries expanded their exports here with the exception of Romania. Hungary and Poland were especially successful, increasing their exports to the OECD area with the strongest growth in each case with the European Community though of course imports have also been sucked in at high rates.[62]

Western free market proponents have made much of this expansion of exports to the advanced West. Even the United Nations Economic Commission for Europe writes that 'it is tempting to draw attention to the perfect correlation between the progress of reforms in these countries and the strength of their export growth' and that the 'recent export performance suggests that there is room for cautious optimism about the... export prospects'.[63] But such comments obscure the total transformation that is occurring. Trade with the two areas characterised by a higher industrial content has contracted whilst trade with the area with a lower industrial content has expanded. The net effect of this has been three fold. In the first place the overall level of trade whether measured in value or volume terms has fallen. This is a process that has been accurately characterised as one of trade 'destruction'. Secondly, the Eastern European countries are being turned much more into exporters of agricultural goods, raw materials and semi or low level manufactures. Thirdly, the trade balance has sharply deteriorated as these countries must now pay for the larger part of their trade in hard currencies. During the 1980s, when only a part of the trade was in hard currency, it had been possible to more or less balance trade. Now current account deficits exist which can only be dealt with by more austerity or borrowing.[64]

The prospects for changing this new pattern are far from good. There will no doubt be success stories in Eastern Europe but they are unlikely to have much impact on the emerging trade pattern. These economies are being forced to compete by adjusting downwards into areas where there is both substantial world market competition already and considerable barriers to trade. For example 25-30 percent of the OECD exports of Hungary, Poland and Czechoslovakia and an even higher share of their European Community exports are in the areas of agriculture, textiles, iron and steel and chemicals.

> These products are subject to significant non-tariff barriers—quotas, voluntary export restraints, price surveillance, anti-dumping measures and countervailing procedures—which are an important obstacle for central and Eastern European countries in their effort to integrate into the multilateral trading system.[65]

It is quite possible that some concessions will be made so that any discrimination is not too obvious. This is what has already begun to happen with the European Community. But it is highly unlikely that these barriers will be removed wholesale and especially not if growth becomes more difficult in the world economy. Already considerable furore has erupted over increased agricultural exports from Eastern Europe to the West. Eastern Europe's agricultural exports have been worth some 7 billion dollars but only 2 billion dollars have gone to the European Community in the past. To expand these is an obvious possibility, especially as such imports make up only around 1 percent of EC output. Yet the agro-capitalist lobby has managed to forge a powerful alliance with many poorer farmers and peasants. Despite representing an area of diminishing importance to European capital this alliance has proved capable in the past of extracting enormous concessions and subsidies and resisting any major opening up to the world market.[66]

Capital—the missing boom

THE HOPE that the Eastern European economies would be able to adjust upwards rather than downwards was largely based upon the belief that foreign capital would flood into the region, bringing with it new techniques. On some accounts this is happening. In particular 1990 saw what has been called a 'joint-venture euphoria' in which private capital appeared to be seizing the initiative. The United Nations Economic Commission for Europe recorded the formation of nearly 14,000 joint ventures by the end of 1990 of which 11,500 had been formed in that year alone with a total 'commitment' of 7.3 billion dollars.[67] Journalists puffed up every private initiative. At the state level, heads of state and heads of international institutions like Jacques Attalai of the newly formed European Bank for Reconstruction and Development (EBRD) encouraged the most optimistic interpretations. If a new Marshall Plan was not to be forthcoming there would nevertheless be Know-How Funds, Enterprise Funds, economic aid and food aid that would help put Eastern Europe on the right track.

All of this has been at best wishful thinking and at worst disingenuous manipulation of the record. To see this it is only necessary to put the real flows into perspective. After the Second World War the Marshall Plan involved the transfer of some 200—300 billion dollars (in today's prices). Currently some 50 billion dollars are being transferred from West Germany to East Germany with the credit to the Treuhand (responsible for keeping what is left of the East German economy afloat) running at almost 20 billion dollars. Estimates of the amounts needed to help keep Eastern Europe afloat vary. If we exclude Yugoslavia and the former USSR, the World Bank estimated that (on its optimistic scenario) some 20 billion dollars a year would be needed to maintain the economies at their earlier levels. To refurbish them would require levels of aid similar to, or in excess of, that in the Marshall Aid programme. Include the old USSR and the figures leap again.

Given the fact that huge sums have been committed once in the past at a time when the world economy was much less productive there is no question that a rationally organised system could provide what was necessary to help rebuild Eastern Europe. But over the past decades similar possibilities have existed for helping the poorer countries of the world and they have been spurned. The same is now happening in the old Eastern bloc. The real inflow of capital has been a trickle and, as in the Third World, it is in danger of being swamped by a massive outflow as these economies are forced to honour the debts of the old regime. For more realistic observers the immobility of Western states and capital in the face of the dimensions of the problem is a tragedy:

> the politicians and officials who take refuge in the sole-cisms of self-help stand among the pygmies of this century—from the architects of German reparations to the proponents of appeasement—as being unable to grasp the seismic challenges before them, and to exercise just a little statesmanship.[68]

Briefly such commentators hoped that the failed coup in the USSR in the summer of 1991 might lead to a significant revision of policy but it was soon back in its old tracks with only minor changes of commitment behind the rhetoric.

But the reason for this is not any failure of imagination—it lies in the real situation in the West. In the first place, the advanced West has problems enough of its own which restrain any willingness to bail out Eastern Europe. In the second place, in 1945 the United States dominated the world economy and could therefore afford to encourage recovery safe in the knowledge that its own economy would benefit substantially. Today economic power is much more evenly distributed and the situation more competitive with no state prepared to give another a free ride. One reflection of this changing balance of power is the European Bank for Reconstruction and Development which is the first major world financial institution created since 1945 which is not effectively controlled by US capitalism. More centrally, aid is now the responsibility of the Group of Seven (G7) leading industrial countries in which each state tries to push another to the front while telling everyone how committed they are to helping their 'eastern brothers'. In the third place, a realistic appraisal of

Eastern Europe's prospects suggests to any sensible investment analyst that too much good money has already been thrown after bad to warrant any further profligacy without cast-iron guarantees of reform and an eventual payoff, in terms of interest paid or growth, in return for aid.

As with the analysis of trade prospects it is important not to be misled by any selective presentation of parts of what is happening. To see the totality of the situation we must begin with debt. The debt burden for 1990 is set out in Table 10. With a total net debt of 123 billion dollars the outflow of interest payments in 1990 was 12 billion dollars which dwarfed any actual inflow into the area in that year. In other words these increasingly poverty stricken countries acted as capital exporters to the banks and states of the advanced West rather than vice versa. Even if more real aid is given rather than promised this problem is likely to remain.

Table 10
Eastern European debt, debt ratios and payments in 1990.[69]

	Net debt $bn	Net debt/ export	Net interest as %	Debt service ratio	Net interest payment ($bn)
Bulgaria	9.8	468	43	77	0.9
Czechoslovakia	6.3	111	10	25	0.6
Hungary	20.3	343	35	65	2.1
Poland	41.8	418	41	71	4.1
Romania	1.3	38	1	10	0.03
USSR	43.4	139	14	29	4.4
Total	122.9	211	21	39	12.1

Making sense of debt measures

Net Debt	total borrowing minus reserves in Western banks
Net Debt-export ratio	described by the OECD as 'the best indicator of overall indebtedness'. Net debt as percent of annual exports. A figure of less than 100 shows low debt, 100-200 medium, 200+ high debt.
Net interest as percentage exports	shows the burden of annual interest payments in relation to export earnings.
Debt Service Ratio	shows the burden of interest payments and debt repayment in relation to export earnings.
Net Interest Payments	shows the total capital transferred to the advanced West.

What Table 10, columns 2 to 4, also shows is that the capacity to sustain this outflow is at a limit. Some of these countries are on the verge of state bankruptcy or, in the more elegant words of the OECD, 'virtually all the central and Eastern European countries are highly vulnerable to a loss of market confidence'.[70]

Another aspect of this vulnerability is, of course, that reform has made these countries more unstable politically and there is now much less confidence that private loans will be repaid. The result is that Western banking capital has virtually suspended loan activity in the bloc. In 1990 private bank lending to Eastern Europe fell by 65 percent and the resulting low level of lending will be maintained in the short to medium term.[71] The irony here, of course, is that Western banks were prepared to back the old regimes to the hilt because they believed that repression in the region was good for business. Economically the strong central control meant that it always appeared possible to manage things so that debt would be paid back. This indeed was what Ceausescu achieved in Romania for his own reasons in the late 1980s. Politically the repression meant both that there were few of the populist pressures evident in the Third World for debt defaulting and at the bottom the working class and peasant protest could be eliminated as a threat.

That is why the West shed crocodile tears whenever revolt broke out and continued to lend. 'It would be a good thing', said one banker in December 1981, of Poland, 'if Russia invaded, because then she would be obliged to honour Poland's debts'. Another was quoted the next day, in the midst of moves for martial law as saying, 'if a few people are shot in the cause of getting the (Polish) economy moving again, then it would be a small price to pay'.[72] Thus in the late 1980s, while Western banking capital was cutting back its lending elsewhere after having its fingers burned in the Third World, it continued to lend to the rulers of Eastern Europe. In fact Eastern Europe not only recovered its credit rating after a fall in the early 1980s, it actually rose and 'international financial markets became increasingly bullish towards the region'. How different the situation is today! Take Poland, for example, 'no Western banker in his right financial mind would consider lending fresh money to Poland right now'.[73]

Thus inflows of capital are primarily taking the form of lending and aid by Western states and international institutions and direct private capital investment. So far as loans and aid are concerned the problem is the already high level of debt. Western policy has been to insist that debt is honoured partly as a weapon against the bloc itself and partly out of fear that too much generosity in Eastern Europe will increase demands to do more than tinker with the debt structure in the rest of the world. The big exception to this has been Poland which in the spring of 1991 was granted what the OECD called 'unprecedented debt reduction' of 50 percent of its inter-state debt (which made up around two thirds of its total debt). Just how unprecedented this was can be illustrated by the fact that the largest previous debt write off was only of one third for the poverty wracked economies of Africa south of the Sahara.[74] But it was made clear that the reduction in the Polish case was a reward for good behaviour— unlike in Bulgaria which had been financially punished in 1990 for both getting the wrong election result and failing to honour its own debts with sufficient enthusiasm.[75]

Measuring the totality of flows to Eastern Europe from international and state agencies is not easy. This is partly because of the sheer variety of initiatives but also because it is important to distinguish between rhetoric and reality. Much attention, for example, was given to Jacques Attalai and the EBRD but within a short time of its creation it had become 'a by-word for corporate extravagance' with 'a resplendent City headquarters and a stratospheric expense bill for hotel and air fares' and before long Attalai had departed in disgrace.[76] In reality the organisation has relatively few funds at its disposal compared to other agencies. Any assessment of Western aid must therefore take into account i) the real amount committed; ii) the amount actually disbursed ie given out each year; iii) the terms of the loans (for there are few gifts!); iv) the nature of the possible impact—for example, some EC funds are designed to deflect and dump Eastern European agricultural exports onto the countries of the former USSR creating another set of problems as one set appears to be solved.

If these issues are explored then the rhetoric is quickly deflated. Table 11 shows one example of this by looking at the total loans approved and disbursed by the main international bodies for Eastern Europe (excluding the former Soviet Union). Readers should compare these figures with the minimum inflows noted earlier that were considered necessary for stability.

Table 11
Value of IMF, World Bank and Group of 24 loans to Eastern
Europe June 1989 to summer 1991 ($bn)[77]

	Approved	Disbursed
Bulgaria	1.9	0.2
Czechoslovakia	4.3	0.7
Hungary	9.0	1.4
Poland	13.3	1.7
Romania	2.5	0.9
Total	31.0	4.9

What then of the much lauded private investment boom from Western business? The answer is that it hardly exists beyond a few sectors. High profile investment has certainly taken place in the services sector but there are three particular reasons for this. One is that Eastern Europe is potentially a large market with an already existing level of pent-up demand backed by sufficient money to make investment worthwhile for producers and dis- tributors of relatively low priced Western goods. The second is that at the world level in the retailing and consumer sector 'in the battle for markets, market shares and profits, the Western mar- kets are very close to global consolidation'.[78] It is these two fac- tors which account for the speed with which MacDonalds, Burger King, Pepsi, Marks and Spencer, Benetton and similar groups have moved into Eastern Europe. The third is that Western banks, finance houses, accountants and consultants can make large prof- its not by bringing in investment, but by telling Eastern European governments how they can make their economies attractive—by selling their dubious expertise at inflated rates.

The rest of the story is quite different. In the heat of 1989 it was certainly true that some Western capital got carried away by the promise Eastern Europe appeared to offer. Some 40 per- cent of early West German joint ventures, for example, were not preceded by any feasibility study.[79] Even now companies are pre- pared to speak with great enthusiasm about possibilities but their real strategy has been much more cautious. Commitments have been made on three bases. The first has been to snap up the East- ern Europe 'jewels in the crown' as quickly and cheaply as pos- sible. The second has been to grab the most attractive greenfield locations and the third has been to make strategic investments as pre-emptive moves against possible rivals. But in each instance the rule has generally been to make limited commitments. 'Given the risks... it may be best to try to obtain a strategic option in this region without investing too much', writes one leading investment consultant who goes on to urge that 'business decisions... should be even more cautious than usual' and that the best investment at the moment is of a minimal 'sleeping' kind.[80]

We can pull these arguments together by noting that the Group of Thirty Study on Financing Eastern Europe *on the most optimistic scenario* saw the total inflow of capital into Eastern Europe rising from 13.5 billion dollars to 19.8 billion dollars (with private capital growing from around 12 to only 25 percent) in the years 1991-1995. And this optimistic scenario assumed rapid reform.[81] It is also only the inflow side against which must be set the outflow of interest payments, repayments of debt itself and the repatriation of profits.

But if much of the discussion of foreign investment and joint ventures has been hot air it has served a useful purpose of providing a distraction from the way that some of the acquisitions that have been made by Western multinationals have been on the basis of virtual give aways by Eastern European states. The 'Skoda-Volkswagen Joint Venture', in reality Skoda's acquisition by Volkswagen, is a major case in point, especially as it has been much lauded as a model agreement. The whole deal, however, has been subjected to a devastating analysis by a London based Czechoslovakian financial analyst who argues that the then Czechoslovak government allowed itself to be persuaded by its consultants—Price Waterhouse, Credit Suisse, First Boston and the Investment Bank Prague—that the only choice was between two inadequate deals offered by Renault and Volkswagen.

In the event Volkswagen acquired the most advanced car maker in Eastern Europe with the best record in the West for a song. Whether the government acted out of stupidity, ignorance or naivety is not clear but if what the analyst claims are his conservative estimates are correct then Volkswagen has acquired Skoda for less than the price it would have fetched as a bankrupt concern in the West. In real terms Volkswagen appears to have paid no more than 200 million marks for assets worth possibly 3 billion marks—15 times as much. Such estimates are necessarily speculative but that is the point because virtually no information on costings has been published. 'The price of the factory was not determined by market forces, it was set arbitrarily by a small group of Czechoslovak officials and politicians'. And in its turn the reaction to the critique was telling—so strong was the ideological consensus in favour of such a deal that the new media refused the discussion publication. The issue was then taken up with the government by a Prague weekly which was advised against publication since 'Volkswagen could sue ... for damaging its reputation and the reputation of the new joint venture [sic] company'.[82]

Migration—'Keep them out'

WE HAVE already seen that one of the consequences of the pattern of state industrialisation was a tight control over the movement of labour across international frontiers and between East and West. Fully opening up Eastern Europe will therefore give workers an opportunity to move freely but this, of course, is hardly an attribute of the market that proves attractive to the right. In fact already in the 1980s the gradual breakdown of the old system was allowing freer movement. Between 1981 and 1988, for example, emigration from Poland was equivalent to virtually the entire increase in the population of working age. The general pressure in Eastern Europe increased in 1989. 'Ethnic Germans' moved to Germany from Eastern Europe, 'Turkish Bulgarians' moved to Turkey. Between 1978 and 1988 185,000 left but in 1989-90 the figure was 310,000. Albanians fled to Greece and Italy, well over 100,000 Romanians left voluntarily and emigration from the Soviet Union rose steeply too.

To see the scale of the potential movement of labour and people it is helpful to follow a European study which divides potential migrants into three groups. The first consists of 'ethnic migrants' who might be tempted to migrate to what they consider their 'homelands' or stronger communities elsewhere in the world. There are still some 3 million 'ethnic Germans' who might move. The Soviet Jewish population is another example and a third would be the Armenian population living in Georgia and Azerbaijan who, left to their own devices, might prefer to migrate to join the American or French Armenian communities. A second group of potential migrants would be those affected by political migration due to persecution. There are some 1.6 to 2.5 million gypsies, for example, in Eastern Europe who have a history of suffering oppression. In addition there are the unknown numbers who might become victims of the increases in national tension and violence in Yugoslavia. The third group is potentially the biggest of all—the economic migrants. The logic of the market is that people should move in search of better jobs and higher wages.[83] This is what freedom of labour means and for peoples denied that freedom for generations and facing worsening conditions in their own countries both the push of poverty and the pull of higher living standards in Western Europe will encourage them to move. Unless, that is, troops are set to control the borders and a new iron curtain is pulled down. And this is what is happening.

It is important to understand what is at stake. Even if several tens of millions were to try to move there is little doubt that they could be accommodated. That has occurred in the past. Moreover, internal population growth is stagnating in Western Europe as the birth rate has fallen to below or near replacement levels. But for those in power this is not the point. Unlike in the 1950s and 1960s Western capital is not looking for a massive increase in unskilled labour flows. It already has access to large existing pools of such labour within Europe and from legal and illegal flows from its existing periphery. Thus while nationalistic and racist arguments about 'cultured central Europeans' might lead capital to prefer Hungarians to Turkish workers, in the immediate future Western European capital is more interested in particular flows than large scale movements from either area. A spokesman for Citroen in France has made this point well,

> we no longer hire—as we did in the past—a large number of immigrant workers who only speak their native language and are often illiterate. We're not worried about finding enough workers in the future, it's finding enough qualified workers that concerns us.[84]

In other words while industries like building might find Eastern European migrant labour attractive, in general big capital's interests will be in a much more selective 'middle' and 'top' level 'brain drain'. As one Russian journalist has put it,

> if you're the *creme de la creme* they will welcome you with open arms. Otherwise they are keen to prevent floods of Soviet emigrants pouring over their borders... Soviet people categorised as 'especially useful' have no problems... apart from the independently wealthy these may

include defectors from the KGB or Soviet military intelligence, sports stars, outstanding scientists, artists, musicians etc. There are also good chances for Soviet people under 30... if they are well-educated... a 26 year old computer programmer with a good knowledge of English or an electrical engineer of similar age...[85]

Such needs dovetail well with the political pressures on governments from the right and short-sighted sections of the labour movement. They also fit well with governments' own desires to use an internal European 'race' card to their political advantage. By the early 1990s this card had begun to be played in every country as the flames of racist violence and immigration scares were being fanned.[86]

The unequal crisis—the escape of the ruling class

THE CONSEQUENCE of this analysis of what is happening in terms of integration with the world economy is to suggest that Eastern Europe is unlikely to experience vigorous growth. But this does not mean that the costs of transition will be shared equally. It is precisely because that burden will be unequal that those at the top have been engaged in supporting change.

We have already argued before 1989 there was a ruling class in control which was determined to hang on to its power and that it was already making significant moves to accommodate itself to the 'winds of change' blowing in the bloc. It is now time to analyse how this ruling class has shifted its base in order to retain its grip on power.

Analysing the contours of a modern ruling class requires a sensitivity to the real distribution of power in both East and West. Marxists have frequently shown themselves to be hamfisted in both areas. In the case of Eastern Europe this hamfistedness had three common expressions. One was the simple identification of class with legal property ownership rather than effective control of the means of production. A second was a woeful ignorance of the real scale of the inequalities that arose as a consequence of the real distribution of control. A third, which flowed from the first two, was a tendency to focus only on the narrow party political, administrative elite at the top rather than see this group as a component of a wider ruling class. The real power of this wider class in Eastern Europe was expressed through its effective control of the economic, social and political assets of society and it is this that it has sought to hang on to through the transition while certain of the party and security groups within it have been beheaded. Even amongst these groups, however, what is often striking is their resilience and the jails have hardly been bulging with those responsible for the old order.

Commentators on Eastern Europe have made much of the fact that in Warsaw the old Communist Party headquarters has been turned into the Stock Exchange. But the real irony of the joke runs rather deeper than they have allowed because what this better illustrates is a fundamental continuity of power. This is not so much because the communist bureaucrats have all become stockbrokers, though some certainly have. Rather what we see here is an expression of the basic continuity in class relations of exploitation.[87] It is not possible in the space available to trace this across the whole of the ruling class so here our attention will focus on those holding the economic levers of power.[88]

Before 1989 the Eastern European economies were state run in the sense that legally most property was nationalised and economic activity was administered from the centre through the central planning network. In reality the 'plans' expressed the central planners' attempts to direct the enterprise within the economy along lines determined by the competitive international networks in which these economies were imprisoned.

The top planners in the various central planning offices and the factory managers formed part of the ruling class alongside those controlling the state machine, the media, party and so on. Their effective control of the means of production was expressed in similar ways to those found in the West amongst managerial and bureaucratic sections of the ruling class. That is, not only did they control society and act as the agent of accumulation but they also benefited personally in terms of high incomes, wealth accumulated on the side and an ability to pass on their general class position to their children and wider families. Indeed the more that is revealed about the contours of power and the way that these societies structurally reproduced it over time the more obvious it becomes that the class rates of social mobility, income and wealth distributions were little different from those in the West. It was the Hungarian sociologist Hankiss who again painted one of the clearest pictures of this concentration of power in an analysis of Hungary. Here he wrote, those at the top,

> created their fiefs, pacified and protected their subjects, developed their patron-client networks, siphoned off more and more resources out of society, built their castles, socialised at hunting parties, enjoyed the comfort of their luxurious holiday centres, sent their children abroad, poured huge resources into wasteful mega-projects, financed their power by huge loans from abroad, and hid their claws in velvet gloves or behind the smiles of paternalistic benevolence.[89]

If we focus particularly on the economic core of this ruling class then in its heyday in the old society greater power lay with those in the central institutions rather than the enterprises. In the last decades, however, there is evidence that the balance was changing as managers became more professional and, under the impact of partial reform and crisis, there took place what has been called 'the shrinkage of central planning'. Those who half saw the way in which change was going took opportunities to move sideways from the party, state or planning structures to the business and commercial ones. In Hungary the shift was so obvious that it was given the name 'parachuting'. In the transition this shift in power to the enterprise bosses and the financial system has become even clearer as the old central structures have been partly dismantled.

The dismantling has been partial because, of course, although central planning is disappearing the state continues to play an important role. As a result many of the old personnel continue to be needed. At the same time the old personnel have been ideally placed to make the sideways step to the more market based structures. Thanks to the investigations of a Hungarian journalist we can see clearly how this has worked in the Hungarian Finance Ministry. Consider first the case of Mihaly Kupa, the Finance Minister. Under the old regime Kupa was Head of the Fiscal Policy Unit in the Ministry of Finance. He left the state in May 1990 to organise the Hungarian office of an American-Japanese firm only to return in the early summer as the new Finance Minister of the Antall government. Kupa's case is by no means untypical of what has occurred, 'those who held middle level positions in the economic administration shifted to managerial posts at Hungary's big companies, and one time government experts can be found in the management or board of directors of almost every Hungarian bank'.

In the Finance Ministry, with the new government, all five deputy ministers and nine out of 11 section heads resigned. The former Finance Minister and Deputy Prime Minister went to work for the Hungarian branch of the French banking group Paribas. One deputy finance minister went to work for London firm James Capel; another became Chief Executive of Reviconsult, a Hungarian Accounting Company co-operating with James Capel; a third deputy minister became President of the Hungarian Industrial Bank; a fourth, President of the Agrobank. The President of the National Bank of Hungary became a manager of the Vienna based Indosuez investment group, the chief economic adviser to the former government became head of Central European Economic Research and Counselling Ltd, a company working for Hungarian banks and Western investors in which a former justice minister was also a partner. The Kadar regime's banker, Janos Fekete, who had appeared regularly in the West and helped to build up Hungary's debt, went to work for the Israeli Bank Leumi in Hungary and so on.[90]

These sideways movements or circulation within the existing ruling class are taking place not simply at the visible level of the ministries but below them at the level of enterprise management. In the first place we should note that large chunks of industry will continue to remain in state hands with little or no change in the nature of their management groups.

The proposed privatisation schemes were unrealistic on any scenario. A Polish minister put it this way, 'the task is colossal. The totality of privatisation made in the world in France, Great Britain, Argentina, Mexico... only represents 11 percent of the privatisation to be carried out in Poland'.[91] When attempts were made to begin this process a cluster of technical issues arose—ownership squabbles, legislative problems, accounting difficulties, lack of personnel, inexperience and so on. But the more fundamental problem is simply that few enterprises could survive on their own. 'A change in ownership of deeply troubled enterprises will not make much difference: what is needed is capital—that's the critical issue', is how Jan Vanous of the American PlanEcon consultants has put it. But this argument has found little favour with other Western consultants and even less with those like Sachs who see the solution as dumping whole sections of industry, 'the idea is to privatise and then to solve the problems of enterprises, not the other way round. British state privatisation is an illusion. It's an expensive and slow way whose sole virtue is solving the unemployment problem in the City of London'.[92] Given that Western privatisation advisers are charging up to 20 percent of the value of the flotation it is not difficult to sympathise with this last point. But neither offloading chunks of industry or giving away shares to the population will work if enterprises cannot survive. Share markets throughout the world depend upon institutional investors to support them and few institutional investors will be attracted to privatised Eastern European companies in any form in the immediate future.[93]

Smaller scale privatisations have taken place but these have usually involved effective 'management buy-outs' or they are examples of what has been called 'nomenklatura privatisation' after the nomenklatura lists of the old regime which indicated people acceptable for the top positions.

Much the same applies to the development of new companies in the private sector. As with other aspects of the transition much nonsense has been talked about the emergence of new entrepreneurs. Crisis and austerity has certainly led to the proliferation of Third World style informal sectors but this is no more relevant to future economic development than the proliferation of car boot sales in Britain in the last decade. Beyond this there has certainly been a dramatic rise in small scale business activity. In 1990 and early 1991 516,000 new enterprises were created in Poland, 300,000 in Czechoslovakia and 250,000 in Hungary but the vast majority of these were examples of self-employment.[94] Undoubtedly there will be examples of rags to riches stories from this sector but these will be no more a guide to the real process of class reproduction than the rise of the occasional Alan Sugar is to the dynamics of class in the West. What is important here is to take out the significant new companies—the larger ones and these are defined by the way that their owners have been able to establish themselves through access to education, knowledge, capital and contacts, ie through using their existing position in the system, their class position. This is most obvious in terms of 'nomenklatura privatisation' which also takes the form of the sponsoring of new companies alongside the state ones, but let the President of the Warsaw Economic Association explain how it works,

> The state and party apparat are interested in founding as many companies as possible. They see chances for themselves to sit on various company councils and even to hold stocks... The apparat is only whetting its appetite for profits that companies can provide them with, and so not only is it not trying to hamper the growth of entrepreneurs but it is even making life easier for companies by opening up a protective umbrella over them... The first companies have already been founded at the initiative of the apparat, and even of people representing medium-level Party authorities, and some of those new companies are chaired by people from the top echelons of power in Poland.[95]

But it is not just formal nomenklatura privatisation that is important here. What matters is also the way in which those at the top have the capacity to reproduce themselves as a whole both in the state and the private sectors. One Hungarian study, for example, has shown that the entrepreneurial, intellectual and managerial groups in that country have all been recruited from 'people of more or less the same origin'. In the case of new entrepreneurs in the private sector,

> only one fourth or fifth of the total number of those participating in enterprises come from the lower social groups. All this indicates that this group of self-employed entrepreneurs has successfully taken advantage of the parents' socio-economic position making use of the opportunities provided by the 1980s.[96]

One reason for this is that it is only these people who were able to accumulate money and convert it into and out of foreign currencies to maintain and increase its value. Andrea Gallai, for example, a Hungarian businesswoman running a chain of artshops and identified by *Business Week* as one of the new generation of entrepreneurs 'poured $80,000 of private savings into her first venture... "Everyone has stashed away some wealth", says Gallai'.[97] But not the equivalent of $80,000 in either Hungarian or even less hard currency. To get this you had either to be a member of the existing ruling class or serving it through the black market.

And finally when Western companies move in they are

interested in building on existing unequal social relationships. At the top they hand out jobs 'for the boys' as we saw in the case of the Hungarian Finance Ministry but below this level they draw on the existing managerial groups and especially the younger managers serving their 'apprenticeships'. These people are then retrained in house or in the country concerned on Western style programmes or, for a select few, they are taken abroad for training. Even in the former East Germany this has been true. Western capital has not been interested in re-equipping the old productive assets of Eastern Europe but it has put itself behind the re-equipping and reskilling of the management stratum of the ruling class. This is how Axel Osenberg of the leading German financial conglomerate Deutsche Bank puts it:

> We are training the staff we took over from the East. In the first six months they took part in more than 6,000 seminars. More than 1,000 people attended training courses in the West. We now have more than 700 apprentices, 130 of whom we took over from Staatsbank. Our East German staff are highly motivated... they clearly identify themselves with the objectives of our bank.[98]

What all of this evidence points to therefore is a process involving a recomposition of the ruling class as a whole with some groups experiencing downward mobility and new groups being co-opted. The power of the class as a whole is surviving and so is that of many of its individual members. This process of co-option provides a safety valve through which those with an understanding of what is happening can be integrated into the new. Ironically this has included Elemer Hankiss who moved from being the sharp-eyed observer to a fully integrated new head of Hungarian television until he became the victim of new media wars.

This recomposition is not a chance happening. It is a reflection of deeper social processes which have created the opportunities for movement. These social processes are rooted in the structural characteristics of the Eastern European societies. It is precisely because both sides of the transition show the same structural features that individual opportunism on the scale we have analysed has been possible. We are not merely looking at class societies, but class societies rooted in a common mode of production where what has been changing has been the form rather than the essence. Unless this is understood it becomes impossible to understand how, beneath the turnover at the top, the same people, the same families, the same social networks are still toasting their good fortune in the 1990s as they had toasted it in the 1980s. It is true that as they chatter and socialise they might on occasion spare a thought for some of their absent friends but they will not lose sight of the greater whole—that they are still on top despite the transition. Beneath them is the same working class, still carrying the burden of their wealth, privilege and their incompetence as it has done in the past.

The unequal crisis—making the workers pay

IF WE TURN to the other side of this process we can now trace how the working class and (to a lesser extent) the peasants of Eastern Europe are being made to pay for the crisis through increased unemployment, a falling standard of living and increased exploitation.

Identifying the full rise in unemployment is difficult because the statistics are only just beginning to be created and they do not measure the real rise. Right wing critics have argued that official figures overstate real levels because people are being encouraged to register for benefits. This argument has already led to a tightening of regulations especially in Poland. In this sense one level of controversy about real levels of unemployment is exactly the same as that in the West where similar accusations of 'scrounging' and 'moonlighting' are made. But the problem is compounded in Eastern Europe by the way that the labour markets in these societies worked before 1989.[99]

Contrary to what their supporters often claimed these regimes did have real unemployment, but it is true that in the past the drive to compete created a general labour shortage which led to high participation rates especially amongst women. The crisis is therefore acting not only to restructure production but also to restructure the labour force and this means squeezing women and the old either out of the labour force altogether or into part-time work. The official figures in Table 12 therefore do not really capture the true extent of the change. Nevertheless they still paint a telling picture of who is experiencing the burden of transition.

Table 12
Percentage Unemployed in Eastern Europe (end period)[100]

	1990	1991	1992	1993*e*	1994*p*	1995*p*
Bulgaria	1.6	11.7	15.6	17	17	16
Czechoslovakia	1.0	6.8	5.1			
Czech Rep.			2.8	4	8	8
Slovak Rep.			10.4	15	18	18
Hungary	1.6	7.5	12.3	13	13	12
Poland	6.1	11.5	15.0	17	16	14
Romania		2.7	6.2	9	15	15

(*e* indicates estimate, *p* indicates projection)

Problems also arise with the measurement of the fall in the standard of living. It is the case that the old official figures overstated the standard of living (though by how much is less clear). Simple comparisons of pre- and post-1989 can therefore overstate the fall but the evidence of a real decline in the standard of living is so clear that no amount of revision can disguise its nature.[101] Initially the most extreme case was that of Poland where the average standard of living was cut by around a third when the shock programme was introduced. This decline was probably the greatest sudden reduction in a peacetime standard of living through 'normal' economic processes anywhere in recent world economic history. It was much greater, for example, than in the crisis of the 1930s and comparable only to the collapse in the standard of living of the Soviet worker that was brought about by the introduction of the first five year plan between 1928 and 1932. Subsequently, the collapse of the standard of living in the successor states of the old USSR was as—if not more—dramatic. The comparison with 1928-32 is an important one for it shows the way in which both the birth and death of regimes built around state directed competitive industrialisation were undertaken at the expense of the working class.

A third element in the pressure on the working class has been the attempt to tighten work discipline in order to improve profitability which has meant a cut in absenteeism, improvements in productivity and so on. This process is being quite consciously manipulated with the approval of Western agencies and advisers. Lipton and Sachs (advisers to Solidarity remember) boast that 'with workers afraid of job losses, sick leave has dropped sharply according to unpublished government surveys... wages pressures have abated' and they quote one commentator describing how, 'in industry, sick leave decreased by 80 percent.

I discovered that it became nearly impossible to lure even my most devoted friends out for a chat during their office hours: with the threat of unemployment looming, skipping work became too risky'.[102] Which is fine, save that these workers will no more be the direct beneficiaries of this productivity drive than they were under the old regime. Rather we can taste here the logic of General Jaruzelski who said in May 1990, in an interview with a Western journalist, 'we tried economic reforms time and again. But it always met with public resistance and explosions. It is very different now. Now with a government that enjoys public confidence, it has become possible to demand sacrifices'.[103]

The disorientation of the left

ALL OF THIS raises the question of where the left is in Eastern Europe? An active left concerned to fight both against the old system and the new one for a real alternative that reflected the real potential of 1989—the power of the workers who struck and demonstrated on the streets, the optimism and the hope that affected the crowds of protesters—could now be making a substantial difference. The success of the transition, the escape of the ruling class, demands the complicity of workers. To take but one example, 'privatisation will not be possible if employees resist: who will buy a company where the employees are on strike?'[104]

Unfortunately the left is encouraging this complicity at the moment. Throughout Eastern Europe the left has also drawn the conclusion that socialism equals state and the market equals salvation. Nowhere has there been an attempt to confront the real nature of the old regime. The result is that the arguments on the left have been moralistic rather than political. The result is what Havel called in Czechoslovakia 'a coalition of sacrifice'. But it is the right which has set the agenda to such an extent that many on the left fear to discuss socialism and prefer instead to identify themselves as 'Western', hoping to indirectly defend a less harsh transition through an argument for 'successful Western social democratic models'.

This disorientation is general but its impact is clearest at the level of trade union organisation. Here a precondition of any attempt to defend workers' interests is independent organisation. But there has been a real failure to build alternative union structures that really represent workers and can displace the old Stalinist structures that in the past were simple transmission belts for the policies of the regimes themselves. In most countries these old 'company unions', for that is what they were, still have significant followings.

This is even true in Poland where Solidarity has failed to re-emerge on its earlier scale and today has only around one fifth of its peak membership. There, although its working class membership appears to be less than that of Solidarity, the old official National Trade Union Alliance (OPZZ) has managed to remain a force and, untied to the government, has found it easy to sound radical. This reflects the second aspect of the problem which is that the leaders of the new union structures often see their task as defending what is emerging on the grounds that there are only two alternatives. This is clearest in the case of Solidarity where the new government sprang from the organisation and where, despite more recent changes and separations, the Solidarity Trade Union organisation still has to carry what its Chairman called, at its third Congress in February 1991, 'the burden of co-responsibility of reform'.

Such views make it hard to develop a resolute defence of workers against the impact of the transition. But this is not to say that the material is not there. In Eastern Europe today small disputes proliferate and occasionally break out into larger ones. In the autumn of 1990, for example, the whole of Budapest was brought to a halt by a taxi drivers' strike. Despite the unpromising nature of the group taking action the strike briefly became the focus of more general resentments about the government that found no echo through the more conventional organisations.

But there has been no real leadership from those whose arguments might have had some resonance because of the positions they had established in the opposition in the past. In Poland, for example, leaders like Adam Michnik and Jacek Kuron have not only made themselves responsible for defending the transition, they have even fought shy of vigorously taking up issues like the power of the Catholic Church for fear of weakening their own positions.

The result has been an astonishing wilting of popular interest in formal politics especially in Poland and Hungary. In the case of Poland it had been Solidarity's striking electoral victory in 1989 that had forced the hand of the old government and led to its replacement by a new Solidarity government. By 1990, however, in the two rounds of the presidential election in the autumn, Solidarity's voting strength had fallen. Partly this was a result of the drift to other candidates like the maverick Tyminski and, partly, because of a simple refusal to vote at all which led to a dramatic decline in electoral turn out. This was continued into the autumn of 1991 as parties proliferated and in the first major free elections in Poland the main winner was apathy. But Poland is in no sense alone. In Hungary in the first round of the parliamentary elections on 25 March 1990 65 percent voted, in the second round in April the figure was down to 45 percent. A year later, in April 1991, two by-elections had to go to the second round because of poor turn out. In one, a Budapest seat, there was a 3 percent increase in turn out the second time to take the number of voters over 25 percent, enough for it to count. In the second case, a rural seat, the elections were abandoned after an 11 percent turn out. But studies of voting patterns in Hungary, notwithstanding the latter by-election, show that it is manual workers who are less likely to vote, not because of apathy but because they do not see that the existing choice has any meaning for them.[105]

If the economic collapse has been one of the most spectacular in history, this collapse into indifference is its political parallel. A huge vacuum has opened up in the political system.

But the fact that such a vacuum exists confirms in a distorted way the thrust of our analysis: that what has been at stake has been a change in the form of class society and not a shift to a class society. Those who argued that what existed in Eastern Europe before 1989 was some form of socialism, however degenerate, were never able to fully confront the scale of exploitation and alienation under the old regimes and their difficulties were compounded with the rise of Solidarity which organised the majority of the working class against one such regime. The subsequent events of 1989 and after have intensified these problems, for workers have shown no interest in defending the old forms. This still emerges strongly today despite the evidence of growing crisis in a material sense.

The evidence clearly points to the belief that it is better to be poorer but freer than better off in an unfree society. And this is a view that deserves every support from socialists for in that freedom lies the ability to organise and fight for new ideas and real change. But it is also clear that no real commitment exists to the societies that are emerging the other side of the transition. Rather what is happening is that those on the left who have been seduced by the new order are not building a consensus of legitimacy, they are sowing confusion when they should be building resistance from below. To say this is not to argue that simple sloganeering is sufficient—it clearly is not. The effect of the association of the old regimes with the name of 'socialism' has been enormous. 'In my country', said Havel in late 1989,

> for ages now, socialism has been no more than an incantation that should be avoided if one does not want to appear suspect... socialism... was transformed long ago into just an ordinary truncheon used by certain cynical, parvenu bureaucrats to bludgeon their liberal minded fellow citizens from morning till night, labelling them 'enemies of socialism' and 'anti-socialist forces'.[106]

To overcome this heritage of distrust the starting point must be different, it must be the practical question of the nature of class power that we have posed here. The urgency of this question is simple. Vacuums do not exist indefinitely. As the crisis intensifies then people will look for answers and it is already clear that the existing rulers will try to supply them in increasingly nationalistic and divisive forms in order to divert blame from themselves.

Nationalism and the political vacuum

THE EXTENT of the lurch towards nationalism has been another aspect of the Eastern European situation that has shocked many people. It should not have. The problem is not, as some have suggested, that there has been a simple return to the petty nationalisms of the inter-war years. There is no transcendent logic of nationalism in Eastern Europe any more than there is in the rest of the world. Rather nationalism has become such a potent force because it was carried and reproduced by the old 'communist' regimes. This was so in the negative sense, that these regimes failed to confront the structural conditions that gave rise to nationalism and, in the positive sense, that their policies were informed by nationalism and they were prepared to use it and some of its equally unpleasant relations, like anti-semitism, for their own ends.

The most fundamental aspect of this was the way in which the ideology of development—'socialism in one country'—was national in its objectives, an expression of the interests of a national ruling class. At the same time the competitive drives which determined development also limited the real effort that could be directed towards eliminating regional and 'national' differences within countries. In this way policies of 'regional' development experienced the same difficulties faced by their counterparts in the West. It was possible to moderate but never eliminate national and regional inequality because such uneven development was built into the logic of the competitive world economy where resources have to be allocated to ends and areas that yield the greatest returns.

So long as the Eastern European regimes boomed nationalism could stay in the background though, whenever difficulties emerged, those at the top often had easy recourse to it. In some countries it went beyond this. In Poland, for example, 'instrumental anti-semitism' was often used against the opposition. In Romania Ceausescu similarly extolled his vision of the Romanian past and present (including making a hero of Vlad the Impaler) against 'internal enemies' in the form of gypsies and the Hungarian minority. But nationalism also came from below in that, given the unequal development and the absence of a clearly articulated alternative explanation, people looking for answers sometimes found them in the existing ideas.

Since nationalism was always there in some form, nurtured and reproduced by the old order, it is easier to understand why it should have become such a strong force for the larger part of the political spectrum in Eastern Europe today, often expressed most intensely by former Communist Party members. This nationalism is occupying the vacuum and pushing country against country and pulling them towards 'national models' in the West that the leaderships admire. More disturbingly it is fracturing internal politics wherever there are significant national minorities. In Czechoslovakia, for example, (which many imagined to be one of the most stable countries) the uneven impact of crisis has forced home the lesson of the uneven development of the Czech and Slovak lands and played into the hands of politicians using nationalism to build their constituency, allowing them to split the country apart in a way that most Czechoslovaks thought impossible a few months before. It is in the continuity of the inequality of exploitation and oppression in Czechoslovakia, and Eastern Europe more generally, that we find the answer to Vaclav Havel's plaintive question posed as the second year of the transition began, 'why is our political climate systematically poisoned by demagogy, by political, ethnic and racial intolerance?'[107]

The contradictory power of religion is to be explained in the same way. The fact that the old regimes were rooted in class society meant that they could never eliminate the forces which pushed people towards the church as a source of hope and salvation. Instead, after a period of trying to suppress religious observance, the regimes moved to a tacit 'concordat' with the various national churches as useful allies helping them to keep stability. Ever the opportunists, the official churches seized their chances to negotiate an area of limited freedom. But this also made them centres which the opposition could use. The pattern is a familiar one and by no means restricted to Eastern Europe. It can be found in Latin America and South Africa. In the Eastern bloc it was most obvious in Poland where the Catholic Church maintained an uneasy stand-off between the regime and Solidarity with 'a finger in both pies'. Now, as the late Jan-Josef Lipski, a long time social democratic oppositionist, put it shortly before his death, 'the Church is presenting its bill for the support of Solidarity'.[108]

The bill is not one over which there is agreement. In Poland the Church has also suffered a loss of support since the heady days of 1989. But it is still insisting on payment in terms of religion being taught in schools, an end to abortion and a general commitment to traditional, conservative, national values. Moreover, even in decline, the Polish church remains a powerful national symbol commanding a significant and vocal minority support. For Walesa it is part of his natural constituency of support. And on the left his opponents are reluctant to challenge the Catholic Church openly for fear of losing support. Yet such a calculated 'electoralism', for that is what it is, usually ends up producing what it most fears. By ducking the debate, refusing to challenge, the initiative is left with those pushing the 'centre ground' ever more to the right.

In this way the mixtures of nationalism and religion feed off real difficulties. But their targets are at a tangent to the real causes of the problems and their solutions, non-solutions. This is most obvious in the widespread development of anti-semitism.

It should hardly need saying that anti-semitism does not depend on Jews for its success. In inter-war Germany less than 1 percent of the population was Jewish. It is not Jews that define the problem but the problem that defines Jews. This was well expressed by Karl Luegar, a leading late nineteenth century anti-semitic Mayor of Vienna who attacked the 'corrosive influence' of Jews. When asked for the definition of a Jew, Luegar's response was simply to say that he would define who was a Jew and who was not. This was the view taken by Hitler.

Today in Eastern Europe we find similar processes at work. In Poland, for example, Lech Walesa has found the hint of anti-semitism part of the natural vocabulary of his populist nationalism. He, at least, is '100 percent Pole going back generations'. As Marek Edelman (a veteran of the Warsaw Uprising and Solidarity) has put it, 'Walesa is not an anti-semite, he's a populist. But he doesn't tell people to stop this shouting'.[109] One of the less attractive reasons for the defeat of the Mazowiecki government (over which, for other reasons, few tears should be shed) was the widespread impression that Mazowiecki (a Catholic) himself was a Jew and surrounded by 'leftist Jews'. In fact Hitler had already seen to it that there were few Jews left in Poland—some 4,000 compared to a pre-war community of 3 or 4 million. But this did not matter and nor does it matter in Romania where only 18,000 of the pre-war Jewish community of 800,000 are left. Nevertheless for Cornelieu Vadim Tudor, once a leading Ceausescu supporter and now responsible for a virulent nationalist and anti-semitic political programme, 'in parliament and in the government, it rains Jews by the bucket'.[110]

Yet there are grounds for optimism. For all the way that nationalism and its relations feed off crisis they still need to be kicked into full gear and this can be resisted. This is the ironic lesson of Yugoslavia where in 1991 they took such an apparently firm grip. There is a real sense in which the previous decade reflected a race between growing opposition from below, expressed in a dramatic rise in industrial conflict, and attempts at the top to divert discontent into nationalistic channels. It took a long time to achieve this and the power of those at the top was frequently under challenge. It should be recalled that the Yugoslavia which erupted into bloodshed in the middle of 1991 was that same Yugoslavia where, earlier in the year, there had been huge strikes, demonstrations and even an invasion of parliament protesting against the policies that were to produce the conflict. The problem was that no political organisation of the left had been created of sufficient size and with sufficient clarity in its politics that could allow it to expose the old regime for what it was—exploitative and oppressive—and challenge the non-solutions being offered. In Eastern Europe there is the opportunity and necessity of avoiding that mistake.

Big tasks and small beginnings

NO ONE should be under any illusion about the scale of the economic and political crisis in Eastern Europe and the problems this poses for building a real alternative. The dissident movement that existed before 1989 was always brave but weak in numerical terms. Its isolation drove it together for mutual support and suppressed the full articulation of political differences. At the same time it was easy for those in the West to have influence as it looked anywhere for sustenance. Now that open organisation is possible—in part because of the brave efforts of these people—the movement has fractured completely while some of its members have been absorbed into the new regimes and others remain as marginalised today as they were yesterday, displaced by those who had tacitly supported the old and now are seizing their opportunities to do well in the new.

In these terms the real socialist tradition in Eastern Europe is having to be built again from the bottom up by people who are arguing on the ground in ones and twos, in the same way that socialists began their movement in the nineteenth century. It is easy in this context to look for short cuts. There are none that do not lead to dead ends. The old regimes subordinated their populations to the needs of their rulers, they forced the pace of accumulation at the expense of the working class in order to be better able to compete with the rest of the world. Today the forms are changing but that same logic prevails. The difference is that people now have an opportunity to have these arguments and to organise openly in however small a fashion without the fear of arrest.

This has been the great advance of 1989, the opening that has been created. In that opening there is now the possibility of building an alternative based upon a defence of workers' interests against the old and new forms. On the success of these small beginnings depends not only the future of real socialism in Eastern Europe but also how long that democratic opening remains. As in the West a vigorous and independent left wing working class movement, based in the workplace, with strong trade union roots and a political party to represent it, is the only basis for an effective fight to defend workers' interests in the present and to keep the democratic opening open in the face of a ruling class prepared to consider alternative solutions. Indeed it is on the basis of such a defence that movements are built that offer the real prospect of change East and West.

The return of the national question

CHRIS HARMAN

Introduction

IT HAS become almost an orthodoxy to say that the great divide in the world today is between nationalisms. The talk of 'a new world order' and 'the end of history' may not have lasted long. But what has replaced it does not seem to have been class politics, but rather the rivalry of reborn—or sometimes completely new—nationalisms.

Yet those who speak in these terms have great difficulty in defining what makes up a 'nation'. It cannot just be those people who inhabit a certain geographical entity—otherwise what sense are we to make of minorities declining to be part of the 'nation' of the majority among whom they live? It cannot just be language—or what are we to make of Serb, Croat and Bosnian speakers of a single language declaring themselves to be separate nationalities, or of the founders of India attempting to impose Hindi, their own recently sanitised version of a regional dialect, Hindustani, as the 'national language' of a whole subcontinent? It cannot be that fashionable catch-all 'culture', since everywhere differences in culture, or ways of living, are greater between the rich and poor, or the workers and peasants, within a national state than they are between neighbours from the same class on different sides of national borders.

There is no single objective criterion by which to determine whether a group of people—or their would be leaders—will decide they should constitute a nation. On this, at least, such diverse authorities as 'old left' academic Eric Hobsbawm,[1] 'new left' academic Benedict Anderson,[2] liberal academic Ernest Gellner[3] and former editor of this journal Nigel Harris[4] are in agreement. Nations are, in Anderson's words, 'imaginary' entities—although in this case imagination in power can use all the nastiest weapons of the state to impose its beliefs on those who dissent from them.

The ideologists of nationalism nearly always try to trace the ancestry of their particular nation back many hundreds of years—as when English history is said to begin with King Alfred and his burnt cakes and Ethelred the Unready, when Tudjman's government speaks of 'the thousand year old Croatian nation', when the Serbian government invokes the battle of Kosovo in 1389, or Romanian nationalists claim a continuity going back to the Roman Empire's settlement of Dacia.[5] But these claims are invariably based on fictitious histories. For nations as entities have not always existed.

The modern nation, with its ideal of a homogeneous body of citizens, enjoying equal rights, expressing loyalty to a single centre of sovereignty and speaking a single language, is as much a product of relatively recent history as capitalism itself. It is a notion as out of place in any serious account of the pre-capitalist societies which dominated the whole world until the sixteenth century, and more than 90 percent of it until little over a century ago, as that of the motor car or machine gun.

In fact, it is the connection between the rise of the nation state and the rise of capitalism which enables us to understand the strength of the myths that lead people to slaughter each other—as always with wars, most of the slaughter being of the poor by the poor, not the rich by the rich.

Capitalism and the nation

THE CLASS societies that existed before the rise of capitalism were organised through states. But these states were external to most of the activities of the great mass of people. They robbed them through taxation and pillage and they coerced or bribed them into joining their armies. But they left untouched their basic everyday activity of getting a living, which took place mainly through subsistence agriculture even if a small portion of their output was traded. The peasantry were, of course, heavily exploited and subject to vicious legal repression but it was by particular lords and particular clerics (often the same people), who themselves owed only a distant and fragile allegiance to any central state.

In such a society the situation which existed in the twelfth century monarchy called England (in fact made up of modern England, much of western France and parts of Wales, Ireland and Scotland) was typical, with the military rulers using one language (Norman French), the literate elite of administrators using another (medieval Latin), and the mass of the population using a variety of disparate dialects (various forms of Anglo-Saxon, French, Welsh and Gaelic).

The state in such a society might be centralised and powerful or weak and fragmented. But in neither case was it a national state as we understand it today. Whatever else its subjects thought, they did not think of themselves as citizens speaking a common language or owing an undivided loyalty to a single geographic entity.

Under capitalism things are very different. The market impinges on every aspect of everybody's life, from the work they do through the food they eat and the clothes they wear to how they amuse themselves. And with the growth of the market there is a massive growth of administration, both within individual companies and in the state.

The ideological mythology of capitalism claims it needs only a minimal state. But, in fact, the market can only function on an extensive, enduring basis if it is backed up by an equally pervasive state—issuing money, ensuring debts are paid, limiting the scale of fraud, building roads and ports, keeping the poor from getting their revenge on the rich, engaging in wars and, above all, enforcing regular taxation on the mass of people.

But an administrative apparatus cannot operate efficiently without an easy means of communication between its functionaries, a language in which they are all fluent. It also prefers this to be the language of most of those who live under it: it makes the prying of the secret police and the tax collectors so much easier, the cohesion between those who give orders at the top and those who enforce them at the bottom so much more efficient.

The first national states

CAPITALISM first began to develop fully in Holland and England from the sixteenth century onwards—although market relations and, with them, the first nuclei of capitalist production, were already present in parts of fourteenth century

Italy and Flanders, and sixteenth century Germany, France and Bohemia. In each case the rise of the market began, spontaneously, to give rise to the elements that were to come together to create the national state.

The spread of trade caused people in different regions to have increasing direct and indirect contact with each other. Traders from the towns travelled through the countryside, buying, selling and talking to people in the most remote villages, picking up the bits of dialect they needed to make themselves understood and mixing them into the colloquial idiom of the town, creating, without thinking about it, new standard forms of communication which it was an advantage for everyone connected with the new commerce to learn. Along with the traders went itinerant preachers—often out to profit their pockets as well as their souls—and recruiters looking for men for the new mercenary armies. Meanwhile, the poorest in the villages would leave for the towns in search of work, and the richest to cut out the middleman and to trade directly themselves. While in rural France, the average peasant never travelled more than about five miles from his or her home in a lifetime of toil, by the late seventeenth century one in seven of England's population would pass at least part of their life in London.[6]

Spontaneously, unconsciously, trading networks started to become linguistic networks. It was then that the administrators of the state, keen to tax the profits of trade, saw the point in carrying out their transactions in the language of the market, not that of the court or the church. It was then, too, that the innovative writers saw that using the new colloquial tongue was the way to win an audience—as Dante did in early fourteenth century Florence, Chaucer in England half a century later, and Luther and Rabelais in sixteenth century Germany and France.

The change took a long time to complete—even as late as the seventeenth century, Hobbes in England and Spinoza in Holland could still write major works in Latin—but where capitalism conquered, so did the new tongues. By contrast, where capitalism had a false start and then succumbed to a revival of the old order, so too the new languages suffered: the increasing refeudalisation of late Renaissance Italy meant much literature was in Latin rather than in Dante's Italian[7]; the smashing of Bohemian Protestantism by the armed counter-reformation at the battle of the White Mountain in 1618 was also the destruction of

Czech as a written language for nearly 200 years; Latin continued to be the language of adminstration in the Habsburg empire
until the 1840s.

What became the first nations began their life as networks
of trade, adminstration and language which grew up in the hin-
terland of major cities. Everywhere in Europe the administrators
of late feudal monarchies tried to increase their power over members of the old feudal ruling class by allying themselves with
the traders and manufacturers of the towns. These 'burghers'
were often already at the centre of geographically compact networks of trade and language. Some of the administrators could
see great advantage to themselves in making the language of the
burghers the language of the state, so cementing the alliance and
beginning to create a linguistically homogeneous state, able as
none previously had been to insist on the allegiance of all those
who lived within its boundaries.

The growth of the new linguistically based state had great
advantages for the rising bourgeoisie. It made it more difficult
for traders from elsewhere, who spoke 'foreign' languages, to
challenge their 'home' markets. And it made the administrators
of the state increasingly subject to their influence and eager to
pursue their interests, especially when it came to helping them
compete with rival groups of traders on world markets—as with
the state backed struggle for control over the East India trade between the English and Dutch chartered companies in the seventeenth century. Even where the form of the state remained feudal,
as in seventeenth century France, it was increasingly attentive to
the interests of the nascent capitalists.

But if the creation of the national state began spontaneously,
elements of consciousness were soon involved as well. Political
philosophers from the time of Machiavelli (at the very beginning
of the sixteenth century) onwards began to urge policies on states
which would speed up the spontaneous process.[8] Political economists elaborated the 'mercantilist' doctrines, which identified
the interests of the state with the accumulation of trade surpluses
by its merchant class. Playwrights, poets and pamphleteers began
for the first time to celebrate what would later be called 'national' traditions.

The new 'national' state proved in practice to have an additional advantage for those who ruled over it, whether they
came from the old aristocracy or from the rising class of capi-

talists. It provided an apparent tie between the exploiters and the exploited. However much they differed in their incomes and lifestyles, they had one thing in common: they spoke a language which others could not understand. This became particularly important to a section of the middle class who, knowing the language and proving their loyalty to the state, could get jobs in the state machine itself which were denied to national minorities at home and colonised populations abroad.

The drive to create new national states

THE SPREAD of capitalism through the globe was characterised by combined and uneven development. The first centres of capitalist accumulation in Britain and Holland had a double effect on the rest of the globe. They robbed and impoverished whole regions. But they also drew them into a worldwide network of market relations and so eventually encouraged the rise of new groups of capitalists—or of new middle classes who saw their future as lying with capitalism.

But these groups found themselves in a world already dominated by existing capitalists using national states to protect their interests. If new centres of capitalism were to develop beyond a certain point, they needed states of their own to fight for their interests. So it was that French mercantile interests looked to the absolutist state that had grown out of feudalism to fight for its interests in a war for global influence with Britain, that land owners and traders in the North American colonies began to resent the dictates of the British state and create state structures of their own in opposition to it, and that sections of the middle class in Dublin and Belfast began to mutter about their own 'right' to independence from Britain.

Those who looked to the creation of new national states to advance their interests could not wait hundreds of years for spontaneous economic and social developments to bring such states into being. The path forward was at least partially blocked by the existing capitalist nation states, particularly Britain, on the one hand, and by the old absolutist, pre-capitalist states on the other. Conscious revolutionary action was required if they were ever to emulate, let alone out-compete, British capitalism. And revolutionary action had to be motivated by an ideology that laid out, in however confused a way, the key points about the sort of state they wanted.

The French revolutionaries went furthest in this direction,

with their proclamation of 'the French republic, one and indivisible'. They forcibly replaced the old administrative divisions, with their plethora of differing taxes and privileges, by a centralised structure run through government appointed prefects. They imposed a single standard of citizenship, demanding the allegiance of everyone, an allegiance which found expression in the universal conscription of young males to fight for 'the nation in arms'. They established a single national educational system, and used it to propagate a single language in place of the regional dialects of the southern half of France, the Breton of the west and the Germanic tongue of the northern frontiers.

Theirs became the model of what the national state should be for all those who sought to make the breakthrough to a 'modern', capitalist development of society elsewhere in the world. Soon young revolutionaries were striving to copy it in Ireland, Latin America, Greece, Italy, Germany, Poland, Hungary and Spain. By the beginning of the twentieth century there were carbon copy nationalisms in the Czech speaking regions of Austro-Hungary, the Balkans, Asiatic Turkey, China, India, the Ukraine and the Russian Caucasus. The next half century saw their spread through the empires of Britain and France, which between them controlled all of Africa and most of South Asia and the Middle East.

Nation, language and religion

THE NEW nations were conscious products, in a way that the earlier ones had not been. There were Italian and German, Greek and Czech, Indian and Indonesian national movements long before the nation states themselves were established, whereas in the earlier English, American and French cases the idea of nationality had only taken hold as, or even after, the national state was coming into being. However, life was usually much harder for the creators of the new nations than for their predecessors. Not only did they often encounter vicious persecution from those in charge of the states they wanted to replace or reform, but the raw material—the people—from which they wished to construct a nation, was far from ready.

Centuries of long drawn out capitalist development had created in north west Europe—and in its transplant in North America—fairly large geographic regions in which single languages predominated: in most of England and part of Scotland, in much of northern France, even in Germany as a result of Luther's success in establishing a church which used a single local dialect. By contrast, in southern and eastern Europe, in Asia and Africa, the late arrival of capitalism meant the task of linguistic homogenisation had hardly begun.

It was still quite usual to find the same picture as in medieval Europe: a state administration using one language, a church another, local landlords a third, the peasantry a fourth and often the inhabitants of the towns a fifth. Thus in any particular part of the Balkans, the religious language would be a dead language—Latin, Old Church Slavonic, archaic Greek or classical Arabic. The language of administration would be German, Hungarian, Turkish or Greek. The language of the peasantry would be a Slav or occasionally a Romance or Hungarian dialect, and the language of the towns quite likely a German dialect. What is more, the language of the peasantry would vary from village to village, or sometimes from household to household within the same village.

This did not lead to any great problems so long as pre-capitalist forms of production dominated. The peasants would know enough of the languages of administration and of the towns to cope in their limited number of transactions with them and indeed would often switch from one language or dialect to another without difficulty as the occasion demanded. They might not have been able to achieve examination level standards of competence—particularly written competence—in any of them, but they could cope very well without doing so.

But this plethora of languages and dialects was a headache for the modernising nationalists, with their aim of achieving linguistic homogeneity not only in the spoken language, but also in the written forms required for the advance of the market and the modern state. The only way they could achieve their goal was to pick on one or other spoken idiom and proclaim this was the 'national' language that everyone had to learn, not merely to speak, but to read and write.

The choice was not always completely arbitrary. Capitalist development, however slow, usually meant there were sections of the peasantry already in continuous contact with part of the urban population, with a dialect that was already more influential than others. So for instance in early nineteenth century Prague there was already a growing Czech speaking petty bourgeoisie that could act as the link with the peasantry that the nationalists wanted. But there was often a powerful, arbitrary element to it—as when Italian nationalists finally opted for the Tuscan dialect [9] (spoken by only 2.5 percent of the population of the peninsular) as the 'national language', or when the first Indian nationalists decided the regional dialect of Delhi, Hindustani, could be the national language once it was purged of all words of Persian origin, or when South Slav nationalists residing in Vienna rejected the idea of using Old Church Slavonic as the national language and instead gave the accolade to the Stokavian dialect (spoken by sections of both Croats and Serbs, but not by all of either) which they baptised 'Serbo-Croat'.[10]

But deciding what was the national language was only the beginning of the problem. The mass of people then had to be persuaded to accept it. Here again, things were much harder with most late arriving, more economically backward nations than with their predecessors. For where capitalist development was successful, providing markets for peasants and jobs for growing urban populations, it was not that difficult to get people to put up with the discomforts of not being fluent in the official language. In France most of the non-French speaking minorities embraced the revolution and the nation because it seemed to offer them a better life. In the US generation after generation of non-English speaking immigrants treasured their new nationality, even if they could not speak its language very well. By contrast, in Spain Catalans resented having to speak the language of economically more backward Castille and Andalusia, in Romania Hungarians and Saxons insisted on using their own languages, in Ireland a mass of inducements by the state could not stop the people of the far west abandoning their native Gaelic for the economically much more useful English, and in India the peoples of the south simply refused to accept the Hindi of the north.

The latecoming nationalists had similar problems when it came to the question of religion. The model for nationalists was strongly secularist. For religion was a product of the pre-capitalist societies they were trying to transform. It usually encouraged them to take on obligations that cut right across the new state boundaries they were trying to establish. And it often encouraged divisions among the people they were trying to win to a sense of a single national identity. So nineteenth century South Slav nationalists wanted the unity of Catholic, Orthodox and Muslim; Indian nationalists of

Hindu and Muslim; Irish nationalists of Catholic and Protestant; Arab nationalists of Muslim and Christian.

But the temptation was always to compromise with religion so as to find a base among a mass of peasants who were still fairly remote from the market and the modernising schemes that went with it, and who found the 'national language' incomprehensible. So the leaders of the Irish national movements always combined talk of secularism with attempts to win at least limited support from the Catholic Church, the Indian National Congress's most popular figure, Gandhi, sought to compromise with peasant prejudice by adopting the garb of a Hindu saint, and the founder of the Arab nationalist Ba'ath party, Afleck, converted to Islam towards the end of his life.

These problems over language and compromises with religion had very important effects. The founder nationalists did not usually identify with one ethnic group against another, and did not embrace what today is euphemistically called 'ethnic cleansing'. Their aim was to unify the population of a particular region so as to enable them to 'modernise' it in a capitalist sense. They were ready if necessary to force a certain language and culture on people, and if necessary to use the full power of the state against those who resisted—as the French Revolution did in Brittany, or the combined forces of the English and Scottish bourgeoisies did in the Highlands. But their aim remained to unite the whole population, not to use one section to eradicate another.

However, they began to move away from this aim every time they picked on one minority dialect as the national language or identified with one particular religion. The national movement became based in one part of the population, not the rest. And it was very easy to make a virtue of necessity—to see the German speakers as excluding themselves from the Czech nation, the Protestants from the Irish nation, the Muslims from the Indian nation, the Catholics and Muslims from the Serbian nation.

The class base of nationalism

NATIONALISM grew up as part of the ideology of capitalist development. The idea of the nation is inseparable from a range of other ideas associated with the bourgeois revolution. If nationalism has conquered the globe, with every individual anywhere in the world today slotted into one national identity or another, it is because capitalism has conquered the globe.

This does not mean, however, that the pioneers of nationalism have necessarily been capitalists themselves. There have been such cases. For instance, the first nationalist party in Catalonia, the Lliga, was the party of the Catalan capitalists.[11] More commonly, however, the promoters of new nationalisms have come from sections of the middle class frustrated by the stagnation and backwardness of the society in which they have found themselves. They have seen the only way out as being to turn their country of origin into a 'nation' like every other nation, and using that to encourage economic advance. Since every other nation is capitalist, this involves, in reality, encouraging capitalist development, however much it is dressed up in talk of the virtues of the traditional way of life: the Celtic twilight may have inspired Irish nationalists of a century ago, but the programme of the founder of Sinn Fein, Arthur Griffiths, was to create 'a Gaelic Manchester'[12]; Mahatma Gandhi may have preached the virtues of homespun cloth, but his Congress was financed by the big Indian capitalists and the building up of heavy industry was central to its economic programme; Nkrumah of Ghana may have praised African 'communalism', but on gaining control of state power he set about trying to build modern industry.[13]

The nationalists were more often middle class intellectuals—poets, playwrights, teachers, lawyers—than big capitalists. But their programme depended on the encouragement of capitalism, even if this meant turning some of their own number into state capitalists by the establishment of new nationalised industries. Before being able to do any of these things, the nationalists had to find a base of support in society at large.

The middle class itself, or, rather, certain sections of the middle class, was usually an important part of the base. The backwardness of society was reflected in the feebleness of career opportunities for the literate middle class, especially when state power was in the hands of a pre-capitalist ruling class or some already existing foreign nation state. Then an obvious way for the middle classes to improve their chances in life was to fight for their own right to work in the state machine—using their own language if this was a problem—and to go even further and fight for a revolutionary reconstitution of the state machine under their own 'national' control.

In a similar way the small shopkeeping, trading and petty

manufacturing bourgeoisie could rally behind the nationalist course. They did not have the ability to extract concessions from a pre-capitalist or foreign state machine which big capital sometimes had. The creation of a new national state would provide them with influence over political decisions and with the government contracts and protected markets that went with it.

Finally, the peasantry and the incipient working class were always possible allies for the national cause. They suffered from the general backwardness of society and faced continual humiliation and repression from those who ran the old state machine. Nationalist agitation could act as a focus for a mass of discontents and stir the lower classes into action.

But there was always a problem for the nationalists in relying on the workers and peasants. Their discontent was not merely with pre-capitalist forms of exploitation or the behaviour of the old state; it was also with the new, rising forms of capitalism, often presided over by the new 'national capitalists', and with the privileges of the 'national middle class'. A movement of workers and peasants which began with hostility to the old rulers and exploiters could all too easily spill over into confrontation with the new, home born variety. This could destroy all the plans of the nationalist leaders. That is why the history of nationalist movements often involves spells of agitation among workers, but these spells have always been brought to an end with a sharp turn to placate 'national' propertied interests, even if the price of doing so is to derail the national movement itself. Hence the 'betrayals' of Germany in 1848-9, Ireland in 1921-2 or China in 1925-7.

The workers' movement may be a temporary ally for the nationalists. But it cannot constitute a firm and reliable base for their schemes. For this they have to look to sections of the bourgeoisie or petty bourgeoisie.

Reactionary nationalist movements

THE CLASSIC nationalist movements were part of the bourgeois revolution which swept Europe and the Americas in the eighteenth and nineteenth centuries. Later nationalist movements were often associated with the struggle of colonial peoples to throw off imperialist rule. To this extent they involved a challenge to existing oppressive state structures—even if they intended only to replace them with new oppressive state structures.

But from very early on movements arose which seemed to have certain 'national' characteristics, but which served to protect, not undermine, the old structures. One such movement was that of Highlanders who joined the reactionary risings of the Stuart pretenders to the British throne in 1715 and 1745 in the belief that this would protect them against the new, bourgeois organisation of society being imposed by the Lowlanders and the English. Another was the *chouan* movement in Brittany in the 1790s, with priests and royalists manipulating the fears of Breton peasants about threats to their traditional way of life so as to ignite a counter-revolutionary revolt. A third was the Carlist movements of northern Spain in the 1830s and 1872, with Basque and Navarese peasants expressing resentment at the loss of traditional rights by fighting under the leadership of the most reactionary forces (their first demand was the restoration of the Inquisition!).

In the same league, although with a rather different social base, was the Orange Order in Ireland—consciously established by the British state around the slogan of Protestant supremacy to help smash the Irish national movement in the late 1790s, and revived for the same purpose in 1832, 1848, 1884, 1912 and 1920-1. These movements did not proclaim themselves to be national, although some present day nationalists have claimed them as precursors. But a movement which emerged during the revolutions of 1848 did present itself as part of the more general nationalist upsurge. This was the movement of the Slavs living within the Austro-Hungarian Empire. Its leaders aimed to create new national entities for the Czechs, the Ruthenes (western Ukrainians) and the South Slavs (the common name for Serbs, Croats and Slovenians). But with the partial exception of the Bohemian Czechs, these peoples were still in their overwhelming majority economically backward peasants, speaking mutually incomprehensible dialects, with the idea of any common national ties restricted to a handful of urban intellectuals. The mass of peasants could not be drawn into battle to replace the old traditions of economic backwardness and local parochialism by some new model of national unity. But some of them could be persuaded to play the role of the Bretons and the Basques—to fight in defence of the old feudal order against the challenge to it from the German and Hungarian nationalists. So in 1848 they fell in behind the counter-revolution and helped the Habsburg monarchy to crush the revolution in Vienna. As Marx wrote at the time, 'In Vienna we have a whole swarm of nationalities which imagined the counter-revolution will bring them emancipation'.[14] No wonder, 'in those months all of Europe's democracy came to hate the small Slavic nations...'[15]

As 'nationhood' became the established, generally recognised symbol of legitimacy in an increasingly bourgeoisified world, so not only movements fighting the old order but those striving to reinforce it inscribed 'national' slogans on their banners. By the second half of the nineteenth century even the dynastic empires which had previously been the most bitter opponents of national movements began to redefine themselves in nationalist terms. The Prussian monarchy took over the German nationalist ideology. The Habsburg monarchy split its domains into two halves, in one of which Hungarian replaced Latin as the official language, in the other, German. The 'Tsar of all the Russias'—whose court had spoken French and relied to a considerable extent on German speaking administrators—for the first time began to encourage a Great Russian nationalism, which regarded other ethnic groups as innately inferior. 'It was not until Alexander III (1881-94) that Russification became official policy.'[16]

The absolutist monarchies, which had established themselves in the late middle ages by using the urban burghers as a counterweight to the feudal lords, were now trying to prolong their life by renegotiating terms with sections of the bourgeoisie and petty bourgeoisie. The monarchy would give privileges to traders, bankers, manufacturers, gentry and literate intelligentsia which spoke one language, if they would ally with it against its enemies—inducing those sections of the bourgeoisie and petty bourgeoisie who spoke other languages.

But it was not only the old absolutist monarchies who adopted the policy of pushing one nationalism and oppressing others. So did the already capitalist states which were dividing the whole of Africa and most of Asia between them. The second half of the nineteenth century saw a new celebration of 'British' nationalism, with the establishment, for the first time, of a state run educational system that indoctrinated children in the glories of 'national' history, the writing of nationalist popular novels, plays, poetry and songs by literary admirers of the empire and the conscious invention of traditions aimed at encouraging popular identification with the monarchy. For the middle classes the identification with 'nation' and empire was not to be simply ideological but contained crude material incentives: the bureaucracy that administered the empire was English speaking, and the career structures in it were open to the middle class English or Scots in a way in which they were not to the Irish Catholic or the Australian, still less the Indian or African.

The use of reactionary nationalism was combined with the deliberate exploitation of linguistic and religious differences to weaken movements against British rule in the colonies. Just as the Orange slogans of Protestant ascendancy had been used with effect in Ireland, in India the British sought to play the Muslim card against the incipient national movement by splitting Bengal along religious lines in the early 1900s, in Palestine they encouraged European Jewish immigration at the end of the First World War to undercut the power of Arab resistance to British rule. In Cyprus they recruited the police force mainly from the Turkish speaking minority, and in Ceylon (present day Sri Lanka) from a section of the Tamil speakers.

Contradictory nationalisms and communalism

THERE WAS one further twist to the spread of the national ideal across the whole world from the late nineteenth century onwards. Rival nationalities were soon battling for the same territory.

The model of the early nationalists assumed they would easily be able to absorb minorities into their new national states. And so it was with many of the first national states: the English did succeed in getting the Scots to identify with 'Britain' and the empire, the French did absorb the southerners who spoke the Occitanian dialect and even gained the support of many German speaking Alsacians, the German empire did win the allegiance of Saxony, Thuringia, Hanover, Hamburg and Bremen (although separatist currents persisted in Bavaria and the Rhineland).

But things were very different with many of the later developing nationalisms. As we have seen, the late arrival of capitalism meant there was rarely one predominant language or dialect among the people who were supposed to make up the new nation. The nationalists might be able to gain support from one section of the population by declaring its language the new national tongue—but only by antagonising other groups.

Even where a degree of capitalist development did take off, it did not always make things easier. For it drew new sections of the peasantry, not fluent in the national tongue, into market relationships and created a new petty bourgeoisie from among them. Intellectuals from this milieu began to codify peasant dialects into new tongues, to fight for official status for them and eventually for nation states based on them. Thus, as a continual influx of former peasants transformed Prague from a mainly German speaking city into a mainly Czech speaking one, so the demand grew to establish a new Czech state out of the Austrian provinces of Bohemia and Moravia. But at least by the late nineteenth century there was a clear Czech speaking majority in Prague. In many major east European, Balkan and Caucasian towns all the competing linguistic groups grew, without any one necessarily predominating: Hungarian and Romanian speakers in Transylvania; Italian and Slovene speakers in Triest; German and Polish speakers in Silesia; Lithuanian, Polish and Yiddish speakers in Vilnius; Ukrainian, Yiddish and Polish speakers in the western Ukraine; Turkish, Greek and Armenian speakers in Istanbul; Greek and Slav speakers in Macedonia; Russian, Armenian and Turkish speakers in Baku.

The capitalist world was a world organised into linguistic nation states, and so, as each ethnic group was drawn into this world, its petty bourgeoisie wanted its own language and its own state. But it had arrived too late on the scene to get this through the long drawn out, spontaneous processes that had brought linguistic homogeneity to England, Holland, France or Germany. The different nationalisms could only achieve their goals if they waged bloody wars against each other as well as—or sometimes instead of—against the old absolutisms.

What this meant was shown in all its horror with the Second Balkan War of 1913, as the rival national states of Romania, Serbia and Greece ganged up against Bulgaria and sliced Macedonia in two, causing some half a million deaths. It was shown again in 1915 when, in an effort to draw behind them the Turkish and Kurdish speaking populations of the old Ottoman Empire, nationalist 'Young Turk' officers organised the extermination of the great majority of the empire's Armenian speakers; in 1918-19 when rival Azer and Armenian nationalist groups murdered each other in Baku; in 1921-2 when the war between Turkey and Greece led to each army expelling hundreds of thousands of civilians of the other nationality. In eastern Europe, the Balkans and the Caucasus the point had been reached where nationalism came to mean 'ethnic cleansing'—pogroms, forced expulsions and even extermination camps.

Classical Marxism and the national question

MARX AND Engels were part of the revolutionary movement of the 1840s. They began their political life on its extreme liberal democratic wing, but came to realise very quickly that human emancipation could only be achieved by a movement that went further and looked to working class revolution. Such a revolution would end 'national differences and antagonisms among peoples':

> In proportion as the exploitation of one individual by another is put an end to, the exploitation of one nation by another will also be put an end to. In proportion as the antagonism between classes within the nation vanishes, the hostility of one nation to another will come to an end.[17]

This did not mean, however, that they abstained from the struggle of bourgeois democratic forces against absolutism. They threw themselves into the revolutionary upheaval of 1848-9, criticising from the left the attempts of the bourgeois democrats to conciliate the old order. A key role in the upheaval was played by the four major national movements: the struggles to unite Germany and Italy as bourgeois national states in place of the various monarchies that divided them, the struggle to free Hungary from the Habsburg dynasty based in Vienna, and the struggle to free Poland from Tsarism, the gendarme of reaction right across Europe. A success for any one of these movements was, in the context of 1848-9, a gain for the revolution as a whole, and a defeat for them was a victory for the counter-revolution. Marx and Engels therefore looked to revolutionary war to establish new national states in Germany, Hungary, Italy and Poland, and to inflict a final defeat on the last remnants of feudalism in Europe. Among the enemies who would have to be fought in this war were those Slav politicians in the Austro-Hungarian Empire who used the phraseology of nationalism to justify their support for absolutism. Their defeat would be part of the process of clearing the ground for the full development of bourgeois democracy and so for the struggle of the working class against the system.

Marx and Engels did not require any particularly sophisticated analysis of nationalism to see what needed to be done in such a situation. And their time was absorbed, remember, not only in engaging in revolutionary agitation, but also in elaborating a completely new view of history and society. So Engels, in particular, simply took over the terminology of Hegel's philosophy of history and distinguished between different national movements on the basis of whether they represented 'historic peoples' who had a long and dynamic history, or 'non-historic peoples' who were doomed to be marginalised by historical development. At this stage neither Marx nor Engels seem to have grasped what a new historical phenomenon the nation was,[18] how it differed from previous states or ethnic groupings, and how distant most of the movements they condemned were from sharing the characteristics of modern national movements.[19]

They began to shift their position on national movements in the 1860s, faced with a renewal of the agitation against British rule in Ireland. Previously they had opposed British repression in Ireland, but had looked to revolutionary change in Britain to bring it to an end. They now changed their views. Marx wrote to Engels:

> I have done my best to bring about a demonstration of the English workers in favour of Fenianism... I used to think the separation of Ireland from England was impossible. Now I think it is inevitable, although after separation there may come federation.[20]

> What the Irish need is... self government and independence from England... Agrarian revolution... Protective tariffs against England.[21]

And to Kugelmann:

> The English working class... will never be able to do anything decisive here in England before they separate their attitude towards Ireland quite definitely from that of the

ruling classes, and not only make common cause with the Irish, but even take the initiative in dissolving the Union established in 1801. And this must be done not out of sympathy with the Irish, but as a demand based on the interests of the English proletariat. If not the English proletariat will for ever remain bound to the leading strings of the ruling classes, because they will be forced to make a common front with them against Ireland...[22]

In his approach to the Irish issue, Marx was making a very important point: the nationalism of workers belonging to an oppressor nation binds them to their rulers and only does harm to themselves, while the nationalism of an oppressed nation can lead them to fight back against those rulers. What is more, he was supporting the struggle of a nationality which could never be included in the list of 'the great historic nations of Europe'. However, it was not until after Marx's death that Engels began to present a new, historical materialist account of nations. An unfulfilled plan to rewrite *The Peasant War in Germany*—about popular unrest during the Reformation—led him to study the transformation of society at the end of the Middle Ages and to see material factors as giving rise to the beginnings of the nation state as a new historical phenomenon. He stressed that as the towns grew in prominence and allied with the monarchy against the rest of the feudal ruling class, 'out of the confusions of people that characterised the early middle ages, there gradually developed the new nationalisms'. But this was in a manuscript that remained unpublished until 1935.[23]

Deeper historical materialist analysis of nationalism did not begin until the end of the nineteenth century, when new political developments suddenly made it an urgent issue.

The growth of the socialist movement in the German empire was followed by a similar growth in Austria (which then included the present day Czech lands of Bohemia and Moravia, and present day Slovenia), and many of the best known German language Marxists came from there: Otto Bauer and Rudolf Hilferding were Austrians, and Karl Kautsky a Czech. But just as the Austrian party was enjoying its first real successes in the 1890s it was plunged into bitter arguments by the growing nationalist agitation among Austria's Slavs.

Otto Bauer tried to resolve the disputes by making a new analysis of nationalism. He argued that the nation is 'a community of culture' or 'a community of destiny', which causes all those who belong to it to experience things differently to those who belong to a different nation.[24] The nation gives all its members certain character features in common, so that an English person and a German, making, for instance, the same journey would experience it differently. This diversity of culture meant that even when people spoke the same language, as with the Danes and Norwegians or the Serbs and Croats, they remained separate nations.[25] 'It is the diversity of culture which rigorously separates nations, despite the mixing of blood.'[26]

Bauer argued that national culture went through three historic stages. It began with the period of primitive communism, when 'all the compatriots are related as much by community of blood as by culture', then went through a period of class society, in which it was bound together by the culture of the ruling class, and finally would be 'represented by the socialist society of the future'.[27] So the 'nation' can be seen in terms of the development of the productive forces, as constituting 'what is historical in us',[28] as a 'condensation of history'.[29]

He went on to attack, in the most forthright terms, those who did not see the value of the nation and instead opted for 'proletarian cosmopolitanism', 'the most primitive taking of position by the working class as against the national strife of the bourgeois world', for instance talking of 'Czech and German speaking comrades' rather than 'Czech and German comrades'. They were falling into the trap of 'rationalist, enlightenment' thinking, of 'an atomistic-individualistic conception of society' which failed to see that 'the individual man is himself a product of the nation'.

Bauer's conclusion was that socialists should embrace the idea of nation as an important social and historical factor in human existence, and tell the different nationalities that only under socialism would national culture reach its full development. 'Socialism announces to all nations the realisation of their aspiration to political unity and freedom. It does the same for the German nation.'[30] Such support for cultural nationalism, he argued, would enable socialists to prevent the fragmentation of the large states which were, in his view, necessary for economic development.

The Austrian socialists drew up an elaborate programme, based in part upon Bauer's views,[31] which promised all the different peoples of the Austro-Hungarian Empire their own national institutions within the existing imperial state structure. A national grouping in any particular locality would be given autonomy over educational and cultural affairs, and then would federate with groupings in other localities so as to form a single 'autonomous' structure right across the empire. There would be no official language, although 'whether a common language is required, a federal parliament can decide'. The whole structure was intended to encourage 'the nurturing and development of the national peculiarities of all the peoples of Austria'.[32]

The practical outcome of such a scheme was to encourage the members of the socialist movement to make continual concessions to those who stressed cultural differences within the working class, until first the socialist party and then the unions split into different national organisations—something which must have been rather gratifying to those employers, whether German or Czech speaking, who exploited linguistically mixed workforces.

The first theoretical onslaught against Bauer's position was led by Karl Kautsky. He had already begun to deepen the materialist analysis of the origins of modern nationality in the late 1880s, and went on to write numerous articles dealing in one way or another with the same issue. These were the starting point for other Marxists like Lenin. As George Haupt has noted, 'Kautsky, who formulated theories, opened parentheses and made distinctions, without engaging in systematisation, remained the indispensable reference point for a long time'.[33] His disagreement with Bauer was 'the confrontation between two conceptions of nations, to be labelled by Lenin the "psychological-cultural" and the "historical-economic".'[34]

Kautsky recognised the virtual impossibility of defining what a nation is:

> 'Nation' is a social formation difficult to apprehend, a product of social development, that rules have never been able to transform into a precisely defined social organism. Nationality is a social relation that transforms itself ceaselessly, which has a different signification in different conditions.[35]

But he nevertheless insisted it could be understood in relation to economic development. 'The concentration and separation of societies into nation states was one of the most powerful levers of economic development'.[36] This alone, he argued, explained why German speakers in, say, northern Bohemia regarded themselves as part of the German nation, while those in Switzerland did not.[37] Because of its role in economic development, 'The classical form of the modern state is the nation state. But classical forms exist in general only as a tendency. It is rare that they are developed in a perfectly typical fashion'.[38] What is more:

> To the extent that economic antagonisms deepen, each economic region tries to develop its own urban and rural industry, but can do this less and less without hurting the industry of its neighbours. The different Austrian regions tend to separate, and the 'reconciliation' of nations becomes more difficult.[39]

He criticised Bauer for downplaying the importance of language. There was, he said, only one example of a nation that included more than one 'linguistic community', the Swiss. As for the cases where different nationalities shared the same language—he mentions the English and the Irish, the Danes and Norwegians, the Serbs and Croats—'this does not prove that each national community is a linguistic community, it simply proves that sometimes a linguistic community can comprise two nations, that linguistic community, is not the sole distinctive sign of a nation'.[40] In fact, 'the powerful role of language in social life can make us understand a good part of the force of national sentiment'.[41]

He went on to ascribe the rise of the national state to a series of factors. First, the bourgeoisie's desire to provide itself with a market for its own commodities, free from the hindrance of feudal territorial divisions or from interference by old state structures. Second, the growing importance of administration in modern society, which gives unprecedented importance to the language question: 'The bureaucracy is a structure that finds it difficult to function without a single language'. Third, the way in which the 'commercialisation of society' laid the ground for linguistic unification by increasing the frequency of intercourse between people in different localities and produced a more uniform language: 'uniformisation rarely succeeded just through the channel of education, but through the development of commercial relations at the interior of the state'.[42]

It was this, finally, which explained the rise of rival nationalities within a single state. Where the economic forces were not powerful enough to get the speakers of different tongues to learn the national language, government attempts to enforce uniformity increased the divisions between different linguistic groups. Some gained material advantages from the official status given to their language: it gave them preferential chances of promotion into and up the ranks of the state bureaucracy. But others suffered and tended to turn to national identities of their own in opposition to the official one:

> When, in professional life or in front of a tribunal, the dominant language was spoken, the members of the other nations were at a disadvantage... Promotion of the children of artisans and peasants into the bureaucracy was made very difficult for nations which did not speak the official language.[43]

Kautsky thus provided an account of the rise of rival nationalisms that was more historical and more materialist than Bauer's—which is perhaps why Bauer receives the praise today from those who damn Marxism for being 'reductionist' and not taking account of 'ethnicity' and 'gender'.[44] But there was an unresolved problem with Kautsky's own analysis. He saw capitalist economic development as leading to a withering away of national struggles, despite his insights into how minority groups could turn to new nationalisms. In his early writings he argued that capitalist development doomed the Czech nation to disappear. And even after he had dropped this view he still saw national conflicts as dying away as capitalist commerce became increasingly international:

> As [social] intercourse grows with economic development, so the circle of people using the same language must grow as well. From this arises the tendency of unified languages to expand, to swallow up other nations, which lose their language and adopt the language of the dominant nation or a mixture...
>
> The joining of nations to the international cultural community will be reflected in the growth of universal languages among merchants and educated people...[45]

There was an important insight here which led him to denounce Bauer for encouraging national antagonisms among socialists:

> Never was a purely national culture less possible. There-

fore it strikes us as very strange when people talk always of only a national culture, and when the goal of socialism is considered to be the endowing of the masses with national culture... When socialist society provides the masses with an education, it also gives them the ability to speak several languages, the universal languages, and therefore to take part in the entire international civilisation and not only in the separate culture of a certain linguistic community.[46]

But the insight was buried within a wider analysis which vastly underrated the way in which capitalism provokes national antagonism at the same time as creating the possibilities of overcoming it.

Luxemburg and Lenin

ROSA LUXEMBURG began from a different starting point to Bauer and Kautsky. She was trying to build a revolutionary party in Poland, where the socialist movement split in the 1890s between those—like the future Polish dictator Pilsudski—who were moving increasingly in a nationalist direction and those who stood resolutely for internationalism. Yet when her party attended the congress of the International in the 1890s and of the Russian Social Democratic Labour Party in 1903, it found the majority of delegates embracing the right of Poland to independence in a way which seemed to her to give solace to her nationalist opponents at home. Right up to her death in 1918 she was to argue vehemently against any 'right' of nations to self determination and against any involvement of socialists in national uprisings.

She backed up this position with arguments that combined elements of Kautsky's view with elements of Bauer's. She located the origins of nationalism squarely in economics—in the economic needs of this or that ruling class. Her interpretation of Kautsky's account of the rise of nationalism in countries like Germany and Italy puts all the stress on the role of the big bourgeoisie.[47] She argues that its desire for domestic markets led it to promote the national movement, and gave this a realistic character. She then goes on to use this 'economistic' analysis to tear late nineteenth and early twentieth century Polish nationalism apart:

The material base of Polish national aspirations (in the first half of the nineteenth century) was determined not as in central Europe by modern capitalist development, but on the contrary by the nobility's idea of its social standing, rooted in the natural feudal economy.

The national movements in Poland vanished with these feudal relations, whereas the bourgeoisie, as the historical spokesman of capitalist development, was with us, from the beginning, a clearly anti-national factor. This was due, not only to the specific origin of the nineteenth century bourgeoisie, alien and heterogeneous, a product of colonisation, an alien body transplanted on to Polish soil. Also decisive was the fact that Polish industry was from its beginning an export industry... Export to Russia... became the basis for the existence of and development of Polish capitalism... and the basis of the Polish bourgeoisie. As a consequence, our bourgeoisie showed political leanings... towards Russia... The class rule of the bourgeoisie in Poland not only did not demand the creation of a united nation state, but, on the contrary, it arose on the foundations of the conquest and division of Poland. The idea of unification and national independence did not draw its vital juices from capitalism: on the contrary, as capitalism developed this idea became historically outlived... In Poland there arose an opposition between the national idea and the bourgeois development, which gave the former not only a utopian but also a reactionary character.[48]

For her, if the bourgeoisie did not want a nation state somewhere, since that state was part of capitalist development, the idea was both doomed and reactionary.

Her argument arose out of the Polish context. But she extended it further. She argued, correctly, that Kautsky was wrong to see the needs of capitalism for international trade leading to a peaceful growing together of national states. Instead, she insisted, there would be increasing conflict between states, and these states would increasingly not be states with a homogeneous national population, but rather states which forcibly annexed whole peoples against their will:

Historical development... lies... not in the tendency toward the idea of a 'national state' but rather in the deadly strug-

gle among nations, in the tendency to create great capitalist states... The form that best serves the interests of exploitation in the contemporary world is not the 'national'
state as Kautsky thinks, but a state bent on conquest. When
we compare the different states from the point of view of
the degree to which they approach this ideal... we look to
the British and German states as models, for they are based
on national oppression in Europe and the world at large—
and to the United States, a state which keeps in its bosom
like a gaping wound the oppression of the Negro people and
seeks to conquer the Asiatic people.

This, she concluded, destroyed any possibility of a new,
viable national movement emerging:

The development of world powers, a characteristic feature
of our times growing in importance along with the progress
of capitalism, from the very outset condemns all small nations to political impotence... 'Self determination', the independent existence of smaller and petty nations, is an
illusion, and will become even more so... Can one speak
with any seriousness of the 'self-determination' of peoples
which are formally independent, such as the Montenegrins,
Bulgarians, Romanians, the Serbs, the Greeks...? From this
point of view, the idea of 'insuring all the nations the possibility of self determination' is the equivalent of reverting
from great capitalist development to the small medieval
states, far earlier than the fifteenth and sixteenth centuries.[49]

The characteristic feature of this part of her argument is
the way in which she moves from a brilliant, dialectical account
of the economic and military trends in capitalism to a completely
mechanical view of the political consequences—big capital does
not want national struggles and national insurrections, therefore
these count for nothing.

This did not mean that her position was one of simple opposition to nationalism. For she combined her ultra-Kautskyite
analysis of the roots of the nation state with a Bauerite attitude
to cultural nationalism. She praised the Austrian party's Brno
programme, with its scheme to divide the population into autonomous national groupings. She referred to 'national senti-
ments' as among 'the higher forms of psychic phenomena', and
foresaw the survival of 'Polish national identity' as socialism

led to 'the opening up of new vistas for the deliverance of Polish national culture'.[50] She claimed that 'the cause of nationalism in Poland is not alien to the working class—nor can it be', on the grounds that 'the working class cannot be indifferent to the most intolerable barbaric oppression, directed as it is against the intellectual and cultural heritage of society'.[51] She believed, 'The proletariat can and must fight for the defence of national identity as a cultural legacy, that has its own right to exist and flourish', but the 'national identity cannot be defended by national separatism'.[52]

By far the most theoretically sophisticated of the classic Marxist theorists of nationalism was Lenin.[53] The analysis of the new nationalisms being thrown up by the continued development of capitalism was not, for him, some academic exercise. The Russian Empire was an even more ethnically mixed state than Austro-Hungary and it was a much more explosive mixture. The revolution of 1905 was to be as much a revolution of the national minorities as of the workers, the peasants and the liberal bourgeoisie. If his party got the national question wrong its whole revolutionary strategy would be in tatters. This led him to a sharp conflict with the positions of both Bauer and Rosa Luxemburg.

Lenin's analysis of the rise of nations is based on Kautsky's materialist interpretation. Writing early in 1914, Lenin argues:

> Throughout the world, the period of the final victory of feudalism over capitalism has been linked up with national movements. For the complete victory of commodity production, the bourgeoisie must capture the home market, and there must be politically unified territories whose population speak a single language, with all the obstacles to the development of that language and its consolidation in literature eliminated. Therein is the economic foundation of national movements. Language is the most important means of human intercourse. Unity and unimpeded development of language are the most important conditions for genuinely free and extensive commerce on a scale commensurate with modern capitalism, for a free and broad grouping of the population in all its various classes as, lastly, for the establishment of a close connection between the market and each and every proprietor, big or little, and between seller and buyer.
> Therefore the tendency of every national movement is to-

wards the formation of national states, under which these requirements of modern capitalism are best satisfied... Therefore, for the whole of Western Europe, nay, for the entire civilised world, the national state is *typical* and normal for the capitalist period.[54]

The spread of capitalist relations internationally would mean the throwing up of more and more national movements:

The greater part of Asia... consists either of colonies of the Great Powers or of states that are extremely dependent and oppressed as nations. But does this shake the undoubted fact that in Asia itself the conditions for the most complete development of commodity production and the speediest growth of capitalism have been created in Japan, ie only in an independent national state?... It remains an undoubted fact that capitalism, having awakened Asia, has called forth national movements everywhere in that continent too; the tendency of these movements is towards the creation of national states in Asia; that it is these states that ensure the best conditions for the development of capitalism...
The national state is the rule and the norm of capitalism... From the standpoint of national relations the best conditions for the development of capitalism are created by the national state. This does not mean, of course, that such a state, which is based on bourgeois relations, can eliminate the exploitation and oppression of nations. It only means that Marxists cannot lose sight of the powerful economic factors that give rise to the urge to create national states.

By 1916 he was developing the analysis, to attack those who, in the manner of Rosa Luxemburg,[55] used the argument about the connection between the development of capitalism and the growth of the national state to draw the conclusion that national demands were 'utopian' and 'reactionary' once the most advanced capitalisms began to spread beyond their old national boundaries. This, he said, was to fall into 'imperialist economism', to try to reduce politics to a direct mechanical product of economics. Economism, he said, is the argument: 'capitalism is victorious, therefore political questions are a waste of time', the new theory was that 'imperialism is victorious, therefore political questions are a waste of time. Such an apolitical theory is extremely harmful to Marxism'.

What is more, he no longer maintained the old, Kautsky-ist view that the proponents of national capitalist development had to be the capitalists. He noted that the Irish uprising of 1916 had involved 'street fighting conducted by a section of the urban petty bourgeoisie and a section of the workers...' He drew the conclusion that:

> To imagine that social revolution is conceivable without revolts by small nations in the colonies and in Europe, without revolutionary outbursts by sections of the petty bourgeoisie with all its prejudices, without a movement of the politically non-conscious proletarian and semi-proletarian masses against oppression by the landowners, the church and the monarchy, against national oppression, etc — to imagine all this is to repudiate social revolution.

He drew sharp practical conclusions from his analysis. He defended the slogan of the right of self determination against Rosa Luxemburg and those with similar views, like Karl Radek and Nikolai Bukharin. And he rejected the Bauerite programme of 'cultural national autonomy'.

There were two components to his defence of the self determination slogan. The first was concerned with the political consciousness of workers having the same nationality as those who ran the oppressing state:

> If, in our political agitation, we fail to advance and advocate the right to secession, we shall play into the hands, not only of the bourgeoisie, but also of the feudal landlords and the absolutism of the oppressor nation... When, in her anxiety not to 'assist' the nationalist bourgeoisie in Poland, Rosa Luxemburg rejects the *right* to secession in the programme of the Marxists *in Russia*, she is in fact assisting the Great Russian Black Hundreds. She is in fact assisting the opportunist tolerance of the privileges of the Great Russians... The interests of the freedom of the Great Russian population requires a long struggle against such oppression... The long centuries-old history of the suppression of the movements of the oppressed nations and the systematic propaganda in favour of such suppression coming from the upper classes have created enormous obstacles to the cause of freedom of the Great Russian people itself, in the form of prejudice... The Great Russian proletariat cannot

achieve its own aims or clear the road to its freedom without systematically countering these prejudices...

In Russia, the creation of an independent national state remains, for the time being, the privilege of the Great Russian nation alone. We, the Great Russian proletarians, who defend no privilege whatever, do not defend this privilege either.[56]

Against the claim that this encouraged a split in the workers' movement along national lines, Lenin replied insistently that it did the opposite. So long as the workers in the oppressed nation could see no one defending their right to national equality among the people of the oppressing nation, they would fall for the nationalist demagogy of their own bourgeoisie and petty bourgeoisie. But if they found the workers' party in the oppressing nation standing full square for the right to self determination, then they would see it as standing for their interests and turn their back on their own bourgeoisie and petty bourgeoisie. He used the example of Norway's secession from Sweden in 1905 to back up his argument. Rosa Luxemburg had argued the secession was reactionary, simply replacing one monarchy by another. Lenin acknowledged that the outcome was no great step forward for the workers. But he insisted that the attitude of the Swedish socialists, who had supported the Norwegian right to secede, ensured it was not a step backwards either:

The close alliance between the Norwegian and Swedish workers, their complete fraternal class solidarity, gained from the Swedish workers' recognition of the right of the Norwegians to secede. This convinced the Norwegian workers that the Swedish workers were not infected with Swedish nationalism, and that they placed fraternity with the Norwegian workers above the privileges of the Swedish bourgeoisie and aristocracy.[57]

By standing by the right of self determination, socialists in the oppressor country encouraged internationalism among both their own working class and that in the oppressed country: 'In reality, the recognition of the right of all nations to self determination implies the maximum of democracy and the minimum of nationalism'.[58]

Lenin's first reason for advancing the slogan of the right to self determination was, then, to do with the principle of fighting against reactionary ideas within the working class of the oppressing country. This did not mean he ruled out exceptional situations. He admitted there were situations in which the slogan could be misused (as Marx claimed the Czechs and South Slavs had misused it in 1848):

> There is not one of these (democratic) demands which could not serve and has not served, under certain circumstances, as an instrument in the hands of the bourgeoisie for deceiving the workers... In practice the proletariat can retain its independence only by subordinating its struggle for all democratic demands to the revolutionary struggle for the overthrow of the bourgeoisie... On the other hand Marx... put the fundamental principle of internationalism and socialism in the foreground—no nation can be free if it oppresses other nations.

So Lenin's first argument was of a general, if not completely unconditional, character. But he combined with it a second argument, about the impact of the fight for self determination by the oppressed nation in certain concrete situations. This was an argument about revolutionary strategy and tactics rather than principle.

Supporting the right to self determination was not inevitably to favour the secession of a particular nation from the state. The socialists in the oppressor country could fight for the right for secession as a way of fighting against reactionary ideology, while the socialists in the oppressed country could argue for workers to oppose the practice of secession—just as the right of divorce leaves it open to the married couple to decide freely that they want to stay together:

> This demand [for the right of self determination] is not the equivalent of demand for separation, fragmentation and the formation of small states... The closer a democratic state system is to complete freedom to secede, the less frequent and the less ardent will the demand for separation be in practice...[59]

But there were situations in which the fight of the national movement of an oppressed nation aided the international working class struggle, even if the national movement was under bourgeois or petty bourgeois leadership. For it weakened the dominant states and their ruling classes. This, Lenin believed, was the case with the Irish uprising of 1916 and with the risings among the various other peoples oppressed by the Tsarist regime and the Western imperialisms which he rightly expected the impact of world war to bring about. For this reason not only should socialists in the oppressing countries support the right to self determination in these cases, but socialists in the oppressed countries should be part of the struggle for secession. 'If we do not want to betray socialism, we must support every revolt against our chief enemy, the bourgeoisie of the big states, provided it is not the revolt of a reactionary class'.[60]

However, there were situations when socialists had to oppose nationalist agitation—as with the Polish national movement in the concrete circumstances of the First World War, when it became intricately connected with the struggle of German imperialism against British, French and Tsarist imperialism.

> The bourgeoisie, which naturally assumes the leadership at the start of every national movement, says that support for all national aspirations is practical. However, the proletariat's policy in the national question (as in all others) only supports the bourgeoisie in a certain direction, but never coincides with the bourgeoisie's policy...
>
> The demand for a 'yes' or 'no' reply to the question of secession in the case of every nation may seem a very 'practical' one. In reality it is absurd... in practice it leads to subordinating the proletariat to the bourgeoisie's policy.
>
> The proletariat... assesses any national demand, any national separation, from the angle of the workers' class struggle.[61]

> It is impossible to estimate beforehand all the possible relations between the bourgeois liberation movements of the oppressed nations and the proletarian emancipation movement of the oppressor nation.[62]

This point leads on to the other central feature of Lenin's position on the national question—the one which has often been forgotten by supporters of national movements who have quoted him at length in defence of the right to self determination. He condemns Otto Bauer's scheme for 'national cultural autonomy'—and Rosa Luxemburg in so far as she is favourable to it—for making concessions to bourgeois nationalism.

The argument had first arisen in the Russian socialist movement at the time of the Second (effectively the foundation) Congress of the Russian Social Democratic Labour Party in 1903. At that point the socialist movement was still more advanced among the pockets of Jewish workers in the western Russian Empire than among the mass of other workers. Some of those involved in organising the Jewish workers had founded an exclusively Jewish socialist party, the Bund, which argued that Jewish workers had to have their own separate organisations and concentrate on agitating for separate Jewish schools and cultural organisations. They were opposed, not just by Marxists of Russian nationality, like Lenin and Plekhanov, but by many of the best known Jewish Marxists such as Martov and Trotsky. Martov, for instance, argued that to accede to the Bund's demands would be to weaken socialist organisation in every workplace and locality:

> We cannot allow that any section of the party can represent the group, trade or national interests of any section of the proletariat. National differences play a subordinate role in relation to common class interests. What sort of organisation would we have if, for instance, in one and the same workshop workers of different nationalities thought first and foremost of the representation of their national interests.[63]

Lenin extended these arguments into a challenge to the whole Bauerite approach, by making a sharp distinction between the fight against every element of discrimination against any group on the basis of their language or culture, and exaltation of particular national cultures.

The opposition to discrimination against and oppression of those with particular national cultures meant that socialists had to fight for the children of every group to be taught in their own language, for courts and other tribunals to hear cases in that language, and to reject any idea of the dominant language being the 'official language' to which others should bow down. 'Whoever does not recognise and champion the equality of nations and languages, and does not fight against all national oppression and inequality, is not a Marxist; he is not even a democrat.'[64]

This meant that socialists should be for any measure that would guarantee equality. They should be for 'the hiring at state expense of special teachers of Hebrew, Jewish history and the like, of the provisions of state owned premises for lectures for Jewish, Armenian, or Romanian children, or even for the one Georgian child (in one area of St Petersburg)'.[65]

At the same time socialists should not identify with any national culture, even that of the oppressed:

To throw off the feudal yoke, all national oppression and all privileges enjoyed by any particular nation or language, is the imperative duty of the proletariat as a democratic force, and is certainly in the interests of the proletarian struggle which is obscured and retarded by bickering on the national question. But to go beyond these strictly limited and definite historical limits in helping bourgeois nationalism means betraying the proletariat and siding with the bourgeoisie. There is a border line here which the Bundists and the Ukrainian nationalist socialists often completely lose sight of.

Combat all national oppression? Yes, of course! Fight for any kind of national development, for 'national culture' in general? Of course not!

The development of nationality in general is the principle of bourgeois nationalism; hence the exclusiveness of bourgeois nationalism, hence the endless national bickerings. The proletariat, far from undertaking to uphold the national development of every nation, on the contrary, warns the masses against such illusions, stands for the fullest development of capitalist intercourse and welcomes every kind of assimilation of nations, except that which is founded on force or privilege.[66]

There are two nations within every modern nation — we say to all nationalist socialists. There are two national cultures within every national culture...

If the Ukrainian Marxist allows himself to be swayed by his quite legitimate and natural hatred of the Great Russian oppressors to such a degree that he transfers even a particle of this hatred... to the proletarian culture and proletarian cause of the Great Russian workers, then such a Marxist will get bogged down in bourgeois nationalism.

The Great Russian and Ukrainian workers must work together... towards a common or international culture of the proletarian movement, displaying absolute tolerance in question of language in which propaganda is conducted... All advocacy of the segregation of the workers of one nation from those of another, all attacks upon Marxist 'assimilation', or attempts where the proletariat is concerned to counterpose one national culture as a whole to another allegedly integral national culture and so forth is bourgeois nationalism, against which it is necessary to wage a ruthless struggle.[67]

The slogan of working class democracy is not 'national culture', but the international culture of democracy and the world wide working class movement.[68]

The elements of democratic and socialist culture are present, if only in rudimentary form, in every national culture, since in every nation there are toiling masses whose conditions of life inevitably give rise to the ideology of democracy and socialism. But every nation also possesses a bourgeois culture (and most nations a reactionary and clerical culture as well) in the form not merely of 'elements', but of the *dominant* culture.

In advancing the slogan of the 'international culture of democracy and of the world wide working class movement', we take from each national culture only its democratic and socialist elements; we take them only and absolutely in opposition to the bourgeois culture and the bourgeois nationalism of each nation.[69]

Lenin pointed out that the socialist in an oppressor country had to be very careful how he or she saw the issue of 'assimilation':

If a social democrat from a great, oppressing, annexing nation, while advocating the amalgamation of nations in general, were for one moment to forget that 'his' Nicholas II, 'his' Wilhelm, 'his' George, etc also stands for amalgamation by means of annexation — such a social democrat would be a ridiculous doctrinaire in theory and an aider of imperialism in practice...

It is our duty to teach the workers to be 'indifferent' to national distinctions... But it must not be the indifference of the annexationists.[70]

It was precisely to hammer this point home that Lenin was so insistent on defending the right of self determination and secession. At the same time, however, he insisted, 'a social democrat from a small nation must emphasise in his agitation... "voluntary integration" of nations. He may, without failing in his duties as an internationalist, be in favour of both the political independence of his nation and its integration with the neighbouring state of X, Y, Z etc. But he must in all cases fight against small nation narrow mindedness, seclusion and isolation...'[71]

These considerations led Lenin to bitterly oppose talk of 'national cultural autonomy'. He argued that separate school systems for each national group would split workers one from another:

> On the boards of joint stock companies we find capitalists of different nations sitting together in complete harmony. At factories workers of different nations work side by side. In any really serious and profound political issue sides are taken according to classes, not nations. Withdrawing school education and the like from state controls and placing it under the control of the nations is in effect to attempt to separate from economics, which unites the nations, the most highly ideological sphere of social life, the sphere in which 'pure' national culture or the nationalist cultivation of clericalism and chauvinism has the freest play.[72]

Nationalism since the First World War

THERE CAN be little doubt that Lenin was right in his argument against Rosa Luxemburg and others, that the development of capitalism was leading to a proliferation of new nationalisms.

Far from these being 'utopian', nationalist movements contributed to the break up of all the great empires. The Russian Revolution of 1917, like its precursor in 1905, involved the seizure of power by nationalist movements around its periphery as well as by workers and peasants at its centre. The collapse of the Austro-Hungarian war effort in October 1918 led to rapid secession by the Czechs, the Romanians of Transylvania, the Croats and the Slovenes, leaving behind separate rump Hungarian and Austrian states. Even the victorious British Empire was shaken by a revolt in Ireland, which succeeded in gaining independence for three quarters of the country, by the first massive demonstrations in India and the first revolutionary upsurges in China. The weakening of the European colonial empires as a result of the Second World War was followed by independence for India, Pakistan, Burma and Ceylon, Indonesia and then, after a bloody war, North Vietnam, Laos and Cambodia, to be followed by Ghana, Nigeria, Malaysia, Kenya, Uganda, Morocco, Tunisia, most of French Africa, the Congo, Zambia, Malawi, and after further bloody wars, Algeria, Aden, the rest of Vietnam, Angola, Mozambique, Guinea and finally Zimbabwe. By this time virtually every member of the world's population would define themselves as a citizen of one or other of 194 national states,[73] with the USSR remaining the only sizeable multinational empire. Just as market, commodity production and capital accumulation had conquered the whole world, so had the national state as the archetypical form of organised political power.

The formation of new nations did not always throw the old empires into convulsions: Britain finally abandoned India, Holland abandoned Indonesia and Belgium abandoned the Congo without being thrown into any great domestic crisis. But on occasions it did, with the wars in Indo China and Algeria shaking metropolitan France, the war in Vietnam throwing the US into a deep political crisis, and the wars in Angola, Mozambique and Guinea leading to political revolution in Portugal. To this extent too, Lenin was vindicated.

Indeed, the vindication often went further than he himself could ever have imagined. So much has the ideal of the national state become part of the ruling ideology throughout the world system that it was taken up by movements that differed in some important respects from those he had known.

The movements which fought against the old colonial empires were usually based in the administrative divisions created by those empires themselves. These divisions ignored whatever boundaries there might once have been between groups with different languages or traditional cultures. They separated like from like, and threw like together with unlike. Yet it was within these divisions that those who took over from the colonial empires attempted to create new nations—in India and Pakistan, Burma and Ceylon, Indonesia, Malaysia and the Philippines, and throughout black Africa—without a common language for the whole country and sometimes without even a unified market.

Alongside these there have been cases of minorities reacting to their oppression by seeing themselves as a nation, even though they do not live in any defined territory or share a separate common language. This was true by the 1930s of many of Europe's Jewish minorities and by the early 1970s of very many black Americans.

Finally, precisely because the notion of nationhood was so

central to the ideology of the system, people's reaction to the economic and political crisis of one existing national state was to look for a way out through the creation of a new nation, based on different criteria to the old—as with the attempts to carve a Biafran national state using the Ibo language out of Nigeria in the late 1960s, Catalan and Basque states out of post-Franco Spain, an Akali state based on the Sikh religion out of the Indian province of the Punjab, or Serb and Croat states, based on the same language but different religions, out of what used to be Yugoslavia.

In each case, those who preached the nationalist project seemed far less 'utopian' and far more 'practical' than those who turned to class politics. The nationalists were, after all, cutting with the ideology of nationhood that had come to dominate the world with capitalism.

Nationality and culture today

THE PROFUSION of nationalities has been accompanied everywhere by a stress on the differences of cultures. In the advanced Western countries the ideology of biological racism has, to some extent, given way in the last quarter of a century to what might be called cultural racism. This does not talk in terms of biological inferiority of non-whites, but of the 'cultural backwardness', or at least the 'cultural difference' of those who come from non-British, non-French, non-German—or more generally non-European or non-Western—backgrounds.

So it was that back in 1978 Margaret Thatcher played the race card shortly before an election, claiming British people were being 'swamped by people of a different culture'.

In a slightly less extreme form the argument goes, 'everyone has their own culture, so we naturally identify with ours, and other groups with theirs'. Such thinking underlies the stress of the right wing ideologues who increasingly dominate the content of the national teaching curriculum in Britain on 'British history', 'English literature' and the Christian religion. Interestingly, these ideologues are pressing for the right of both evangelical Christians and Islamic fundamentalists to set up their own schools.[74]

The argument is, at least in part, accepted by some of those usually regarded as being on the left. Many liberal intellectuals stress that everyone must value their own culture, and even go so far as to show concern about the 'bastardisation of cultures'.[75] And many of those who react against the disguised racism of the various forms of cultural supremacism do so by asserting a cultural separatism of their own—which in a few cases becomes an inverted form of cultural supremacism. They argue that because they are of Irish, Jewish, Armenian, Asian, Arab, Muslim, African, etc ancestry, then they have to fight to preserve the purity and independence of their 'indigenous culture'. They justify their stand with references to the 'fight against cultural genocide' and 'cultural imperialism'.

Yet all these different stresses on maintaining the separation of cultures—whether from the conservative right or from those who see themselves on the anti-racist, anti-imperialist left—rest on the same fallacy. They all assume that the growing proliferation of nationalities and nationalisms rests upon a growing diversity of cultures. But the modern world is, in fact, marked by a growing together of cultures, by a trend towards a homogeneous world culture—a trend enormously more marked than when Marx and Engels noted how 'the intellectual creations of individual nations become common property, national one sidedness and narrow mindedness becomes more and more impossible, and from the numerous national and local literatures, there arises a world literature',[76] or than when Kautsky and Lenin wrote about the merging of cultures 90 or so years ago.

The word 'culture' has two different meanings, one broad and one narrow. In its broad meaning it refers to the totality of people's social practices including such things as the way they get a livelihood, their religious practices, the relations between the sexes, their moral attitudes, their sense of time, their treatment of old people and children, their cooking, and, drawing all these activities together, their language. The more restricted meaning refers to art, music and literature.

The two meanings are connected. For culture in the narrow artistic sense is an expression of culture in the wider, way of life, sense. Art grows out of the soil of the wider culture and displays certain of the elements within it in a form that can bewitch or delight, thrill or frighten. When people like a certain artistic product, they do so because they find in it something which, in one way or another, gives expression to their own lives and dilemmas.

It is this which enables 'culture' in the narrow sense to provide a sense of identity to people from a particular society, something to which they can try to cling at moments of social crisis. This is why conservatives of all sorts seek to extol what they claim is the 'traditional' national culture. They are endeavouring to appeal to past ways of living so as to oppose any challenges to the old society. It is also why those who seek to establish new nations under their own hegemony search for what they claim are radically different counter-traditions.

But culture in the narrow sense can never be more than a partial expression of people's wider way of life in a class society. For in such a society there is not one way of life, but different ways of life for each class. And art and literature tend to express the way of life of those classes who alone have the resources and the leisure to sustain artistic production—the privileged exploiting classes. Even though the best artists are those who attempt to reflect the total social experience, which includes elements of the experience of the oppressed and exploited, they do so from the point of view of those who depend on the oppressors and exploiters for sustenance, even when they are not themselves from the ruling classes.

When we talk of British art, Russian art or Chinese art, we are talking of the art of the rulers of those societies, art which may say something about the exploited classes, but only in an indirect oblique way. This is even true when we talk about Aztec art or much art from pre-colonial Africa, for specialisation in artistic production was not possible on any scale until there was at least the beginning of a polarisation into classes.

What is more, as society changes, so culture changes. It cannot be a changeless fixed thing. Any attempt to treat it as such is, in reality, a fiction, an ideological device used to bind people to certain approved patterns of behaviour. This is especially true in the modern world, a world which has been changed utterly by the development of capitalism. Everywhere on the globe people's lives have been transformed as they have been subordinated to market relations and dragged from the relative isolation of rural life into contact with vast population centres.

When people talk of 'traditional culture' of any sort, they are harking back to something which no longer fits the reality of their lives anywhere. This is true of attempts to force us to live a traditional 'English culture', most of which was historically created by and for leisured gentlemen living in a predominantly agrarian society. It is true too of those who, out of a justified revulsion against such cultural reaction, would have us turn to 'Celtic culture', 'Indian culture', 'African culture', 'Islamic culture', or any other.

In fact, the forms of culture that dominate in every part of the world are products of very recent history, even when the conservatives claim an ancient lineage for them. It was, for instance, only a century ago that Celtic literature was reborn at the hands of modern, bourgeois—and usually Anglo-Irish—intellectuals like Lady Gregory and Yeats, or that modern petty bourgeois nationalists sought to create a Hindi speaking culture in opposition to that of the plebeian market language of the Delhi region, Hindustani, and the courtly version of it, Urdu.

The contemporary 'national' forms of both high art and popular art are very much the products of the recent, capitalist, period of human existence—thus with the different forms of popular music that tend to dominate different regions of the globe. As an authoritative study of non-Western popular music tells, these are all relatively recent products, based on the drawing together of elements from different cultures:

> The most conspicuous form of acculturation involves Western influence—especially the adoption of Western musical elements (such as instruments, harmony and vocal style) by non-Western musical cultures... The Western disco, rock and slow ballad have become international styles, promoted by a network of multinational corporations.[77]

But, of course, Western music itself was not a product of the European peoples alone. A central component of it came into being as 'descendants of African slaves in the Americas developed dynamic, hybrid musics synthesising African-derived rhythms and Western melodic and harmonic patterns.'[78]

Similarly, in parts of the globe new regional styles have been based on a synthesis of traditional and Western forms. Thus Indian film music—which today has a multinational audience stretching from Vietnam and Indonesia to the former Yugoslavia,[79] is formed by a merging of local styles from south and north India, using 'Western harmony in its own distinctive way',[80] while modern African popular music arose as 'some... Caribbean... styles—especially the Cuban rumba—became widely popular in the Congo and other parts of Africa from the 1950s on, and generated new hybrids of native African and Afro-Caribbean music'.[81]

The example of popular music shows how advanced the tendency towards the fusion of cultures can be. There may not yet be a single world popular music, but there are a relatively small number of interacting regional styles, with the trend being towards fusion and the conquest of worldwide audiences, not towards separation and narrow national traditions. That is why its impact is resented by the cultural conservatives in every country. Yet popular music is probably the form of artistic culture that most penetrates the life of the great mass of people: its closest rival in terms of popularity, spectator sport, although hardly an 'artistic product', is even more a uniform worldwide phenomenon.

Such cultural growing together should really surprise no one. The dynamic of capitalist accumulation is creating, in fact, a worldwide way of life (or rather contrasting worldwide ways of life for the opposing classes). Significantly, the creators of modern popular cultures are those thrown together in the great cities by the spread of capitalism:

> One of the most remarkable features of the evolution of popular music is its association in numerous cultures worldwide with an unassimilated, disenfranchised, impoverished, socially marginalised class, the lumpenproletariat of hoodlums, pimps, prostitutes, vagrants, sidewalk vendors, drug addicts, musicians, miscellaneous street people and assorted unemployed migrants... It was such groups... that gave birth to such diverse and vital forms as rebetika, modern kroncong, reggae, steel band, the tango and jazz... The lumpenproletariat are city dwellers... They are inherently predisposed to new forms of cultural expression.[82]

But it is not only the creators of an art form who determine its popularity, and therefore who determine what will flourish and what will die out. It is also the consumers, those for whom they perform. And for the mass of workers and the urban middle class (as well as the lumpens) tempos of work, patterns of consumption, styles of dress, forms of recreation, forms of sexual relations and the rest increasingly cut across the old cultural barriers. Languages remain different, but what they say is increasingly the same.

If there is, in this broad sense, increasingly a world culture, it is not surprising that art—both in its popular and its 'high-brow' forms—is increasingly international, with a world audience for films and TV programmes, rock bands and symphony orchestras, for novels and operas.

Just as in popular art there is increasing interaction between regional styles, each the product of capitalist development, so in high art the pre-capitalist forms have been replaced by international, capitalist forms. Thus the novel, which was a literary form created as the bourgeoisie fought for power in Western Europe, has been adopted and mastered by writers from the non-Western world like Ngugi, Achebe, Rushdie, Ben Ochre, Marquez and so on.

Cultural imperialism occurred when dominating powers forced conquered peoples to adopt their language and their view of world history—as the British and French did in various parts of their empires, or as the Russians did first under the Tsar and then under Stalin. It was a by-product of imperialism proper—the bloody and barbaric process by which empires were carved out and whole peoples exterminated.

But the fusion of cultures today cannot be dismissed as simply a product of enforced subjection. Rather, it flows from the irreversible changes wrought by the spread of capitalism. It occurs because throughout the world people are trying to come to terms with living in societies which are moulded by the same world system, which are subject to the same tempos of accumulation. As the forms of exploitation undertaken by ruling classes get more and more alike, so do their lifestyles and their culture. By the same token, as the humdrum everyday lives of the mass of people become ever more dependent on their ability to sell their labour power and to fit into the tempo of work in the factory, mine or office, so their forms of recreation, culture and even dress converge. Rhythms of modern pop, for instance, reflect—even if only by trying to provide an escape from—the reality of urban life and the compulsion to paid labour. The novel form dominates in literature everywhere because it gives expression to the way bourgeois and petty bourgeois intellectuals experience a present day worldwide reality.

Nothing brings home the fact of an increasingly international culture more than the television images of the civil wars between rival nationalities that have broken out in the former Yugoslavia and the former USSR. For the mass of fighters on either side wear the same jeans and the same trainers, listen to the same Walkmans or ghetto blasters, follow the same sports and quite likely watch the same soap operas. This is because, if they were not fighting, they would be living essentially similar lives, working at near identical jobs.

The process of transformation is not of course complete. A large portion of the world's population are still peasants rather than wage labourers. Among the wage labourers there are those who live on the brink of starvation, unable to get anything more than the occasional day's work, and those who are in full time employment in large industry. In many cities there is a very large petty bourgeoisie, often merging at its lower reaches with a mass of still barely urbanised former peasants, which can still mobilise behind the demand for a return to tradition—as with the Islamic movements in many middle eastern countries or the Hindu supremacist movements in India. Yet the trend towards fusion of cultures is still overwhelming, simply because the pressures of the world system on the lives of everyone within it are overwhelming. That is why the returns to tradition are always phoney: the traditions are manufactured, with the most modern techniques being used to recast the meaning of the oldest texts.

The culture created by modern capitalism is of course a deficient distorted culture. It is the culture of a class society which drains meaning from the lives of millions of people. It is a culture which has condoned slavery while preaching freedom, producing Belsen as well as Beethoven. The point is not to worship this culture in the manner of so many postmodernists, but to recognise it as the only terrain people have to fight on, since the system which created it has made obsolete and destroyed all others.

Modern theories of nationality and nationalism

THE TWO great tendencies of the last 75 years—the proliferation of nations, with many created among groupings that did not fit into the classic nineteenth century model, and the growing homogeneity of culture worldwide in every respect except language—has led to confusion among certain recent writers on nationalism. They see that, although there no longer seems to be any fixed, objective criteria for saying what is a nation and what is not, an identification with 'your own' nation is taken for granted by virtually the whole of humanity.

The result has been a tendency to see nationalisms as arbitrary constructs, detached from the economic development of capitalism. This is the tenor of Nigel Harris's recent book, *National Liberation*. For Nigel, capitalism is by its very nature an international system, based on the free movement of commodities and finance. It grew up within a system of national states, which were being constructed by pressures—the competition between rival absolutisms—other than itself, but today has an innate tendency to break through the boundaries between these states and to establish a new multinational order. All that holds it back is the continuing ability of political forces to get people to identify with the ideology of nation.

Benedict Anderson's very influential book, *Imagined Communities*, makes a greater effort to locate the growth of rival national consciousness in material reality. What he calls 'print capitalism' plays a very important role in his account. And he sees the rising bourgeoisie as playing a vital role in the creation of the first European nations: 'The coalition between Protestantism and print capitalism quickly created large new reading publics— not least among merchants and women who typically knew no Latin—and mobilised them for politico-religious purposes'.[83] The growth of new national consciousness in the eighteenth and nineteenth centuries was possible because of 'a half fortuitous but explosive interaction between a system of production and productive relations (capitalism), a technology of communication (print) and the fatality of human linguistic diversity'.[84]

Once some nations were already established, individuals from certain social groups could imagine establishing new ones, based on giving a printed form to languages, 'The "nation" thus becomes something capable of being consciously aspired to... rather than a slowly sharpening frame of vision'.[85] 'A model of the independent nation was available for pirating'.[86]

The audience for the new printed languages came, by and large, from 'families of ruling classes of nobility and landed gentry, courtiers and ecclesiastics, rising middle strata of plebeian lay officials, professionals, and commercial and industrial bourgeoisies'.[87] So 'in world historical terms bourgeoisies were the first class to achieve solidarities on an essentially imagined basis... In Europe these solidarities had an outmost stretch limited by vernacular legibilities'.[88]

But once the model was established along linguistic lines

in Europe, it could operate if necessary without them. The European powers established administrations in the colonies that cut across old linguistic divisions. The indigenous middle class that was recruited to fill many lower and middle administrative positions began to imagine themselves taking charge and copying the European model: 'Is Indian nationalism not inseparable from the colonial administrative-market unification, after the Mutiny, by the formidable and advanced of the imperial powers?'[89]

However, Anderson does not succeed in combining these elements into a coherent, total, materialist analysis. For, instead of recognising the nation state as the typical form of capitalist rule, he puts the emphasis on subjective factors that led people to want to 'imagine' new forms of community. These factors first emerged, he argues, when social and economic changes in the late medieval period led to the breakdown of 'cultural concepts of great antiquity' which gave 'a certain meaning to the everyday fatalities of existence (above all, death, loss and servitude)'. From that point, 'the search was on for a new way of linking fraternity, power and time meaningfully together'.[90]

The roots of the nationalist ideology, then, are finally located in existential yearning, not capitalist development, despite the promise of much of Anderson's argument. This becomes clearer in his more recent 'New World Disorder'[91] in which the strength of nationalism is ascribed, not to capitalism as such, but to 'two significant factors' linked to 'the rise of capitalism... mass communications and mass migrations'. 'Print capitalism brought into being mass publics who began to imagine through the media a new type of community: the nation', while 'the mass appearance in settled communities of thousands of immigrants did not, and will not, fail to produce its own ethnicisations... Le Pen's neo-fascist movement in France... the National Front in Britain... "White Power" extremists in the United States...' This is to repeat the old fallacy that immigration is to blame for racism—despite the very powerful evidence that racism is often strongest where there are fewest members of ethnic minorities (as with anti-semitism in Poland today, or with anti-black racism in virtually all-white towns and suburbs in Britain).

The weakness in Anderson's otherwise powerful argument is undoubtedly connected with the starting point of his book. He began to write it, he explains, in the late 1970s under the impact of the first war between what he saw as socialist states—

China and Vietnam. His whole aim was to understand what it was about nationalism that made it a central feature of socialist as well as capitalist societies. By refusing to see China and Vietnam as societies dominated by the dynamic of competitive accumulation—as a state organised variant of capitalism—he was driven to look outside capitalist society for the roots of nationalism, to see these instead in the satisfaction of innate psychological needs.

The result, paradoxically, is that Anderson is blind to something which the non-Marxist, Ernest Gellner, does grasp. Gellner sees the development of history not in terms of primitive communism, slavery, feudalism, capitalism and socialism, but rather of 'primitive' society, agrarian society and industrial societies. Despite the innumerable faults with this approach, it does provide him with one advantage over Anderson when looking at the so called socialist societies of the mid-twentieth century. He does not expect them to be any different in their essentials to capitalist societies, and looks for material explanations for those shared features which differentiate both from previous societies. Thus he is absolutely scathing about attempts to see nations as eternal: 'Nations as a natural God-given way of classifying men are a myth; nationalism which sometimes takes pre-existing cultures and turns them into nations, sometimes invents them and often obliterates pre-existing cultures—that is the reality'.[92]

He argues it is the need of each 'industrial society' for a 'homogeneous' population, literate in a single tongue, that gives rise to the nation:

> It is not the case that nationalism imposes homogeneity...
> It is the objective need for homogeneity that is reflected in
> nationalism... A modern industrial state can only function
> with a culturally standardised, interchangeable population...
> Nationalism is not the awakening of an old, latent, dormant force, though that is how it does present itself. It is,
> in reality, the consequence of a new form of social organisation, based on deeply internalised education-dependent
> high cultures, each protected by its own state.[93]

Just as the nation is a result of objective material realities, so too is the striving after nationhood among the masses. With industrialisation:

> The illiterate, half starved populations from their erstwhile

cultural ghettos who are pulled into the melting pots of shanty towns yearn for incorporation into one of those cultural pools which already has, or looks as if it might acquire, a state of its own, with the subsequent promise of full cultural citizenship, access to primary schools, employment, and all.[94]

When entry into the perks of nationhood is easy, he argues, they will forget their old culture and assimilate—thus explaining the reality that there are around ten times more potential languages in the world than there are nations or aspiring nations. But when they are 'spurned' they will seek some other way to define themselves. 'Nationalism as such is fated to prevail, but not any particular nationalism'.[95]

Gellner can therefore go beyond both Anderson and Harris in seeing why the drive to identify with a nation—and if necessary to try to create new nations—is such a central feature of the modern world:

Nations can be defined only in terms of the age of nationalism, rather than the other way round... When general social conditions make for standardised, homogeneous, centrally sustained high calderas, pervading whole populations and not just elite minorities, a situation arises in which well defined educationally sanctioned and unified cultures constitute very nearly the only kind of unit which men willingly and ardently identify... Only then does it appear that any defiance of their boundaries by political units constitutes a scandal... Under these conditions, and these conditions only, can nations be defined in terms of both will and culture.[96]

But Gellner has a vast blind area of his own. He does not conceive it possible that industrial society could be organised in a way other than it is. To this extent his much more materialist analysis leads to a conclusion very like Anderson's: the nation dominates all existing societies, and we have to like it or lump it. Gellner, who was involved in protests against the descent into rival barbaric nationalisms in Yugoslavia in the summer of 1991, clearly does not like it all that much. But he can point to no other way forward.

Eric Hobsbawm's work *Nations and Nationalism since 1780* takes for granted a framework very similar to Gellner's,[97] although with far more references to the Marxist tradition which, Hobsbawm points out, was the first to grasp that nations are not timeless entities but constructed with the rise of 'modern society'. Most of the work is concerned with fixing a mass of historical material into the framework—so much at times that the reader is in danger of getting lost amidst a mass of fascinating facts, unable to see the wood for the trees. But Hobsbawm departs from Gellner at a number of points.

First, he insists the views of those who align with national movements or national states may not be as clear cut as the nationalist leaders claim:

> If I have a major criticism of Gellner's work it is that his preferred perspective of modernisation from above makes it difficult to pay adequate attention to the view from below. The view from below, ie the nation as seen not by governments and spokesmen and activists of nationalist (and nonnationalist) movements, but by the ordinary persons who are the objects of their action and propaganda, is exceedingly difficult to discover...
>
> We cannot assume that national identification—when it exists—excludes or is always or ever superior to the remainder of the sets of identifications which constitute the social being...
>
> National identification and what it is believed to imply can change and shift in time, even in the course of quite short periods.[98]

Later he elaborates the argument further:

> Men and women did not choose collective identification as they choose shoes, knowing that one could only put on one pair at a time. They had, and still have, several attachments and loyalties simultaneously, including nationality, and are simultaneously concerned with various aspects of life, any one of which may at any moment in time be foremost in their minds, as occasion suggests. For long periods of time these different attachments would not make incompatible demands on a person... It was only when one of these loyalties conflicted directly with another that problems of choosing between them arose.

He provides a graphic example of how social concerns and national loyalties have interacted by quoting Peter Hanak's research on letters from soldiers from different ethnic backgrounds serving in the Austro-Hungarian army during the First World War:

> During the first years there was not much nationalism or anti-monarchism among the correspondents... The years of war, but especially the first Russian revolution, raised the political content of the intercepted correspondence dramatically. Indeed, the censors' reports on public opinions unanimously observed that the Russian revolution was the first political event since the outbreak of war whose shock waves penetrated to the lowest levels of the people. Among the activists of some of the oppressed nationalities such as the Poles and Ukrainians, it even raised hopes of reform—perhaps even of independence. However, the dominant mood was for peace and *social* transformation.
>
> The political opinions which now begin to appear even in the letters of labourers, peasants and working class women, is best analysed in terms of three interlocking binary opposites: rich-poor (or lord-peasant, boss-worker), war-peace, and order-disorder. The links, at least in the letters, are obvious: the rich live well and don't serve in the army, the poor people are at the mercy of the rich and powerful, the authorities of state and army, and so on. The novelty lies not only in the greater frequency of complaints... but in the sense that a revolutionary expectation of fundamental change was available as an alternative to passive acceptance of destiny.
>
> National feeling comes into the arguments only indirectly, chiefly because, to cite Hanak, 'until 1918 national sentiment had not yet crystalised out, among the broad masses of the people, into a stable component of consciousness...' Nationality appears most often as an aspect of the conflict between rich and poor, especially where the two belong to different nationalities. But even where we find the strongest national tone—as among the Czech, Serbian and Italian letters—we also find an overwhelming wish for social transformation... The period when the October revolution made its first impact was the one in which the social element in the public mood was at its strongest...

It was only when the wave of strikes in Austro-Hungary and Germany in January 1918 failed to bring down the regime and force an end to the war that people began to look away from social revolution and to look for their salvation through nationalism: 'But even when, in the course of 1918, the national theme finally became dominant in popular consciousness, it was not separate from or opposed to the social theme. For most poor people the two went together, as the monarchy crashed...' Hobsbawm argues that 'nationalism was victorious... to the extent that the movements which reflected the real concerns of the poor people of Europe failed in 1918. When this happened, the middle and lower strata of the oppressed nationalities were in position to become the ruling elites of the new independent... petty states'.[99]

The second novelty in Hobsbawm's account is that he claims the hold of nationalism is declining, despite the widespread belief to the contrary. He bases his claim on a number of arguments.

First, he denies that most of the new states that have emerged in the ex-colonial world since 1945 can really be counted as national states, since confined within the old colonial administrative boundaries they cannot achieve linguistic homogeneity or gain any real loyalty from the mass of their subjects. Yet this only proves they are unsuccessful — because late coming — national states. All aspire to become the focus of identity of their subjects, and some are successful, even if the identification is not total (but then, Hobsbawm's own analysis shows we should not expect it to be): despite the state's failure to impose a common language, very many Indian citizens do identify with 'their country', even if they also identify themselves as Hindus or Muslims, workers or employers, Brahmins or untouchables. In Africa and the Middle East the fact that state boundaries cross cut linguistic boundaries does not always stop the state becoming a focus of loyalty for the middle classes who depend on it for a livelihood and look to it to 'modernise' society, and who in turn exert ideological influence on the workers, the lumpenproletariat and the peasantry.

At the time of writing he had a second, even more dubious, argument, concerning the 'socialist' countries:

> Inasmuch as such regimes do not, at least in theory, identify with any of their constituent nationalities and regard the interests of each of them as secondary to higher common purpose, they are non-national... It was the great achievement of the communist regimes in multinational countries

to limit the disastrous effects of nationalism within them...
The 'discrimination' or even 'oppression' against which
the champions of various Soviet nationalities abroad protest,
is far less than the expected consequences of the withdrawal of Soviet power.[100]

One only wishes at this point that Hobsbawm would take
seriously his own injunction to look at things 'from below' and
not just in terms of how official spokespersons present them.
He might have asked himself what it meant to be a Tatar or Caucasian temporary worker living in a hostel in Moscow, a Turkic
speaking conscript in a Russian speaking army, or a Kazakh
speaking child in Alma Ata, a city without a single nursery using
the native language. As it is, the realities of oppression are confined to two footnotes, one mentioning the Romanisation of
Ceausescu's Romania (but not persecution of the Turks in Bulgaria, still less the ethnic cleansing which drove Hungarian
speakers from Slovakia and German speakers from Bohemia,
Moravia and western Poland after 1945) and 'the mass transfer
of entire populations on the grounds of their nationality which
took place after the war' in the USSR (but not the glorification
of Tsarist Russia's conquest of the non-Russian peoples that
became the official ideology from that time on).

Whether Hobsbawm likes it or not, all the Eastern European
regimes were seen by everyone who lived in them as regimes
dominated by single nationalities.[101] It is hardly surprising that,
since people have been able to express themselves freely, there
have been revolts of minority nationalities, and attempts — often
orchestrated by remnants of the old ruling parties — to mobilise
the dominating nationalities against them.

But Hobsbawm makes two other points that have rather
more going for them. He argues:

Nationalism... is no longer a major vector in historical development. In the 'developed' world of the nineteenth century, the building of a number of 'nations' which combined
nation state and national economy was plainly a central
fact of historical transformation... In the 'dependent' world
of the first half of the twentieth century... movements for
national liberation and independence were the main agents
for the political emancipation of most of the globe... Both
were typically unificatory as well as emancipatory...

The characteristic nationalist movements of the late twentieth century are essentially negative, or rather divisive.

There is a correct element in this argument. Capitalism
today finds even the biggest existing states too small for its operations. The idea that smaller states will make it easier for
people to cope with the vagaries of the system is absurd. But
this was already true 80 years ago when Rosa Luxemburg used
this argument against Lenin. And in economic terms she was
right: the successor states to the Austro-Hungarian Empire, for
instance, failed abysmally to advance their economies in the
inter-war years,[102] cut off as they were by state boundaries from
their old raw materials and markets. But politically she was
wrong, because millions of people flocked to nationalist movements, tore the old empires apart and created new states anyway.

The fact that nationalism is a blind alley does not automatically stop people going down it, even if it does mean at
some point they are likely to do a U-turn and start coming out
again.

Hobsbawm's final point is that much that is loosely called
nationalism is not concerned with building new states at all, but
rather with mobilising people from certain linguistic or ethnic
backgrounds to exercise political pressure on existing states.
This, he says, is a product of the way in which economic development has pulled vast numbers of migrants from many different backgrounds into the great cities of the world. The degree of
ethnic mixing makes any idea of establishing a new mono-ethnic
state impossible. But it also creates powerful constituencies for
those who want to make political careers by promising favours
to one linguistic, ethnic or religious group rather than another.
In extreme cases the result will be horrendous communal blood-
baths. But even if these groups are organised around nationalist
identification with a distant land of origin, they cannot be considered nationalist in the way the term is usually used.

His case here is very strong. Yet he still overstates it. In conditions of economic collapse, movements demanding the driving out of other ethnic groups can fight for control even of
modern, multinational cities—as we have seen in Bosnia in
recent months. Ethnicity can go beyond communalism and aspire
to impose new ethnic state boundaries using the most barbaric
means.

Some of Hobsbawm's arguments show that the potential

exists for resisting nationalism, that it is not the unstoppable juggernaut many people believe. But they do not show how that potentiality can become a reality. To do that Hobsbawm would have to break with his own watered down Eurocommunism, with its residual admixture of nostalgia for Stalinism, and look to the class alternatives he mentions when writing of the First World War.

Social crises and nationalism today

THE CENTRAL contention of this article so far is that the mystery of the nation state disappears when it is seen as the typical form of political administration associated with the advance of capitalism, from its beginnings in the western fringe of Europe to its present day conquest of the whole world. At each stage those who have striven to share in the gains of this advance, whether they themselves have been capitalists, state bureaucrats or members of the literate middle class, have wanted to have a local national state of their own. The fact that in order to gain such a state they have sometimes had to bend the definition of 'national' almost beyond belief is irrelevant, as is the failure of many of the new states to deliver the economic gains expected from them.

The system of nation states, then, is the political correlate of the full blown capitalist mode of production. It is the political form which, having aided capitalism in its conquest of the world in its youth, persists into its maturity and old age.

The strength of the ideology of nationalism under capitalism is not, then, surprising. It is part of the reflection in people's consciousnesses of the experience of living in a capitalist world. Just as living under capitalism makes the great mass of people take for granted that commodity production, alienated wage labour and competition are more common than co-operation, so it makes them take for granted the necessity of the nation state. And nationalist consciousness makes sense so long as they do not challenge the system as a whole: within it the individual capitalist is in a very weak situation unless he has a state to enforce his interests on others[103]; the individual peasant family hopes the state will protect it against the inevitable ups and downs of the market in foodstuffs; the individual worker knows he or she has to belong to a state to be allowed to work and live freely, and to apply for welfare benefits when necessary.

Marx made the point nearly 150 years ago that the ruling ideas are always the ideas of the ruling class. And one of those ideas is the idea of the nation as a 'natural unit' for grouping together a section of humanity into its 'own' cordoned off part of the planet.

The ruling ideas are not immutable. On this at least Hobsbawm is absolutely right. Great social crises create situations in which ideas and realities move in opposite directions, in which social turmoil and human suffering conflict with old allegiances, in which people find it literally impossible to continue to live according to the old ways, in which the outbreak of sudden confrontations creates new antagonisms and new loyalties.

In such periods people's consciousness is not monolithic, but contradictory, to use Gramsci's description.[104] Old ways of seeing things co-exist with new ways of seeing things. People continue to express themselves using concepts while taking actions which imply completely new ones. In the end the contradiction can only be resolved by breaking with the old or abandoning the new. But the end can sometimes be a very long time in coming.

Thus the development of capitalism in the sixteenth and seventeenth centuries created forms of social behaviour that challenged the whole ideology of medieval Christianity. The logic of this challenge led to the complete rejection of religious ways of thinking by the Enlightenment. But this rejection did not permeate right through into popular consciousness for centuries. In the interim people who identified with the new ways of living tried to reconcile themselves partially to the old ways of thinking by continuing to accept Christianity, but in new reformed versions.

The speed of the onset of crises and the degree of social turmoil is much greater under capitalism than under any previous mode of production, and the stresses besetting old forms of consciousness accordingly that much more acute. Nevertheless, contradictory, hybrid forms of consciousness are an inevitable feature of mentality for the great mass of people at the first stage of any great convulsion: the mass of workers who overthrew the Tsar and established soviets in February 1917 did allow Prince Lvov to head the Provisional Government; the German workers who got rid of the Kaiser and ended the war did, disastrously, allow Ebert, Scheidermann and 'the bloodhound' Noske to maintain the power of the bourgeoisie and the officer corps; the Polish workers who created a huge independent trade union and inflicted the first major defeat on Stalinism in the summer of 1980 did bow down to the Pope and accept the advice of those who preached compromise with their rulers.

It is in this context that we have to explain the sudden rise of new nationalisms. The idea of the division of humanity into nations is etched into people's consciousness under capitalism. If one national state fails them, the easiest thing is to turn to the idea of creating a different national state. It seems so much more 'practical' to rearrange the pieces on the board than to invent a totally new game.

This can be encouraged by the material interests of wide sections of the middle class—especially where a large part of a region's population are fluent in a language other than the official one of the old state. For some of them a separate state—or at least a grant of national autonomy—means improved access to bureaucratic posts. Hence the flourishing of Catalan nationalism in the last couple of years of the fascist regime in Spain, as wide sections of the Catalan speaking middle class joined and exercised influence on a struggle that had previously been spearheaded by mainly Spanish speaking workers. But language is not an indispensable factor: in any formation of a new state identification with the struggle for it can enhance many career prospects.

The directing of discontent into nationalist demands can also be of benefit to important sections of the capitalist or state capitalist ruling class. The most powerful rarely promote nationalism themselves, and they sometimes do their best to resist it as detrimental to their own powerfully established links with the old state. But even then they can come to regard it as the lesser evil compared with the growth of a movement for social revolution. And less powerful elements within the ruling class can see sponsorship of a secessionist state as a very good way of accelerating their own accumulation of wealth. Thus it was not the small Bengali speaking big bourgeoisie who initiated the movement to separate eastern Pakistan from the central state apparatus in western Pakistan in 1971, but some of them managed to profit enormously when separation finally led to the formation of the new national state of Bangladesh.

A final factor is also of immense importance in helping to trigger identification with nationalist slogans—the extent to which the old state carries through policies that can be seen as involving oppression along national lines. The classic form this takes is discrimination against those who speak a certain language—as with the Turkish government's attempts in the 1980s to ban Kurdish or the Sri Lankan government's insistence that Sinhalese, not Tamil, is the official language. Although the middle classes suffer most, workers too face problems every time they come in contact with the state—with its police, its courts, or even its post offices. But discrimination does not have to be formal, as black people in Europe and North America are all too aware. A particular linguistic or religious group can find they are treated as second or third class citizens every time they come into contact with police officers, officials or employers. This was always the experience of the Irish (especially, but not only, the Catholics) under British rule, of the Bengalis under Pakistani rule, and of Kurds under Iraqi rule. The logic of the situation leads to a vicious circle of oppression: the minority protest at the discrimination against them, the state regards them as disloyal, arrests their spokespeople, disbands any representative institutions they possess, censors their press, encourages further discrimination against them, and thus heightens their feeling of alienation from it. What begin as mild protests aimed at securing a better place within the existing state often end up as irreconcilable demands for secession.

But the element of real oppression is not always necessary for a movement to gain mass support. Just as there is usually support of a fairly passive nature for the official nationalism of the state among the majority of its population, so great social and political crises can see that support transferred by a section of the population to its secessionist rival. Indeed, because secession offers change and any change seems like improvement, the loyalty to the new nationalism can be stronger than that to the old—although this increased strength need not last long.

Scotland provides an example of how the nationalism of the non-oppressed can fluctuate wildly.[105] Independence, or at least devolved government, seems on occasions to offer a quick way for people to break from the hold of a Tory government and the grim effects of Britain's long drawn out economic decline. Support for nationalism, and for the Scottish National Party in particular, grows very quickly. Identification with the superficial symbols of British nationalism—the 'national' sports teams, the 'national' flag, 'national' culture and 'national' celebrities—

becomes overwhelmingly an identification with Scottish symbols. But the support remains passive for the great mass of people and when no breakthrough to independence occurs, can die down as quickly as it arose. And then people see no contradiction in identifying with Scottish symbols (the football team) and British symbols (the monarchy, the armed forces, and even the Olympic team,[106] an identification that the Scottish National Party does not challenge!).

This does not mean that the nationalism of the non-oppressed cannot occasionally present problems for the existing state. Fortuitous conditions can turn it into a focus for much wider discontents of a social nature, and the state can react by trying to crush it, so creating oppressive conditions that did not exist before. It is worth remembering that until the mid-1930s Basque nationalism was a right wing force in Spanish politics; it was the actions of the state itself which forced it to align itself with the left and to take up a position of irreconcilable hostility to fascism.[107]

More recently the nationalisms of peoples who are not subject to oppression on the basis of any national characteristics, but who live on different sides of state boundaries drawn by great powers in the past, have had considerable political impact. The movement against the Stalinism of the East German state machine in 1989 transformed itself into a movement for incorporation into the Federal German Republic, while in South Korea much of the reformist left has seen national reunification as the central slogan—even though parties of the conservative right also call themselves 'unification' parties.

In any case, the turn towards nationalism among workers must be regarded as one of the ways the ideas of the ruling class continue to exercise an influence, even when the crisis of the system begins to break people from a conservative attachment to the old order. The extent of this influence depends here, as in other cases, on two factors: the level of collective struggle against the system, and the degree to which socialist organisations exist on the ground, capable of taking up political and ideological arguments in each workplace and locality. Where nationalist influence is greatest is where the crisis results in defeat and demoralisation rather than struggle among workers, and where the ideological crisis of most of the left since the collapse of Stalinism has done most damage.

For the rise of nationalism cannot be separated from the crisis of the left internationally which has accompanied the crisis of the system. There is an enormous vacuum on the left, which often leaves those who preach nationalism (or in large areas of the world, religious fundamentalism) with little socialist competition.

Nationalism since the collapse of Stalinism

THE VACUUM on the left is greatest and the crisis of the system reaping more havoc than anywhere else outside sub-Saharan Africa in the countries that used to be called Communist. It should be no surprise that these have experienced the greatest growth of rival nationalisms in the last few years.

The fate of the former USSR shows how economic crisis—the 'stagnation' that began in the last Brezhnev years giving way to contraction and mass impoverishment in the last Gorbachev years—can create political crises, and political crises find expression in the growth of national movements. It shows how members of the middle class intelligentsia create movements which make the national question the focus through which all other discontents are meant to be focused—the popular fronts in the Baltic states, Moldavia, Armenia and Azerbaijan, Rukh in the Ukraine, and the Round Table in Georgia. It shows how the very real oppression suffered by very large numbers of ordinary people could allow these movements to gain enormous mass followings (a much larger and more active following than the various democratic movements among the Russians). And it shows how at a time of major political crisis important figures within the ruling class itself could switch to nationalism as a way of maintaining their control over part at least of the old state—Kravchuk in the Ukraine, Nazarbayev in Kazakhstan and, most amazingly of all, Yeltsin in Russia who beats the nationalist drum and claims the dominant nationality has been exploited by the others.

But it is the Yugoslav case which is the most revealing—if also so far the most horrific.

The state had been carefully reconstructed after the defeat of the German occupation in the Second World War to balance its main Slav constituents—Slovenes, Serbs and Croats—against each other, so preventing political disruption caused by Croats and Slovenes feeling they were being dominated by Serbs (as in the pre-war monarchy) or Serbs feeling they were dominated by Croats (as under German occupation). To this end the Serbs of Montenegro, the Macedonians (regarded by the Serbs previously as 'southern Serbs') and the mixed Serbian-Croat-Muslim population of Bosnia were all given their own republics separate from Serbia proper, while the mixed Serb and Hungarian speaking area of Vojvodina in northern Serbia was given an autonomous status. All Slavs had an equal chance of rising in the state bureaucracy; the only oppressed nationality was the Albanian speakers of Kosovo, who were denied their own republic and subject to systematic discrimination at the hands of everyone else. But it is important to understand that the structure was not based on any systematic attempt to undermine national allegiances, rather on using each to neutralise the others. Divide and rule was always present.

The structure worked well for its rulers until the late 1960s. The state's cohesion was such that it survived unscathed through the various serious external political crises of 1948, when it split from the Russian bloc, and the economy grew rapidly for the next 20 years. When a loss of economic dynamism led to another political crisis in the late 1960s, with the purging of the interior minister, the weakening of police control allowed discontent to express itself through student demonstrations in Belgrade and a rise of Croat nationalism within the ruling party itself in Croatia. A clampdown succeeded in breaking both movements, but only because it was followed by a growing institutionalisation of the rival Slav nationalisms at the governmental level. The heads of each of the republics were able, to some extent, to head off discontent by giving the impression they were fighting for 'national' interests within the federal government.

Then in the 1980s an economic crisis broke out with a vengeance. There was growing unemployment, growing inflation and a drop in living standards until they were no higher than they had been in the 1930s. There was an explosion of discontent—and much of it on a class basis. The number of strikes leapt from 100 in 1983 to 1,530 in 1987, when there were powerful calls for a general strike as workers broke into the federal parliament. But at this point powerful political figures set out to protect themselves against the growing anger from below and to advance their own careers by deliberately inflaming national hatreds.

The first to do so was Slobodan Milosevic, a rising figure in the Serbian party leadership. He launched a massive campaign against the alleged persecution of Serbs in Kosovo and used huge demonstrations of all the classes in Serbia—industrial managers gave workers time off to attend, where they were joined by student organisations, veterans, members of the academy of science and so on—to take over control of the Serbian leadership and then to impose his nominees on Vojvodina and Montenegro. His efforts were soon matched by others. In Croatia a Titoist general who had fallen from grace, Franjo Tudjman, began courting supporters of the wartime Ustashe regime that had butchered Serbs and demanded that Croats police the Serbian inhabited areas of Croatia. In Slovenia leaders of the old ruling party threw in their lot with what had been the leadership of the liberal opposition throughout Yugoslavia to join together to press for secession.[108]

The rival nationalist campaigns of Milosevic and Tudjman reinforced each other. By bringing down the Vojvodina and Montenegro governments, Milosevic frightened Croats with the spectre of Serbian hegemony over the whole of Yugoslavia. By attacking the rights of the Croatian Serbs, Tudjman drove them into the hands of Milosevic and forces even further to the right. By supporting the Yugoslav army's onslaught on Slovenia and then parts of Croatia, Milosevic encouraged Croats to rely on Tudjman and the paramilitary groups to his right. The horrific logic of what they were both up to was shown when they agreed secretly to partition Bosnia between them and to destroy the harmony that had existed between Serbs, Croats and Muslims in its capital, Sarajevo. 'Uniting the divided nation' became a slogan which authoritarian right wing parties in both Serbia and Croatia could use to draw support behind them.

What Milosevic and Tudjman had discovered was that in a declining economy nationalist slogans could draw sections of the middle class into a fight for rival state machines and the careers available within them, could divert workers from fighting to defend living standards and could give sudden popularity to individual members of the old ruling class. Because nationalism has always been part of the ruling ideology, it always presents a possible safety valve for sections of ruling classes in moments of acute crisis.

But that is not the end of the matter. For if the movement to form new national states cannot open up new economic possibilities for society as a whole, then it cannot provide more than temporary relief for ruling classes. Here the difference between national movements in capitalism's youth, when they advanced the forces of production, and their role today, when they constrain any such advance, is important. Having gained power, the nationalists still have to confront the crisis of the national economy, and this at a time when pressure to placate the nationalist desires of their own supporters exerts pressures on them to seize fresh territory and enlarge 'the nation'. So long as the nationalist frenzy continues its upward path, the economic problems get greater. The moment the nationalist frenzy fades, the economic problems—and with them the class struggle—suddenly move back to the centre of the stage. The very discontents sidetracked by the nationalist agitation then return to haunt those who used it to hoist themselves into power.

As so often in history, war is used to head off class struggle, but the cost of war then heightens the class bitterness in society, and threatens to end in the overthrow of those who promoted it. At the time of writing, nobody can tell what is going to emerge from the bloody morass in former Yugoslavia—or for that matter in Moldova, Azerbaijan and Armenia, or Georgia. But what is very clear is that there is no stable political outcome to a situation in which nationalism can tear states apart but has no economic programme for carrying society forward. Just as general social discontent switched into nationalist hatreds, so national hatred can suddenly switch back into social struggles, particularly as the violence and cost of inter-ethnic struggles produces war weariness and bitterness against those who run the governments.

A war like that in former Yugoslavia necessarily gives rise to vague desires for peace among vast numbers of people and to anti-government demonstrations. If these feelings can be fused with the struggles of workers against the cost of the war and the effects of the economic crisis, then the wave of nationalism can be beaten back. But class politics does not arise automatically. It has to be argued for. Here an enormous responsibility lies with those small groups, who alone of the genuine left have survived the crisis of Stalinism.

Socialists and nationalism

THE LEFT cannot fulfil its responsibilities unless it is clear on the relation between nation and class. Its starting point has to be a clear understanding that nationalism is about the organisation of capitalist society. On this Kautsky and Lenin were absolutely right against Otto Bauer. Internationalism cannot be achieved by the arithmetic addition of different nationalisms, but by a conscious opposition to them all. There are not Serbian or Croat, English or Irish, Russian or Ukrainian socialists, but socialists who happen to live in one or other of these states. Socialists are not proud of their nationality. They are proud of the denial of their nationality. By the same token, socialists do not stand for the maintenance of 'their own' national culture, but for the integration of all that is best in every culture into a new, cosmopolitan, human culture. This is important for those who have been brought up to identify with the culture of oppressor nations—but not for them alone. As Lenin stressed repeatedly, any defence of the separation of cultures ends up in a defence of the separating off of workers from one another, just as the capitalist production process pulls them together. It plays into the hands of reactionaries among both the oppressor and the oppressed nationalities.

At the same time, however, socialists have to understand the only way to bring workers of different nationalities together is to insist on free association. Internationalism does not mean identification with existing states. Workers who regard themselves as having a certain nationality cannot unite freely with other workers within the same state unless they know those workers defend their right to secede if they so wish. Croat workers will not unite with Serb workers unless the Serb workers defend their rights—including the right to secession. Serb workers will not unite with Croat workers unless Croat workers oppose every attempt to discriminate against and oppress the Serb minority within Croatia. Only by the workers of different nationalities defending each others' rights can they create circumstances in which nationality ceases to be of significance to any of them.

There is a difference between oppressor and oppressed nationalities that socialists have to understand. We can fight on the same side, temporarily, as the bourgeois or petty bourgeois leaders of the oppressed nations against the oppressor. We can never be on the same side as the oppressors against the oppressed. And internationalism can never mean simply balancing between one and the other.

But even when we find ourselves on the same side of the barricades as the leaders of a national movement, we have to understand their goals are not our goals, their methods not our methods. They are out to establish new capitalist or state capitalist states, and that will mean them turning against their own workers and if necessary turning their guns on us. We are out to develop the international struggle of workers, to unite workers of the oppressed nationalities with workers who have mistakenly identified with the oppressor in the past.

We are for the right of secession—and, in certain concrete situations, for the struggle for secession—because we are for the unity of workers. Nationalists who are for the same goals are out to break this unity, to put nation before class.

One of the reasons the left is in such poor shape to deal with nationalist challenges like that in former Yugoslavia or the former USSR is that it has not understood these things in the past. It has flipped between wrapping itself in the flags of small 'progressive' nationalisms and identifying with the great oppressor states like the USSR—or even, in the present war in former Yugoslavia, calling for the intervention of the major Western imperialisms. It will indeed be tragic if the left does not learn how to fight for internationalism as people become sickened by the nationalist delirium.

Notes

Marxism and imperialism today

My debt to John Rees's 'Arms and the new imperialism', chapter 2 below, whose subject matter overlaps with that of this essay, should be obvious. Chris Harman has now given a masterly treatment of capitalist development in the Third World in 'Where is Capitalism Going?', *International Socialism*, 2:60 (1993)

1. T Congdon, 'How the City is Making Economic Nationalism Obsolete', *Spectator*,13 Feb 1988, pp. 21, 25.
2. K Kautsky, 'Imperialism', in J Riddell, ed, *Lenin's Struggle for a Revolutionary International. Documents 1907-1916 The Preparatory Years*, New York 1984, p. 180.
3. Ibid, p. 181.
4. AJ Mayer, *Why Did the Heavens Not Darken?*, New York 1990, p. 31.
5. B Warren, *Imperialism-Pioneer of Capitalism*, London 1980, pp. 9, 10.
6. Lenin, *Collected Works*, Moscow 1964, Vol. XXII (hereinafter *LCW*), pp. 266, 267.
7. See, for example, M Kidron, *Capitalism and Theory*, London 1974, ch. 6, M Barratt Brown, *The Economics of Imperialism*, Harmondsworth 1974, ch. 8 and Warren, *Imperialism*, pp. 57-70.
8. *LCW*, p. 298.
9. NI Bukharin, *Selected Writings on the State and the Transition to Socialism*, Nottingham 1982, pp 16-17.
10. Id., *Imperialism and World Economy*, London 1972, pp. 25-6, 125.
11. See my discussion of Lenin and Bukharin in 'Imperialism, Capitalism and the State Today', *IS* 2:35, 1987, pp. 79-88
12. The concept of uneven and combined development is, of course, one of Trotsky's main contributions to Marxism. Without it one cannot explain either the hierarchical nature of imperialism (the domination of the advanced countries) or its instability (the unequal division of resources gives rise to constant inter-imperialist struggles to repartition the world).

13. J Schumpeter, *Imperialism and Social Classes*, New York 1955, pp. 64-5, 94, 96

14. AJ Mayer, *The Persistence of the Old Regime*, New York 1981, pp. 4, 305, 314-15.

15. Id, *Why Did the Heavens Not Darken?*, p. 3.

16. Ibid, p. 456.

17. J Schumpeter, *Imperialism*, p. 69.

18. Ibid, pp. 81, 84, 88.

19. For recent versions of this argument (both of which refer to Mayer), see P Anderson, 'The Figures of Descent', *New Left Review* 161, 1987, and T Nairn, *The Enchanted Glass*, London 1990. Anderson read *The Persistence of the Old Regime* in draft: see ibid, p. x.

20. See, for example, EP Thompson, 'The Pecularities of the English', in *The Poverty of Theory and Other Essays*, London 1978, A Callinicos, 'Exception or Symptom?', *New Left Review* 169, 1988, C Barker and D Nicholls (eds), *The Development of British Society*, Manchester 1988, and on Germany, D Blackbourn and G Eley, *The Peculiarities of German History*, Oxford 1984.

21. For accounts that stress the impact of industrial capitalism, see J Romein, *The Watershed of Two Eras*, Middletown 1978, N Stone, *Europe Transformed 1878-1919*, London 1983, and EJ Hobsbawm, *The Age of Empire 1875-1914*, London 1987. I discuss Mayer's work at more length in *Against Postmodernism*, Cambridge 1989, pp. 39-44.

22. J Schumpeter, *Imperialism*, p. 18, and pp. 7-22 passim.

23. See esp. J Brewer, *The Sinews of Power*, London 1989.

24 . See Tables 4 and 16 in Barratt Brown, *Economics*, pp. 110, 187.

25. J Schumpeter, *Imperialism*, p. 14.

26. See JA Hobson, *The South African War*, London 1900, Part II, and T Pakenham, *The Boer War*, London 1979, Part I.

27. J Schumpeter, *Imperialism*, pp. 72, 73.

28. T Nairn, *Enchanted Glass*, pp. 375-6.

29. J Schumpeter, *Imperialism*, p. 98.

30. See esp. F Halliday, *The Making of the Second Cold War*, London 1983.

31. See E Gellner, *Plough, Sword and Book*, Oxford 1988, A Giddens, *A Contemporary Critique of Historical Materialism*, London 1981, M Mann, *The Sources of Social Power*, I, Cambridge 1986, WG Runciman, *A Treatise on Social Theory*, II, Cambridge 1989, and, for a critique A Callinicos, *Making History*, Cambridge 1987, pp. 157-72.

32. E Hobsbawm, *Age of Empire*, p. 51.

33. WH McNeill, *The Pursuit of Power*, Oxford 1982, chs. 7 and 8.

34. *LCW*, p. 255.
35. M Barratt Brown, *Economics*, ch. 8. All data on foreign investment are from this book.
36. E Hobsbawm, *Age of Empire*, pp. 73-4.
37. RP Dutt, *India Today*, London 1940, ch. VII.
38. Quoted in M Barratt Brown, *Economics*, p. l95.
39. A Offer, *The First World War: An Agrarian Interpretation*, Oxford 1989. The text to this note is a most inadequate summary of a very rich and wide ranging book.
40. R Hilferding, *Finance Capital*, London 1981, p. 307.
41. N Bukharin, *Selected Writings*, pp. 18, 19.
42. C Harman, *Explaining the Crisis*, London 1984, ch. 2.
43. M Wolf, 'The Need to Look to the Long Term', *Financial Times*, 16 Nov 1987.
44. E Mandel, *The Meaning of the Second World War*, London 1986, is the only serious Marxist attempt at a global interpretation, though it is not without its weaknesses, notably Mandel's typically scholastic distinction between several different kinds of war involved in the conflict.
45. See P Kennedy, *The Rise and Fall of the Great Powers*, London 1989, chs. 4 and 5.
46. See esp. G Kolko, *The Politics of War*, New York 1970.
47. LD Trotsky, *Europe and America*, New York 1971.
48. See J Waterbury, *The Egypt of Nasser and Sadat*, Princeton 1983.
49. *Sunday Times, Insight on the Middle East*, London 1974, section IV.
50. P Brogan, *World Conflicts*, London 1992, p. vii; compare VG Kiernan, *The European Empires from Conquest to Collapse*, 1815-1960, London 1982.
51. See M Kidron, *A Permanent Arms Economy*, reprinted London, 1989, and C Harman, *Explaining*, ch. 3.
52. C Harman, *Explaining*, ch. 3.
53. This is, of course, the main theme of Kennedy's book: see esp. *Rise and Fall*, pp. 509-64.
54. M Kidron, *Capitalism*, p. 132
55. World Bank, *World Development Report 1985*, New York 1985, p. 126.
56. See, for example, AG Frank, *Capitalism and Underdevelopment in Latin America*, Harmondsworth 1971, and S Amin, *Unequal Development*, Hassocks 1976, and, among critiques of the theory of unequal exchange, M Kidron, *Capitalism*, ch. 5, and N Harris, 'Theories of Unequal Exchange', *IS* 2:33, 1986.
57. M Kidron, *Capitalism*, pp. 134-7.

58. N Harris, *India-China: Underdevelopment and Revolution*, New Delhi 1974, p. 171.

59. M Kidron, *Capitalism*, p. 162, and N Harris, *India-China*, pp. 173-4.

60. See P Clawson, 'The Development of Capitalism in Egypt', *Khamsin* 9, 1981, and J Waterbury, *Egypt*.

61. See N Harris, *The End of the Third World*, London 1986, and AH Amsden, 'Third World Industrialisation', *New Left Review* 182, 1990.

62. United Nations Department of International Economic and Social Affairs, *World Economic Survey 1989*, New York, table IV. 4, p. 64.

63. Ibid. p. 25.

64. *Financial Times*, 15 Nov 1989.

65. J Petras and M Morley, *US Hegemony under Siege*, London 1990, pp. 197, 198.

66. Ibid. p. 201.

67. See esp. N Harris, *Of Bread and Guns*, Harmondsworth 1983, P Green, 'Nation States and the World Economy', *IS* 2:19, 1983, Callinicos, 'Imperialism', C Harman, 'The Storm Breaks', *IS* 2:46, 1990, and id., 'The State and Capitalism Today', *IS* 2:51, 1991

68. The definitive analysis of the collapse of Stalinism is C Harman, 'The Storm Breaks'; see also A Callinicos, *The Revenge of History*, Cambridge 1991.

69. *Independent on Sunday*, 20 January 1991.

70. See P Green, 'Contradictions of the American Boom', *IS* 2:26, 1985, and M Davis, *Prisoners of the American Dream*, London 1986.

71. J Petras and M Morley, *US Hegemony*, p. 78.

72. Ibid., chapters 1 and 2 offers a recent discussion of these strategies, though one which paints an exaggerated picture of the US ruling class's degeneration into a bunch of thugs and rentiers.

73. See F Halliday, *Cold War, Third World*, London 1989, ch. 3.

74. *Guardian*, 29 July 1988. See, for a more detailed analysis of the war, A Callinicos, 'An Imperialist Peace?', *Socialist Worker Review* 112, September 1988.

75. See, for example, the articles by J Rogaly and E Mortimer, *Financial Times*, 18 January 1991.

76. Ibid, 28 January 1991.

77. *Independent*, 19 January 1991.

78. F Halliday, *Arabia without Sultans*, Harmondsworth 1974, pp. 500, 502. Halliday, however, distanced himself from more extreme forms of dependency theory: see ibid, pp. 498-9.

79. B Warren, *Imperialism*, p. 182; see also ibid, pp. 150, 176

80. 'Themes', *New Left Review* 184, 1990, p. 2.

81. *Sunday Correspondent*, 12 August 1990 (1988 figures).

82. H Batatu, *The Old Social Classes and the Revolutionary Movements of Iraq*, Princeton 1978, pp. 25, 86ff, 99ff, 325ff.

83. P Knightley and C Simpson, *The Secret Lives of Lawrence of Arabia*, London 1971, p. l47.

84. F Halliday, *Arabia*, ch. 2.

85. H Batatu, *Old Social Classes*, p. 268.

86. Arguably the white Dominions (Canada, Australia, South Africa, etc) should be placed in the same semi-colonial category, though their successful campaign for legislative independence, culminating in the Statute of Westminster 1931, reflects the growing autonomy of these developing capitalisms from Whitehall. There is a useful discussion of the concept of semi-colony, criticising Mandel's application of it to the NICs, in A Dabat and L Lorenzano, *Argentina: The Malvinas and the End of Military Rule*, London 1984, p. l68 n. 3.

87. See K. Allen, *Is Southern Ireland a Neo-Colony?*, Dublin 1990, esp. chs. 2-4.

88. Dabat and Lorenzano, *Argentina*, pp. 29, 36-7.

89. Ibid, pp. 37-8.

90. Ibid, pp. l86 n. 30, 103-4.

91. On the latter case, see D Glanz, 'Dinki-di Domination: Australian Imperialism and the South Pacific', *Socialist Review*, Melbourne, 2, 1990.

92. DM Gordon, 'The Global Economy', *New Left Review* 168, 1988, p. 64.

93. See F Halliday, *Iran: Dictatorship and Development*, Harmondsworth 1979, ch. 9; there is a useful discussion of the concept of sub-imperialism on pp. 282-4.

94. D Hiro, *The Longest War*, London 1990, p. 261.

95. *Guardian*, 12 Sept. 1990.

96. See, for example, S Lash and J Urry, *The End of Organised Capitalism*, Cambridge 1987, and D Harvey, *The Condition of Postmodernity*, Oxford 1989.

97. See in addition to the articles cited in n. 67 above A Callinicos, *Against Postmodernism*, pp. l37-44.

98. *Financial Times*, 13 July 1992.

99. Ibid., 11 January 1993.

100. RS Nye, Jr., *Bound to Lead*, New York 1991, pp. 108, 110.

101. MJ Boskin, 'Myth of America's Decline', *Financial Times*, 15 March 1993.

102. Kennedy's most detailed response to his critics can be found in *Preparing for the Twenty-First Century*, New York 1993, ch. 13.

103. *Financial Times*, 21 December 1992.
104. Ibid., 8 February 1993. According to a study by management consultants McKinsey, *overall* US productivity is 17 percent greater than that of Japan. High Japanese productivity in sections like cars, metalworking and consumer electronics is balanced by miserably low productivity in other industries: output per worker in food manufacturing is one third of that in the US. German productivity levels generally lag behind those in the US and Japan. *Financial Times*, 22 October 1993.
105. There is an interesting discussion of the problems of US global military strategy in G Friedman and M LeBard, *The Coming War with Japan*, New York 1991, ch. 9. 106. Ibid., esp. Parts III and IV.
106. Ibid., esp. Parts III and IV.
107. *LCW*, p. 270. Even Bukharin tended to treat imperialism as a policy: see, for example, *Imperialism and World Economy*, ch. IX.
108. Ibid., p. 355.
109. Ibid., pp. 356, 357.
110. *Leon Trotsky on China*, New York 1976, pp. 569-70.
111. F Halliday, 'The Left and the War', *New Statesman and Society*, 8 March 1991., p. 16. This article generated an enormous controversy in subsequent issues. For an overview of the debate on the Gulf War, see A Callinicos, 'Choosing Imperialism', *Socialist Worker Review*, May 1991.
112. F Halliday, 'Imperialism, Peace and War, and the Left', interview in *New Times*, 7 August 1993.
113. Letter in *New Statesman and Society*, 12 April 1991, p. 38, replying to, among others, A Cockburn, 'The War Goes On', ibid., 5 April 1991.
114. Halliday, 'Imperialism'.
115. A Callinicos, 'Intervention: Disease or Cure?', *Socialist Review*, June 1993.

The new imperialism

Thanks to Alex Callinicos, Lindsey German, Chris Harman, Mike Haynes and Ahmed Shawki for comments on the first draft of 'The New Imperialism' when it first appeared in *International Socialism* 48 . Thanks also to Matt Perry for material on the USSR's military strategy.

1. M Beaud, *A History of Capitalism 1500-1980*, London 1984, p. 186.
2. Ibid and, for Russia and Britain, BR Mitchell, *European Historical Statistics 1750-1970*, London 1978, pp. 224-5.

3. P Kennedy, *The Rise and Fall of Great Powers*, London 1989, pp. 454-9.

4. Ibid, pp. 460-1.

5. P Armstrong, A Glyn and J Harrison, *Capitalism Since World War II*, London 1984, pp. 213-4.

6. M Beaud, op cit, p. 186.

7. See M Kidron, *Western Capitalism Since the War*, London 1970, p. 38.

8. P Armstrong et al, op cit, p. 214.

9. Quoted in D Smith, *Pressure—How America Runs NATO*, London 1989, p. 55.

10. Quoted in P Sedgwick, 'NATO. The Bomb and Socialism', *Universities and Left Review* No 7, Autumn 1959, p. 8.

11. Quoted ibid. British troops had been used to crush the Greek resistance movement at the end of the Second World War.

12. Quoted in P Kennedy, op cit, p. 503.

13. P Kennedy, op cit, p. 558.

14. P Armstrong et al, op cit, p. 219.

15. World Bank, *World Development Report 1989*, Oxford University Press, 1989, p. 167.

16. P Armstrong et al. op cit, pp. 225-226.

17. P Kennedy, op cit. p. 558.

18. Ibid, p. 679. A Congressional study reported a slide in the trading surplus on high technology goods from $27 billion in 1980 to $4 billion in 1985. It is this study which predicts a deficit.

19. Ibid, pp. 554-5.

20. See MC Pugh, 'Prospects for International Order'. in M Pugh and P Williams, *Superpower Politics*, Manchester University Press 1990, p. 180.

21. See B Kagarlitsky, *The Dialectic of Change*, London 1990, p. 236.

22. See M Haynes, 'Understanding the Soviet Crisis', *International Socialism* 34, p. 11.

23. Ibid, p. 9.

24. Source: A Aganbegyan. *The Challenge: Economics of Perestroika*, London 1988, p. 2.

25. See J Sallnow, *Reform in the Soviet Union*, London 1988, p. 17, tables 1.1 and 1.2.

26. A Aganbegyan. op cit. p. 204. Aganbegyan claims that the USSR's economy could withstand another round of the arms race, in spite of the fact that all he had said before pointed to the weakness of the economy in the face of such a challenge.

27. Quoted by David Owen in the *Independent on Sunday*, 1 July 1990. Owen's analysis seems far too intelligent to be all his

own work. The likelihood must be that his old friends at the Foreign Office provided him with the information.

28. See RC Plumber, 'Gorbachev and Soviet Defence Policy', in M Pugh and P Williams (eds), op cit, p. l69.

29. According to David Owen, op cit.

30. As Chris Harman has shown in 'The Storm Breaks', *International Socialism*, 2: 46, London 1990 .

31. See the *Economist*, American Survey, 7 April 1990.

32. International Institute of Strategic Studies (IISS), *The Military Balance 1993-1994*, p.19

33. British defence expenditure took 7.7 percent of Gross Domestic Product (GDP) in 1955. See C Harman, *Explaining the Crisis*, London 1984, p. 98. It fell to 4.5 percent in 1978 and then rose as Thatcher followed Reagan's arms boom, to hit some 5.3 percent by 1984. This massive real increase in defence spending has, like the Reagan boom, been curtailed. By 1992-93that figure had fallen to 3.8 percent and is projected to hit 2.9 percent by 1996-97. See M Chalmers, *Trends in UK Defence Spending in the 1980s*, Peace Research Report Number 11, (School of Peace Studies, University of Bradford), Tables 2 and 3 and p. 5 and the *Economist*, 30 April 1994, p.28.

34. See 'At Ease: Disarming Europe', *Business Week*, 19 February 1990.

35. See *Economist*, 28 January 1989.

36. A Kelly, *The Myth of Soviet Superiority*, Peace Research Report Number 14, School of Peace Studies, University of Bradford 1987, fig. 11.

37. See the *Independent*, 31 May 1989.

38. *Economist*, 28 January 1989. Although in March 1990 one of Gorbachev's key military advisers, Marshall Akhromeyev, told a TV audience that in the financial years 1989-1991. 'We have reduced them [military expenditures] by 8.5 percent and in 1990 we shall reduce them by a further 5-6 percent', BBC Transcripts, Soviet Union, SU/0717, 20 March 1990. Thus Gorbachev's 14 percent was probably Akhromeyev's 8.2 percent and projected 5 percent added together.

39. IISS, *Strategic Survey 1988-1989*, London 1989, p. l23.

40. See my 'What would an arms deal mean?', *Socialist Worker*, 5 December 1987.

41. Evidence given to the Congressional Defence Appropriations Committee in the summer of 1989, see the *Sunday Correspondent*, 28 January 1990 and 10 June 1990.

42. The US Armed Services Committee was told in June 1989, 'Recently NATO ministers of defence have approved a

memorandum of agreement that implements the planning process for TLAM/N [Tomahawk Land Attack Missiles with Nuclear warheads] in support of the Alliance.' Quoted in the *Independent*, 4 June 1990.

43. Archie Hamilton, Under Secretary of State for the Armed Forces, to a Labour MP in a written answer to a parliamentary question, April 1990. Ibid

44. *Independent*, 5 June 1990

45. *Observer*, 10 June 1990.

46. Signed in 1972, SALT was supposed to limit intercontinental nuclear missiles. But the treaty only specificd the number of launchers, not the number of warheads, that the superpowers could build. So the US and the USSR developed the multiple independently targetable re-entry vehicle (MIRV). Each launcher could now carry three, eight or 16 nuclear warheads. Each of these was independently targetable. So it was just like having more missiles. The result was that the Strategic Arms *Limitation* Treaty actually presided over one of the biggest ever increases in the nuclear arms race. The Anti Ballistic Missile treaty set a limit of 100 anti-ballistic missile systems for each side. When the treaty was signed in 1972 neither superpower had any operational anti-ballistic missile systems. In the late 1980s they were still racing to reach the total laid down in that arms 'limitation' treaty.

47. Quoted in my 'What would an arms deal mean'?, op cit.

48. *Guardian*, 1 June 1990.

49. Figures from the Arms Control Association, quoted ibid.

50. Figures from the Arms Control Association quoted in the *Independent*, 1 April 1990.

51. P Rogers and M Dando, *NBC 90 The Directory of Nuclear, Biological and Chemical Arms and Disarmament*, Tri-Service Press 1990, quoted in the *Independent*, 26 March 1990.

52. IISS, *The Military Balance 1992-1993*, p.229

53. *Defence Planning Guidance*, quoted in the *International Herald Tribune*, 14 February 1990

54. This was justified by the proposal that the US and the USSR both cut their forces in the 'central zone' to 195,000. But this would have left the US with an additional 30,000 troops in other European countries outside the central zone.

55. Quoted in the *Financial Times*, 2 February 1990.

56. Ibid.

57. Paul Rogers of Bradford University School of Peace Studies, quoted in the *Independent*, 26 March 1990.

58. See the *International Herald Tribune*, 14 December 1990.

59. *Financial Times*, 16 June 1990.

60. See D Clarke, 'The Warsaw Pact Arms Cuts' in *Report on the*

USSR, 17 February 1989.

61. Interview, 'The Army: Parameters of Change' in *Socialism, Theory and Practice*, October 1989.

62. D Clarke, 'Soviet Nuclear Weapons Production' in *Report on the USSR*, 28 April 1989.

63. Ibid.

64. See the *Economist*, 27 January 1990.

65. D Clarke, Warsaw Pact Arms Cuts', op cit.

66. A Kelly. *The Myth of Soviet Superiority*, op cit, p. 29.

67. 'At Ease: Disarming Europe'. Business Week, 19 February 1990.

68. Ibid.

69. IISS, *Strategic Survey 1989-1990*, London 1990, pp. 58-60.

70. Quoted in the *International Herald Tribune*, 14 December 1990.

71. See T Cliff, 'Perspectives on the Permanent War Economy' in *Neither Washington Nor Moscow*, London 1982, Mike Kidron, *Capitalism and Theory*, London 1974, and *Western Capitalism Since the War*, London 1970 and Chris Harman, *Explaining the Crisis*, London 1984. On the connection between the permanent arms economy and state capitalism see Peter Binns, 'Understanding the new Cold War', *International Socialism* 19.

72. Marx argued that all commodities exchanged at values determined by the amount of labour time it took to produce them. Capital goods—machinery, factories and so on—were no different. They simply passed on an increment of their value to the finished goods that they produced, so that if a machine took 100 hours of labour to produce and was worn out after producing 50 items, each item would contain two hours of crystallised labour as part of its final value. The rest of its value would be determined by the depreciation of other machines used in its manufacture and the amount of direct labour time used to produce it.

The value of labour power, being itself a commodity, is determined in the same way. The amount of labour time used to create labour power—the labour used to build homes, provide food, education, health and welfare to a socially determined average—determines the value of labour power. But labour power is a unique commodity, because it can create more value than was used in its creation. If a machine takes 100 hours to make and ends its life after it manufactures 50 items, nothing can make it produce 51 or 52 items. But if it takes 100 hours of labour to keep the average worker healthy and educated enough to work there is nothing to stop him continuing to work after he has produced commodities to the value of 100 hours of labour. He can, within physical limits, be made to work harder and longer and so produce goods worth 110 or 120 hours of labour. Marx called the result of this exploitation of labour power surplus value. It is the source of the capitalist's profits. Indeed living labour is the only source of surplus value, since machines do not create value but simply impart previously expended labour to the goods they manufacture.

In this situation you might expect capitalists to produce using labour intensive methods, so maximising the amount of labour they can exploit. But competition forces them to do exactly the opposite. Each individual capitalist is constantly looking to increase the number of machines that he uses because, so long as he is the first to mechanise or computerise, he will be able to cut his production costs relative to other, less innovative, competitors.

Every other capitalist will then be forced to do likewise or lose markets. At the end of such a round of innovation the result for the whole economy will be that the amount of machines per worker, the ratio of dead to living labour, will have risen. One can see this pattern at work in the local supermarket. Where once there was a simple mechanical or electrical checkout till there is now a huge computerised bar code till, a convevor belt, a cheque printer and credit card facility all linked to an automatic stock control system. Each checkout worker is now surrounded by a mass of machinery which previously didn't exist and which, only a few years ago, was only used in a few hypermarkets.

And whereas the first firms to introduce these systems may have gained some competitive advantage, now all this equipment is simply the average for the industry. The result is that an action which for the individual capitalist is rational, when generalised to all capitalists, actually reduces the importance of the one element in the system which produces surplus value—living labour.

Marx called the tendency for machines to grow as a proportion of total capital the 'rising organic composition of capital'. And he called the consequent decline in the amount of surplus value produced compared with the total capital employed, the declining rate of profit.

73.   See S Melman, *The Permanent War Economy*, New York 1985, pp. 22-23. I am gratetul to Pete Gillard for obtaining this book for me.

74.   Ibid. p. 79.

75. Ibid, p. 92.
76. Source: Ruth Leger Sivard, *World Military and Social Expenditure 1977*, USA 1977, p. 13.
77. See C Harman, *Explaining the Crisis*, op cit, p. 97.
78. P Binns and M Haynes, 'New Theories of Eastern European Class Societies' in *International Socialism* 7, Winter 1980, pp. 43-4.
79. M Gorbachev, speech to the UN in *The Current Digest of the Soviet Press*, 4 January 1989.
80. CG Jacobson, *The Soviet Defence Enigma, estimating costs and burdens*, Stockholm International Peace Research Institute 1987, p. 43. This is not to say that the defence burden has not lessened since the 1950s, but rather that as the effects of autarchy have taken hold the burden has begun to rise from a level which, in any case never fell as far as the US defence burden.
81. R Walker, 'New Thinking and Soviet Foreign Policy', in *Superpower Politics*, op cit, p. 145.
82. For the USSR see J Cooper, 'Soviet Resource Options: Civil and Military Priorities' in T Hasegawa and A Pravda (eds), *Perestroika: Soviet Domestic and Foreign Policies*, Royal Institute of International Aftairs 1990, pp. 144-5. For the US see the *Economist*, 16 June 1990.
83. A Kawato. 'The Soviet Union: A Player in the World Economy' in T Hasegawa and A Pravdi (eds), op cit, p. 122.
84. M Kidron. 'Two Insights Don't Make a Theory' in *International Socialism* 100 (first series). Also see Chris Harman's reply, 'Better a Valid Insight Than a Wrong Theory' in the same issue.
85. E Bernstein, quoted in MC Howard and JE King, *A History of Marxian Economic Thought*, Princeton 1989, p. 92.
86. A Kawato. op cit.
87. IISS, *Strategic Survey 1989-1990*, London 1990, p. 54.
88. Ibid, pp. 54-5.
89. *Financial Times*, 1 October 1989.
90. Quoted in M Simmons, *The Unloved Country, a Portrait of East Germany Today*, London 1989, p. 180.
91. See *International Herald Tribune*, 28 September 1989.
92. Ibid.
93. *Financial Times*, 12 July 1990.
94. Quoted in the *Independent*, 18 July 1990.
95. IISS, *Strategic Survey 1989-1990*, op cit.
96. The memorandum was reproduced in full in the *Independent on Sunday*, 15 July 1990 .
97. Ibid.
98. Germany Survey, the *Economist*, 21 May 1994, p.7-11

99.   See *Economist* survey 'The New Germany', 30 June 1990, p. 11.
100. The *Economist*, 7 May 1994, p. 134.
101. See *Financial Times*, 2 July 1990 and the *Economist*, op cit.
102. See *Financial Times*, 18 April 1990.
103. Bill Bradley, Senator for New Jersey, in the *International Herald Tribune*, 30 March 1990.
104. See Germany Survey, the *Economist*, op cit, p.10
105. Institute of International Finance report quoted in *Financial Times*, 17 April 1990.
106. *Financial Times*, 17 July 1990 and the *Economist* 21 May 1994, p.152.
107. *Economist*, 16 June 1990.
108. A Horvat in the *Independent*, 27 February 1990.
109. Ibid.
110. See IISS, *Strategic Survey 1989-1990*, op cit, p. 139.
111. Ibid.
112. *Far Eastern Economic Review*, 12 April 1990, p. 23.
113. Ibid.
114. Ibid, p. 20.
115. *Economist*, 21 July 1990.
116. *Independent*, 10 July 1990.
117. *Economist*, 21 July 1990.
118. *Economist*, 26 February 1994
119. See L Selfa, 'Imperialism Today', *Socialist Worker*, Chicago September 1989.
120. Source: W Leontief and F Duchin, *Military Spending Facts and Figures, Worldwide and Future Outlook*, New York 1983. The bar chart given here is a representation of the statistics given in the pie chart on p. 6.
121. *Financial Times*, 8 August 1990.

Class and crisis in Eastern Europe

1.   This comment was made in Washington, 18 November 1989. See *The Failure of Communism: The Western Response. An International Conference Sponsored by Radio Free Europe, Radio Liberty Fund*, Munich 1989, pp. 49-50.
2.   Quoted in *Guardian*, 14 December 1990.
3.   On the pre-1914 situation see N Crafts, 'Gross national product in Europe 1870-1910: some new estimates', *Explorations in Economic History*, vol. 20, 1983, pp. 387-401. On the inter-war years see P Bairoch, 'Europe's Gross National Product: 1800-1975', *Journal of European Economic History*, vol. 5, 1976. For detailed discussion of pre-1939 growth rates in Eastern Europe see M Kaser and E Radice eds,

*The Economic History of Eastern Europe, 1919-1975, vol. 1
Economic Structure and Performance between the Wars*,
Oxford 1986, *vol 2, Interwar Policy, the War and
Reconstruction*, Oxford 1987.

4. Quoted in D Aldcroft, 'Eastern Europe in an age of
    turbulence, 1919-1950', *Economic History Review*, vol. XLI
    no. 4, Nov. 1988, p. 593-6.

5. See PN Rosenstein-Rodan, 'Problems of industrialisation of
    Eastern and South Eastern Europe', *Economic Journal*, vol.
    LII, June-Sept 1943. To break out of a situation where 25
    percent of the population were either totally or partially
    unemployed Rosenstein-Rodan advocated a broad state
    directed development push, 'if the industrialisation of
    international depressed areas were to rely entirely on the
    normal incentive of private entrepreneurs, the process would
    not only be very much slower, the rate of investment smaller
    and (consequently) the national income lower... the whole
    economic structure of the region would be different'. p. 206-7

6. See Y Gluckstein, *Stalin's Satellites in Europe*, London 1952.

7. These growth rates are based on the standard Western
    calculations and recalculations for Eastern Europe. See W
    Baumol, 'Productivity growth, convergence and welfare',
    American Economic Review, vol. 76 no. 5, December 1986.

8. One measure of this was the weak development of intra-
    industry trade—one of the major growth areas in the West as
    the underlying integration of the world economy increased. In
    the mid 1980s, for example, only 17 percent of Anglo-Soviet
    trade was on an intra-industry basis compared to 64 percent of
    Anglo-French and 62 percent of Anglo-German trade. M
    Kaser, 'The East European economies in transition', *European
    Management Journal*, vol. 8 no. 3, September 1990, p. 295.

9. Data for West and East Germany from A Yakolev, 'Monopo-
    lizm v ekonomike SSSR i faktorui ego obuslovlivaoushshie',
    Vestnik Statistiki, no. 1, 1991, p. 4. Data for Poland and
    Western sample from D Lipton and J Sachs, 'Creating a
    market economy in Eastern Europe: the case of Poland',
    Brookings Papers on Economic Activity, no. 1, 1990, p. 84.

10. Yakolev, op cit, pp. 3-4. See also IMF et al, *A Study of the
    Soviet Economy*, 1991, vol. 2 chap. IV. 2, pp. 36-40.

11. In an economy like South Korea there is only limited internal
    competition for similar reasons. See the data quoted in ' "Poor
    Man's Burden": A survey of the Third World', *Economist*, 23-
    29 September 1989, pp. 38-39.

12. Quoted in Lipton and Sachs, op cit, fn 9, p. 76

13. OECD, *Financial Market Trends*, Feb 1991, no. 48, p. 20.

14. Lipton and Sachs, op cit, pp. l04-105.

15. *Financial Times*, 12 March 1990.

16. Hankiss has used this example in a number of places. For a short statement see his 'Reforms and the conversion of power' in PR Weilemann, G Brunner and R Tokes eds, *Upheaval against the Plan: Eastern Europe on the Eve of the Storm*, 1991. For his fuller analysis see his *East European Alternatives*, Oxford 1990.

17. A Aganbegyan, *The Challenge. The Economics of Perestroika*, London 1988

18. I Pozsgay, 'Hungary for change', *Marxism Today*, May 1989, p. 27.

19. Elemer Hankiss, *Vilag*, 23 November 1989 quoted in A Gresh, 'Les sentiers escarpes du passage à la démocratie', *Le Monde Diplomatique*, Feb 1990, p. 5.

20. A Maddison, 'Origins and Impact of the Welfare State, 1883-1983', *Banca Nazionale del Lavoro Quarterly Review*, March 1984; A Maddison, *The World Economy in the Twentieth Century*, 1989, p. 71 for later data.

21. The precise balance between these two tendencies has been subject to ongoing debate. See C Harman, 'The state and capitalism today', *International Socialism*, 2:51, 1991, and the references given there.

22. V Tanzio, 'Eastern Europe: the state's role in mobilizing savings', *IMF Survey*, 27 May 1991, p. l66.

23. S Shahid Husain, 'Reviving growth in Latin America', *Finance and Development*, June 1989, p. 2. See also the *Economist* survey 'Poor man's Burden', op cit on state action in the Third World.

24. Husain, op cit.

25. *The Rise of World Poverty*, Socialist Economic Briefing, 1990.

26. M Pastor Jnr, 'The effects of IMF programmes in the Third World: Debate and evidence from Latin America', *World Development*, vol. 15, no. 2, 1987, p. 250.

27. For the critical debate on the impact of such policies see Pastor, op cit; MD Ramirez, 'The impact of austerity on Latin America, 1983-1989: A critical assessment', *Comparative Economic Studies*, vol. *xxxiii* no. l, Spring 1991.

28. For the defensive discussion of the IMF and World Bank on the costs of their programmes see G Pfeffermann, 'Economic crisis and the poor in some Latin American countries', *Finance and Development*, June, 1987; C Humpheys and W Jaeger, 'Africa's adjustment and growth', *Finance and Development*, June, 1989; J Greene, 'The debt problem of

Sub-Saharan Africa', *Finance and Development*, June, 1989.

29.   J Weiner, 'Capitalist shock therapy: the Sachs Plan in Poland' in his *Professors, Politics and Pop*, London, 1991.

30.   This discussion draws heavily on 'Bolivia: the poverty of progress', *Report on the Americas*, vol. XXV no. 1, July 1991.

31.   See J Newsinger, 'The Bolivian Revolution', *International Socialism*, 2.18, 1983.

32.   Quoted in 'Bolivia: the poverty of progress', op cit, pp. 28-29.

33.   *Guardian*, 2 July 1991.

34.   See the report of Sachs' contribution to the 1991 World Bank Annual Conference, *IMF Survey*, 27 May 1991.

35.   Quoted in 'Bolivia: the poverty of progress', op cit, p. l2.

36.   Quoted in Pastor Jnr, op cit, p. 259.

37.   Lipton and Sachs, op cit, p. 75.

38.   See K. Bossanyi, 'An interview with Janos Kornai', *Acta Oeconomica*, vol. 42 no. 3-4, 1990, pp. 315-28.

39.   J Kornai, *The Economics of Shortage, Growth, Shortage and Efficiency: A Macrodynamic Model of the Socialist Economy*, 1980.

40.   A Nove, 'Reforming the Soviet economy', *Dissent*, Winter 1991, p. 11; J Kornai 'The Hungarian Reform Process: visions, hopes and reality', *Journal of Economic Literature*, December 1986 also expresses his disillusion with reform and the possibility of coping with bureaucracy; J Kornai, *The Road to a Free Economy, Shifting from a Socialist System: The Example of Hungary*, London 1990.

41.   Kornai, *The Road*, op cit.

42.   D Lipton and J Sachs, op cit, pp. 77, 138 (their paper is followed by Kornai's comments).

43.   Kornai, *The Road*, op cit.

44.   Bosanyi, op cit, p. 327.

45.   See, for example, the publicity and campaigns of *Labour Focus on Eastern Europe* as well as the individual campaigns of groups all over the world to the left of the communist parties.

46.   See Bush's speech to the IMF-World Bank Annual Meeting, 25 September 1990.

47.   Two older studies of this process are still useful. See Barrington Moore Jnr, 'Some readjustments in communist theory', *Journal of the History of Ideas*, Vol. 6, 1945, pp. 468-482; RV Daniels, 'The State and Revolution: a case study in the genesis and transformation of communist ideology', *American Slavic and East European Review*, vol. 12, 1953, pp. 22-43.

48.   There is much of interest on this ideological shift in B

Chavance, *Le capital socialiste, histoire critique de l'économie politique du socialisme, 1917-1954*, Paris 1980, although it operates with a different conception of state capitalism to that used here.

49.   The conservative role and content of Soviet ideas and their links to Western conservatism were noted by Nigel Harris many years ago. See his *Beliefs in Society*, London 1971. There is a fascinating study of how this conservative mentality, the development of 'bourgeois values', came to be reflected in popular literature in Vera Dunham, *In Stalin's Time. Middle Class Values in Soviet Fiction*, London 1976.

50.   B Crick, *George Orwell, A life*, London 1980, pp. 52-3.

51.   N Shmelev, 'Avansy i dolgi', *Novy Mir*, no. 6, 1987, p. 147.

52.   *Financial Times*, 29 October 1990.

53.   G Akerloff et al, 'East Germany in from the cold: the economic aftermath of currency union', *Brookings Papers in Economic Activity*, no. 1, 1991, p. 1.

54.   Ibid.

55.   *Observer*, 31 March 1991, estimate quoted from German source.

56.   K Schmidt and B Sander, 'Wages, Productivity and Employment in Eastern Germany' in AG Ghaussy and N Shafer Eds *The Economics of German Unification*, London 1993

57.   Ibid.

58.   OECD, *Economic Outlook*, no. 54, December 1993, p.117

59.   Lipton and Sachs, op cit, pp. 101-2.

60.   For most of Eastern Europe the optimistic scenario suggests it will take the next decade to get back to 1989 levels. When this is eventually achieved the relative gap with the advanced world will be wider than in 1989 because it will have moved on even if only sluggishly.

61.   There have been a number of attempts to calculate the scale of these effective subsidies. By way of illustration it is estimated that in the period 1970-1984 each Soviet citizen subsidised East German industry — the most advanced in the bloc — by 270 dollars a year through purchases of lower quality, overpriced manufactured goods, *Financial Times*, 12 March 1990.

62.   OECD, *Economic Outlook*, passim

63.   United Nations Economic Commission for Europe, *Economic Survey of Europe in 1990-1991*, New York 1991, pp. 90-91.

64.   OECD, *Economic Outlook*, no. 49, July 1991, p. 39.

65.   Ibid.

66.   A major expansion of agricultural trade is a significant part of

the Group of Thirty's proposals for Eastern Europe. *Financing Eastern Europe: A Study Group Report*, 1991. (There is a brief summary of its main conclusions in *IMF Survey*, 29 July 1991. Agriculture now produces only around 5 percent of West European output using some 8 percent of the labour force. But agricultural subsidies which go disproportionally to big farmers and the big food processing companies make up some 60 percent of the European Community's budget. Weekly food subsidy costs are estimated to be the equivalent of £14 per family.

67.   OECD, *Economic Outlook*, no. 49, July 1991, p. 37.

68.   Will Hutton in the *Guardian*, 10 July 1991.

69.   OECD, *Financial Market Trends*, no. 48, February 1991, pp. 20-6.

70.   Ibid, p. 29.

71.   Ibid, pp. 30-1.

72.   *Sunday Times*, 13 December 1981. The second banker was quoted on the BBC radio on 14 December 1981. See M Haynes, 'Russia, Eastern Europe and the world economy', paper given to the Critique Conference, London, 15 January 1982.

73.   OECD, *Financial Market Trends*, op cit, p. 16; D Fairlamb, 'Eastern Europe Opportunities for Bankers', Banking World, April,1990, p. 22.

74.   OECD, *Economic Outlook*, no. 49, July 1991, p. 40. The contrast between the treatment of Poland and the poorer countries of the world has not been lost there. In the Philippines, for example, there has been enormous pressure not to default, ' "But then", observed one human rights lawyer, "the Philippines hadn't just overthrown communism (sic); we had merely chucked out Reagan's chum Marcos". Perhaps, some are saying cynically, the way to get debt forgiven is to go communist and then overthrow the government'. J Seabrook, 'Bad Debts', *New Statesman*, 21 June 1991.

75.   See M.Glenny, *The Rebirth of History: Eastern Europe in the Age of Democracy*, London 1990, p. 185 .

76.   *Economist*, 10 August 1991, *Guardian*, 27 August 1991. In its pinstriped junketing 'while the poor starve' the EBRD is following a well established pattern in the IMF and World Bank. See the critique 'Pinstripes and Poverty: Inside the World Bank', *New Internationalist*, December 1990 which should he compared with the *Economist*'s survey celebrating their activities, 'IMF and World Bank Survey', 12 October 1991.

77.   *Economist*, op cit, p. 49.

78.   Boston Consulting Group, 'Eastern Europe—the free market makes its debut', *Director*, November 1990, p. 122.

79.   R Hunerberg, 'Risk and opportunities in Eastern Europe', *European Management Journal*, vol. 8 no. 4, December 1990, p. 518.

80.   Ibid. For similar caution see A Hermann and M Hermann, 'Eastem and Central Europe: opportunities and problems', *European Management Journal*, Vol. 8 no. 3, September 1990; I. Zloch-Christy, 'Political risk assessment in lending to Eastern Europe', idem., Vol. 8 no. 4, December 1990; Boston Consulting Group (footnote 78). Private consultancy advice is even more cautious. One such report, seen by the author, advises Asian business to treat Poland as an 'upfront expense needed to gain a greater share of the market later on' rather than a source of immediate profit. But investing companies should give the appearance of substantial long term commitment so as to 'potentially win more favourable terms for investing in Poland. Such terms might include longer tax holidays, lower taxes thereafter, more favourable initial valuation etc'. Countries like Poland and Hungary are already moving to create the most favourable legal climates in the world for attracting foreign investment.

81.   'Business in Eastern Europe Survey', *Economist*, 21 September 1991, p. 25.

82.   'The Skoda-Volkswagen Merger: Salvation or Steal?', *East European Reporter*, Spring-Summer, 1991, pp. 56-8.

83.   'Is freedom of movement a threat for Europe?', *Forum Council of Europe*, February 1991, pp. 39-41. Interestingly Akerloff et al (see footnote 53), otherwise apostles of the market, try desperately to disprove that migration in eastern Germany is determined by wage differentials in order to support lower wages in the former East Germany.

84.   Quoted in 'Paying guests', *International Management*, February 1991, pp. 39-41.

85.   I Baranshas. 'West erects its own Iron Curtain', *Guardian*, 12 July 1991.

86.   For the thought proccesses of British and Western European politicians and their advisers see N Hopkinson *Migration into Western Europe*, Wilton Park Papers no. 49, London HMSO December 1991

87.   In fact the KGB and other such organisations have been well placed to make this particular shift and have been argued to be prominent in setting up the Soviet stock exchange.

88.   This discussion summarises a wider analysis of 'Class

Recomposition in Eastern Europe' by the author (forthcoming).

89. Hankiss, 'Reforms' op cit, p. 31 (see footnote 16).

90. G Tamas Koranyi, 'Where have all the experts gone?', *The Hungarian Observer*, no. 3, 1991, p. 16.

91. Quoted in I Rammonet, 'Pologne—annee zero', *Le Monde Diplomatique*, December 1990, p. 8.

92. *IMF Survey*, 27 May 1991.

93. The level of individual share ownership varies but in all major countries it is less than institutional share ownership and declining in importance. Between 1980-1988 private share ownership fell from 28.2 to 21.3 percent of all shares in the UK; 50 to 42 percent in the USA and 29 to 23 percent in Japan. See C Breheny, 'Wider share ownership in danger', *Investors Chronicle*, 15 March 1991, pp. 14-15.

94. *Business Week*, 15 April 1991.

95. Quoted in M.Levinson, 'Reforming the economies of Eastern Europe', *Dissent*, Winter 1991, p. 129.

96. T Kuzci and A Vajda, 'The social composition of small entrepreneurs', *Acta Economica*, vol. 42 no. 3-4, 1990, p. 322.

97. *Business Week*, 15 April 1991, p. 21.

98. A Osenberg, 'Deutsche Bank moves East', *Banking World*, June 1991, p. 27.

99. This discussion of unemployment summarises a longer paper M Haynes and M Perry, 'The measurement of unemployment in Eastern Europe and the USSR', Second European Research Conference, Nottingham, April 1991.

100. OECD *Economic Outlook*, no. 54, December, 1993, p.113. The data available does not yet allow a comparison of GDP with earlier periods. Starting the analysis from 1990 therefore understates the fall in some countries. Output as measured by old style material product fell marginally in 1989 in Bulgaria and Hungary. In Romania it fell by some 10 percent in 1988-1989.

101. Lipton and Sachs, op cit, argue that before 1989 Poles had to queue to get little or nothing. Now they know they can afford little or nothing so they do not queue. Thus the real standard of living has improved in this area and therefore the overall fall exaggerated. I have yet to find an Eastern European who I could persuade of the merits of this argument.

102. Ibid, p. 121.

103. *Guardian*, 7 May 1990.

104. J Seddon, 'Privatisation in Eastern Europe', *European Management Journal*, vol. 8 no. 4, December 1990, p. 508. (The author is head of the privatisation unit at Barclays de

Zoete Wedd who offer advice to Eastern European governments).

105. See I Szelényi and S Szelényi, 'The vacuum in Hungarian politics, classes and parties', *New Left Review*, no. 187 May-June 1991

106. *Guardian*, 30 December 1990.

107. *Guardian*, 19 November 1990.

108. Quoted in I Ramonet, op cit, p. 9.

109. *Guardian*, 19 November 1990.

110. *Guardian*, 15 August 1991.

The return of the national question

1. E Hobsbawm, *Nations and Nationalism since 1780*, Cambridge 1990.

2. B Anderson, *Imagined Communities*, London 1991.

3. E Gellner, *Nations and Nationalism*, Oxford 1983.

4. N Harris, *National Liberation*, London 1990.

5. A typical example is S Pacu, *A History of Transylvania*, New York 1990.

6. EA Wrigley, 'London's importance 1650-1750', in I Patten (ed), *Pre-industrial England*, pp. 196-197.

7. A point made by Gramsci, see A Gramsci, 'The Renaissance', *Selections from Cultural Writings*, London 1985, pp. 222-34.

8. Which was why Gramsci could see Machiavelli as a theorist of a rising bourgeoisie, even though he looked to a feudal prince to achieve his goals.

9. The key part in this decision is said to have been played by Alessandro Manzoni, who first wrote his enormously influential novel *I promessi sposi* (The Betrothed) in the Lombard dialect, and then spent 15 years changing it into Tuscan, see for instance DM Smith, *Italy: A modern history*, Michigan 1959.

10. I Banac, *The National Question in Yugoslavia: Origins, History, Politics*, London 1984, p. 81. See also, E Hobsbawm, *Nations and Nationalism since 1780*, op cit.

11. G Brennan, *The Spanish Labyrinth*, London 1960, p. 29.

12. The expression was actually invented by a critic of Griffith, but nevertheless was an accurate summary of his economic nationalism, which was modelled on that of the German Friedrich List. See N Mansergh, *The Irish Question*, London 1965, p. 238.

13. See B Fitch and M Oppenheimer, *Ghana, The End of an Illusion*, pp. 33 and 182-3.

14. 'The Counter-Revolution in Berlin', *Neue Rheinische Zeitung*,

12 November 1848, in *Marx Engels Collected Works*, vol. 8. Moscow 1977, p. 17.

15. O Bauer, *Die Nationalitaetfrage und die Sozialdemokratie*, p. 271, quoted in R Rosdolsky, *Engels and 'non-historic' Peoples*, Critique 1987, p. 35.

16. B Anderson, op cit, p. 87.

17. K Marx and F Engels, *Manifesto of the Communist Party*, in Marx, Engels and Lenin, *The Essential Left*, London 1960, p. 33.

18. This has escaped some writers on the approach of Marx and Engels to the national question. Thus Ephraim Nimni, a follower of the anti-Marxist Laclau, ascribes to them a sophisticated materialist analysis which they did not, in reality, hold at this time. See his *Marxism and Nationalism*, London 1991.

19. The Czech movement was closer to a modern national movement than those of the Ruthenians and the South Slavs. Even as early as 1848 an incipient Czech bourgeoisie and petty bourgeoisie was attempting to unite the Bohemian and Moravian peasantry behind its programme for 'national' capitalist development, in a way which certainly was not true for the Highlanders, the Bretons, and the Carlists. Marx's *Neue Rheinische Zeitung* did show some sympathy for the Czechs, until their leaders threw their weight behind the Austrian monarchy's attacks on the democratic movement.

20. Letter of 2 November 1867, *Marx-Engels Collected Works*, Moscow 1987, pp. 460-1 .

21. Letter of 30 November 1867, in *Marx-Engels Collected Works*, vol 42, op cit., pp. 486-487.

22. Marx to Kugelmann, 29 November 1869, in ibid, vol 43, pp. 390-1.

23. See 'On the Decline of Feudalism and the Emergence of the National States', written at the end of 1884 and now available in *Marx-Engels Collected Works*, vol. 26, Moscow 1990, pp. 556-65. Only two years earlier, in his manuscript 'On the Early History of the Germans' Engels was still speaking of 'the German nation' as existing at the time of Julius Caesar, see *Collected Works*, vol. 26, p. 30.

24. O Bauer, 'The Concept of Nation', from *Die Nationalitaetfrage und die Sozialdemocratie*, available in French translation in G Haupt, M Lowy and C Weill (eds), *Les Marxistes et la question nationale*, Paris 1974, p. 235.

25. O Bauer, ibid, p. 238.

26. Ibid, p. 239.

27. Ibid, pp. 241-2.

28. Ibid, p. 243.

29. Ibid, p. 249.

30. Ibid, p. 264.

31. Although he was critial of certain aspects of it, according to E Nimni, *Marxism and Nationalism*, op cit., p. 145.

32. The programme, adopted at the Austrian party congress in Brno (Bruenn) in 1899 is contained in Rosa Luxemburg, *The National Question*, New York 1976, pp. 104-5,

33. G Haupt, 'Les Marxistes face a la question nationale: l'histoire du problem', in G Haupt et al, op cit.

34. Ibid, p. 49.

35. ' Nationality and internationalism', *Neue Zeit*, January 1908, translated in French, ibid, p. 129.

36. K Kautsky, 'La nationalite moderne', *Neue Zeit*, 1887, translated into French, ibid, p. 119.

37. Ibid, pp. 114-27.

38. Ibid, p. 114.

39. Ibid, p. 116.

40. Ibid, p. 35.

41. Ibid, p. 136.

42. K Kautsky, 'Nationality and internationalism', *Neue Zeit*, 1908, ibid, p. 136.

43. Ibid, pp. 137-8.

44. For a typical example, see E Nimni, *Marxism and Nationalism*, op cit.

45. K Kautsky, 'Nationality and internationalism', quoted in R Luxemburg, *The National Question*, op cit, pp. 126-7.

46. Ibid, p. 127.

47. See 'The National Question and Autonomy', written in 1908-9, available in ibid, p. 159.

48. Ibid, p. 177.

49. Ibid, pp. 129-31.

50. Ibid, p. 93.

51. Ibid, p. 97.

52. Ibid, p. 96.

53. Although on this, as on so many other issues, Trotsky—who had already written brilliantly on the Balkans during the wars of 1912 and 1913—took up Lenin's legacy after he joined the Bolsheviks in 1917 and deepened some aspects of it. Stalin's 'Marxism and the National Question', written in 1913, used to be quoted by many on the left as a classical exposition of the Bolshevik position. Much of it is a straightforward regurgitation of Kautsky's account of the origins of the nation state and of Lenin's argument for self determination and against cultural national autonomy. But it also attempts to define what a nation is using a list of factors. The attempt has

been very influential, but in fact breaks with the general approach of Lenin and gives a lot of attention to psychological and 'national character' factors in a manner that is closer to Bauer than Kautsky and Lenin.

54. VI Lenin, 'The Right of Nations to Self Determination', in *Critical Remarks on the National Question and the Right of Nations to Self-determination*, Moscow 1971, pp. 40-41 .

55. Although most of his polemic was not directed against Luxemburg but against Radek.

56. VI Lenin, 'On the Right of Nations to Self Determination', op cit., pp. 56-7.

57. Ibid, p. 70.

58. Ibid, p. 77.

59. Ibid, p. 101.

60. VI Lenin, 'The Discussion of Self Determination Summed Up', in *Critical Remarks*, op cit., p. 124.

61. Ibid, p. 83.

62. Ibid.

63. *Minutes of the Second Congress of the RSDLP*, London 1978, p. 81.

64. VI Lenin, 'Critical Remarks on the National Question', in *Critical Remarks*, op cit., p. 16.

65. Ibid, p. 31.

66. Ibid, pp. 22-3.

67. Ibid, p. 21.

68. Ibid, p. 10.

69. Ibid, p. 13.

70. Ibid, p. 137.

71. Ibid, p. 138.

72. Ibid, p. 24.

73. Figures for 1984, from M Kidron and R Segal, *The New State of the World Atlas*, London 1984.

74. See *Independent on Sunday*, 2 August 1992, p. 5.

75. In a recent televised discussion between Stuart Hall, former guru of *Marxism Today*, a French new philosopher and Salman Rushdie, only Rushdie showed any sign of understanding that there could be something *good* about a fusion of cultures.

76. Marx and Engels, *The Manifesto of the Communist Party*, in Marx, Engels, Lenin, *The Essential Left*, London 1960, p. 18.

77. P Manuel, *Popular Music of the non-Western World*, Oxford 1988, p. 20.

78. Ibid, p. 20.

79. Ibid.

80. Ibid, p. 21.

81. Ibid, p. 20.

82. Ibid, pp. 18-19.
83. B Anderson, op cit, p. 40.
84. Ibid, pp. 423.
85. Ibid, p. 67.
86. Ibid, p. 81.
87. Ibid, p. 76.
88. Ibid, p. 77.
89. Ibid, p. 63. See also, for an elaboration of his argument, pp. 119-21.
90. Ibid, p. 30.
91. A talk for the Australian Broadcasting Corporation, printed in *New Left Review* 193, March/June 1992.
92. E Gellner, op cit, p. 48.
93. Ibid, pp. 46-48.
94. Ibid, p. 46.
95. Ibid, p. 47.
96. Ibid, p. 55.
97. It was written after both Gellner's and Anderson's.
98. E Hobsbawm, *Nations and Nationalism since 1780*, op cit, pp. 10-11.
99. Ibid, pp. 127-30.
100. Ibid, p. 172-3.
101. With the partial exception of Yugoslavia, where the domination was in the hands of the two nationalities who spoke Serbo-Croat and the third Slav speaking nationality, the Slovenes all of whom united against the non-Slav Albanian speakers.
102. The only, partial, exception was the Czech part of Czechoslovakia.
103. Both Nigel Harris and to a lesser extent, Eric Hobsbawm, make great play of the existence of capitals today that are not tied to national states or are tied to very small ones, like Singapore or Hong Kong. But these capitals are overwhelmingly the exception, not the rule. The great corporations that dominate world production may operate across national frontiers, but they all make sure they have at least one national state to fall back on in emergencies. Even Hong Kong's capitalists are not really an exception: they have relied on the British state in the past, and are now much keener on the statelet merging into the giant Chinese state than are the great mass of Hong Kong people. For the more general arguments against Nigel Harris's view, see my 'The State and Capital', *International Socialism* 2:51.
104. *Il Materialismo storico e lafilosofa di Benedetto Croce*, Turin 1948, p. 38.

105. For the arguments showing the lack of national oppression in Scotland, see C Bambery, *Scotland's National Question*, London 1990.

106. Thus the *Glasgow Herald*, 10 August 1992, could emphasise the 'achievements' of the British team at the 1992 Olympics and print a list of medals under the title 'Britain's Role of Honour', even if some of the emphasis was on the performance of Scottish competitors. At the same Olympics thousands of spectators in the audience showed their double national identity by waving the Catalan flag when a Castillian athlete won a major event.

107. G Brennan, *The Spanish Labyrinth*, op cit, pp. 268, 279-80.

108. For a detailed account of developments up to the end of 1991, see D Blackie, 'The Road to Hell', *International Socialism* 53, Winter 1991.

Index